THE
KABALA OF NUMBERS
PART I

A Handbook of Interpretation

BY

SEPHARIAL

AUTHOR OF "A MANUAL OF OCCULTISM,"
"KABALISTIC ASTROLOGY," "COSMIC SYMBOLISM,"
"A NEW MANUAL OF ASTROLOGY," ETC. ETC.

NEW EDITION
ENLARGED AND REVISED

NEWCASTLE PUBLISHING COMPANY, INC.
P.O. Box 7589   Van Nuys, Calif. 91409

Library of Congress Cataloging in Publication Data

Old, Walter Gorn, 1864-
    The kabala of numbers.

    (Newcastle occult book P-27)
    Reprint of the 1928 ed. published by D. McKay Co.,
Philadelphia.
    1. Symbolism of numbers. I. Title.
BF1623.P906 1974   133.3'35   74-6128
ISBN 0-87877-027-5

A NEWCASTLE BOOK
FIRST PRINTING: SEPTEMBER, 1974
PRINTED IN THE UNITED STATES OF AMERICA

CONTENTS   PART I

THE
KABALA OF NUMBERS

INTRODUCTION

THE science of numbers is of remotest antiquity. Among the Aryans and Greeks, the Assyrians and Egyptians, we find indications of a development which gave to numbers their real significance and employed them in a system of symbolism which had respect to something more than mere enumeration.

While it is true that a figure is a symbol denoting a quantity, it is also a fact that a quantity thus symbolised may denote much more than a mere number, as we may learn from chemical analysis, where two bodies consisting of an equal number of atoms of the same elements are of an entirely different chemical nature. This is the case as between phenylisocyanide and benzonitrile. But here we have a difference in the arrangement of the atoms, the single atom of nitrogen being active in the one and passive in the other molecule. The position serves, however, for a general thesis which regards all bodies as compounded of elements drawn

1

from a single base, their specific differences being due to the domination of one over another element in them. The astrologers affirm that individual character answers to a similar analysis, for whereas all men are constituted from the same cosmic forces, one has more of Saturn in him than others, being born under the dominance of that planet, while another has more of the nature of Mars, on account of its ascendancy or elevation at his birth, corresponding differences of character being observable in them, the one being ponderous, melancholic and taciturn, the other energetic, enterprising and demonstrative. Man, in fine, is a modification of cosmic elements, a composite of cosmic forces, like any other body. But also something more. Behind the coloured glass there is always the light. The intelligence striking through the composite of personal organisation reveals itself as character.

Similarly, behind the cosmos there is an Intelligence which manifests to us through cosmic elements as Nature. God geometrises, and in Nature we have the geometrical expression of the Divine Intelligence. Crystallisation takes place according to definite laws. All the superior metals crystallise at the angle or complemental angle of a regular polygon, which may be inscribed in a circle ; and these angles are those which are indicated by the astral science as operative. Water, which the ancients referred to in a mystical sense as the mother of all things, their material base, crystallises at an angle of 60 degrees. The universe is but the

crystallised ideation of God [...] divine thought-
form. It is by the study [... num]bers, therefore,
that we may learn the la[...] [d]ivine expression,
from the constitution of [... uni]verse down to the
most trivial occurrence i[... evo]lutional progress.
What we call an event [... a] displacement and
rearrangement of the pa[rticula]r sphere of reality.
Changes taking place [... in the] cosmos are accompanied by changes in a[... co]nstituents, and these
changes may converg[e ... ca]taclysm. They may
also produce a show[er ... rai]n, an epidemic, or a
rise of a penny per [... in] the price of wheat.
Admitting man's re[lation t]o the cosmos, and it
would be difficult t[o ... th]em, there is really no
end to the concaten[ated] effects which may arise
from any single cos[mic dispo]sition, as, for instance,
$\odot \, \ooalign{8} \, \mars$, when our [...] in the diameter of the
Martian sphere of [...].

In the study o[f ...]s, therefore, we are not
concerned with [... ol]ogy, or mere symbolism,
but with quantit[ative ... ge]ometrical relations. This
study has its p[... i]ts alphabet, its language
and terminology [... si]gnification. In the course
of these pages I [... end]eavour to show that there
is a significati[on ... belong]ing to numbers which for
lack of a better [... mu]st call occult; for although
it would be a [... relati]vely easy matter to trace a
relationship e[... bet]ween man and the universe,
it would be [... arg]ument of a mystical nature
only that a[... connec]tion between numbers and
events coul[d ...]d. Yet, if I show that this
connection [... the]re will be at least sufficient

ground on which to establish such an argument, from which, possibly, might arise a deeper understanding and wider appreciation of that ancient key to the mysteries of the universe which was rediscovered and partially formulated by Baron Swedenborg in the Doctrine of Correspondences. In this doctrine, Matter is the ultimate expression of Spirit, as Form is that of Force. Therefore, for every spiritual Force there is a corresponding material Form. The whole of Nature thus becomes an expression of the underlying spiritual world, and its physiognomy is to us the chiefest source of inspiration. The laws governing this expression are traceable only in terms of numbers, *i.e.* of geometrical ratios. The moral sense is only a subconscious recognition of the integrity and harmony of natural laws, a reflex of the greater environment. There is an analogy between the laws of Matter and those of Mind. They may arise from a common cause. The science of numbers is the key to both.

CHAPTER I

THE POWER OF NUMBERS

FIGURES are the means employed by us to express definite quantities. They do not express anything of quality. Thus, if we say 2 eggs and 2 eggs make 4 eggs, we leave out of consideration the fact that one or more of them may be bad. From this we learn that 2, or any other number, is potentially good or evil, its quantity being unaffected.

Every number has a certain power which is not expressed by the figure or symbol employed to denote quantity only. This power rests in an occult connection existing between the relations of things and the principles in nature of which they are the expressions.

Revelation first took a demonstrable form when man evolved the numerical sequence 0 1 2 3 4 5 6 7 8 9, by whatever symbols it was expressed.

In this series—

0 stands for infinity, the Infinite boundless Being, the *fons et origo* of all things, the Brahmânda or egg of the universe, the solar system in its entirety ; hence universality, cosmopolitanism, circumambu- lation, voyaging. But also for negation, circum-

ference, limitation, and privation. Thus it is the universal paradox, the infinitely great and the infinitely small, the circle of infinity and the point at the centre, the atom.

1 symbolises manifestation, assertion, the positive and active principle. It stands for the Logos, the manifestation of the Infinite and Unmanifest. It represents the ego, self-assertion, positivism, egotism, separateness, selfhood, isolation, distinction, self-reliance, dignity, and rulership. In a religious sense, it symbolises the Lord. In a philosophical and scientific sense, the synthesis and fundamental unity of things. In a material sense, the unit of life, the individual. It is the 0 made manifest. It is the symbol of the Sun.

2. The number of antithesis; also of witness and confirmation. The binomial, as plus and minus, active and passive, male and female, positive and negative, profit and loss, etc. It stands for the dualism of manifested life—God and Nature, Spirit and Matter, and their relationships. It denotes agreement, also separation, the law of alternation, subject and object, reflection. As uniting in itself opposite terms or principles, it denotes creation, production, fruition, combination. Primarily the two conditions, the manifest and the unmanifest, the explicit and the implicit. The symbol of the Moon.

3. The trilogy; the trinity of life, substance, and intelligence, of force, matter, and consciousness. Creation, preservation, and resolution. The family—father, mother, and child. The three di-

mensions. The three postulates—the thinker, the thought, and the thing. Duality reflected in consciousness, as in time and space, making a trinity of states, as the past, present, and future; therefore, extension of the self; the self-extensive faculty; volition; procedure; penetration. The symbol of Mars.

4. The number of reality and concretion. The material universe. The cube or square. Physical laws; logic; reason. Appearance, physiognomy, science. Cognition by perception, experience, knowledge. The cross, segmentation, partition, order, classification. The swastika, the wheel of the law, sequence, enumeration. The intellect; consciousness, as discerning between the spiritual and material, the noumenal and phenomenal worlds, represented by the higher and lower triad. Hence discernment, discretion, relativity. The symbol of Mercury.

5. Expansion is represented by this number. Inclusiveness, comprehension, understanding, judgment. Increase, fecundity, propagation. Justice, reaping, harvesting. Reproduction of self in the material world, fatherhood, rewards and punishments. The seed-fruit or pomegranate, multiplication. The symbol of Jupiter.

6. The number of co-operation. Marriage, interlacing, a link, connection. Reciprocal action, counterpoise. The interaction of the spiritual and material, the mental and the physical in man, the psyche, psychology, divination, communion, sympathy. Psychism, telepathy, psychometry. Al-

chemy. Conversion. Concord, harmony, peace, satisfaction. Goodness, beauty and truth, as tested by harmony. Attainment, restitution. Intercourse, reciprocity. Connubiality, the relations of the sexes. The symbol of Venus.

7. The number of completion. Time and space. Duration, distance. Old age, decadence, death, or endurance, stability, immortality. The seven ages, days of the week, etc. The seven seals, principles in man, notes and colours. The triad and quaternary; the perfect man, Adam Kadmon; the cycle of evolution; wisdom, perfection, equipoise, balance, rest. The symbol of Saturn.

8. The number of dissolution. It denotes the law of cyclic evolution, the breaking back of the natural to the spiritual. Reaction, revolution, fracture, rupture, disintegration, segregation, decomposition, anarchism. Lesion, separation, divorce. Inspiration following respiration, afflatus, genius, invention. Deflection, eccentricity, waywardness, aberration, madness. The symbol of Uranus.

9. The number of regeneration. A new birth. Spirituality, sense-extension, premonition, going forth, voyaging. Telæsthesia, dreaming, clairvoyance, clairaudience. Reformation, nebulosity, pulsation, rhythm; reaching out, extension, publication; archery, prediction, revelation; a thought-wave, apparition, wraith, mist, cloud, obscurity, exile, mystery. The symbol of Neptune.

These are some of the links in the almost endless chain of associated ideas centring about the nine digits and the cipher. In some systems of interpretation, the cypher is put last, so that the first and last are brought together to form 10, the perfect number in the decimal system; but in the Hebrew scheme, the number 12 has that distinction, being the product of 3 into 4, as 7, another sacred number, is their sum. The foregoing interpretation of the numbers is applied to the unit value of any number, as $731 = 11 = 2$, in which 2 is the unit value. Thus, all numbers have final reference to one of the nine digits.

The following Minor Key to the interpretation of numbers may prove useful, being in many respects more concise and easier of application than the foregoing :—

In this system—

1. Denotes individuality and possible egotism, self-reliance, affirmation, distinction.

2. Relationship, psychic attraction, emotion, sympathy or antipathy, doubt, vacillation.

3. Expansion, increase, intellectual capacity, riches and success.

4. Realisation, property, possession, credit and position, materiality.

5. Reason, logic, ethics, travelling, commerce, utility.

6. Co-operation, marriage, reciprocity, sympathy, play, art, music, dancing.

7. Equilibrium, contracts, agreements, treaties, bargains, harmony or discord.

8. Reconstruction, death, negation, decay, loss, extinction, going out.

9. Penetration, strife, energy, enterprise, dividing, anger, keenness.

B

In this scheme the answering planets are respectively—

1. The Sun.
2. The Moon (New).
3. Jupiter.
4. The Earth or Sun.
5. Mercury.

6. Venus.
7. The Moon (Full).
8. Saturn.
9. Mars.

Although in the Hebraic system the number 12, as already stated, appears to have stood for perfection, the earliest enumeration would seem to have been made from Chaldean sources, which is distinctly decimal. Thus, we have—

1	2	3	4	5	6	7	8	9
א	ב	ג	ד	ה	ו	ז	ח	ט
10	20	30	40	50	60	70	80	90
י	כ	ל	מ	נ	ס	ע	פ	צ
100	200	300	400	500	600	700	800	900
ק	ר	ש	ת	ך	ם	ן	ף	ץ

thousands being indicated by a dot over any of these numeral letters. Here it is clearly seen that the notation of numbers did not have any other than the decimal basis.

The Greeks, according to Liddell and Scott, employed the following system of enumeration :—

1α 2β 3γ 4δ 5ϵ $6=$ 7ζ 8η 9θ
10ι 20κ 30λ 40μ 50ν $60-$ $70o$ 80π $90-$
100ρ 200σ 300τ 400υ 500ϕ 600χ 700ψ 800ω

A stroke to the right, above, raised the power of a

unit by 100; and one to the left, below, raised it by 1000. Thus $\epsilon = 5$, $\epsilon' = 500$, $_{,\epsilon} = 5000$.

The vau $= 6$, and samech $= 60$, of the Hebrew are not represented, nor is the final $\gamma = 900$.

By a slight variation from the above scheme, but by a method consistent in itself, the following kabalism has been developed from the Apocalypse[1]:—

Ὀ Νικων	The Conqueror	= 1000
Ἐπιστημωγ	Intuitively Wise	= 999
Ἰησοῦς	The Higher Mind	= 888
Σταυρος	The Cross	= 777
Ἠφρήν	The Lower Mind	= 666
Ἐπιθυμια	Desire	= 555
Σπειρημα	Serpent Coil	= 444
Ακρασια	Sensuality	= 333

These are the seven principles of the human being, and represent the stages of his evolution from the animal to the divine.

The principles corresponding to them in the esoteric philosophy of the East are—

The Conqueror . . .	Ātmā.
Intuitive Wisdom . . .	Buddhi.
The Higher Mind . . .	Buddhi-Manas.
The Cross . . .	Antaskarana.
The Lower Mind . . .	Kāma-Manas.
Desire	Kāma.
Serpent Coil . . .	Lingam.
Sensuality . . .	Sthula.

[1] *The Apocalypse Unsealed*, by James M. Pryse.

The use of glyphs in the form of literal numbers, for the purpose of veiling certain revelations or teachings not intended for general readers, is a feature peculiar to all Oriental systems. The Hindus have such glyphs, and they also make use of numbers to veil their knowledge. Thus, we have what are called *Mantrams* used as invocations in the ordinary way, but understood by the instructed to cover choice secrets of natural or spiritual knowledge. The *Achāryavāgabhedya* mnemonic gives the number of days expired from the beginning of the Kali Yuga to the beginning of the reformation under Srī S'ankarācharya, namely, 1,434,160, which, being reduced to years, gives K. Y. 3927. But, as the Kali Yuga began in 3102 B.C. (February), we derive the year A.D. 825. The great philosopher was therefore twenty years of age, having been born on the 8th April (O. S.) 805 A.D.[1]

The value of π, which expresses the relations of the circumference to the diameter of a circle, was concealed in the great cycle known as the Age of Brahma, 311,040,000,000,000 years. This age is one hundred years of Brahma, and a Brahmic year is therefore 3,110,400,000,000 solar years. This number is again divided by 360, which gives the value of the Brahmanic Day or 8,640,000,000 years. Then, by adding together the value for the age, year, and day of Brahma, we have 314159, etc., which is the familiar value of π or very nearly, 355 divided by 113.

[1] *Light of Truth* (Siddhāntā Dīpīka), July 1910 *et seq.*   Edited by V. V. Rámanan, Madras.

Similarly, the Hebrews expressed this value in the name of the seven male-female creative powers, Elohim (trans. God), thus—

$$
\begin{array}{llll}
\aleph & a = 1= & 1 \\
\lambda & l = 30 = & 3 \\
\pi & h = 5 = & 5 \\
\cdot & i = 1 = & 1 \\
\square & m = 40 = & 4 \\
\hline
& & \text{Value,} & 14
\end{array}
$$

These 14 correspond to the seven Prajapatis and their S'aktis, the positive and negative, active and passive, principles in the Oriental cosmogony.

These figures being disposed at the angles of a pentagram, the symbol of the Grand Man, the Adam Kadmon of the Kabalists, are found to read 31415.

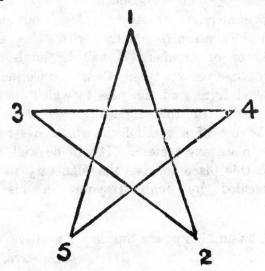

and they express the following geometrical and cosmogonical concept :—

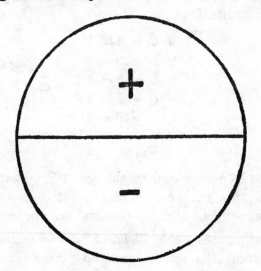

A kabala, as embodying any secret information (Heb. קבל), may assume a variety of forms—literal, numerical, or hieroglyphic ; but as we are now concerned chiefly with the nature and power of numbers, it will be advisable to confine ourselves to these, their connection with the literal form, and the uses to which they may be applied. In this connection we shall have to make use of a symbolism which has relation to the planetary system. It will be well, therefore, in this place to give the planetary numbers as revealed by John Haydon in his *Holy Guide* :—

The number of the Sun is   1 positive.
      "   "   4 negative.

The number of the Moon is 7 positive.

       ,,   ,,   2 negative.

That of Saturn is   8

That of Jupiter is   3

That of Mars is   9

That of Venus is   6

That of Mercury is 5

It will be seen that an extension of these numbers according to their cosmic order yields the glyph of the divine number 15, which, as expressing the name יה Jah, the Hebrews replace in their enumeration by טו, *i.e.* 9 and 6. Thus, we have the signs of the zodiac and the planets ruling them, with their numerical values—

♒	♓	♈	♉	♊	♋	♌	♍	♎	♏	♐	♑
♄	♃	♂	♀	☿	☽	☉	☿	♀	♂	♃	♄
8	3	9	6	5	$\frac{2}{7}$	$\frac{4}{1}$	5	6	9	3	8

Then the sum of the five planetary numbers, plus half the value of Sun and Moon together =positive 35, and negative 34. The sum of these is $69 = 15$, and $+35 - 34 = 1$. Hence the saying: "Jehovah elohanu, Jehovah achad," has reference to this one source of all creations, for achad $= 1814$ $= 14$, the Bi-septenary of Powers employed in the creation.

It will be necessary for the reader to bear in mind the numerical values of the planets, and also the days of the week ruled by them :—

Sunday	ruled by	☉ Sun.
Monday	,,	☽ Moon.
Tuesday	,,	♂ Mars.
Wednesday	,,	☿ Mercury.
Thursday	,,	♃ Jupiter.
Friday	,,	♀ Venus.
Saturday	,,	♄ Saturn.

In the course of this study of the Kabala of Numbers we shall have frequent occasion to refer to these values.

The values given by Haydon appear to be without any or due foundation, and those who have used these planetary numbers have hitherto offered no reason for attaching particular values to the several planets.

In the course of the following exposition I have supplied this deficiency and have given the paradigm from which Haydon derived his values, which are traditional among the Kabalists.

It may be well to note that, among the various alphabetical systems of enumeration, the most commonly in use is the Hebraic ; but that which is capable of the most universal application is the phonetic, which is related to the planetary values.

CHAPTER II

GEOMETRICAL RELATIONS OF THOUGHT

BEFORE we can begin to understand how numbers may have any symbolical meaning or any necessary significance in our daily life, we must consider the geometrical relations of our thought.

The unit idea of Being is expressed in the form of a circle, which is zero, of indefinite dimension, being either the infinite totality or the smallest particle. When we posit Being we include all within the circumference of our thought and perception. When we posit *a* being, we place the point within the circle. We know that that, or any other of its kind, is the centre of its own circle. Thus every unit of life has its own universe, its sphere of influence, and its relations with the things of its sphere of existence. It is a microcosm, a centre of cosmic energy, a reflection in time and space of the One.

If we trace the action or direction of this unit of life we follow a definite line of thought, or sequence of events, involved in its progress. The point has been put in motion, has been given a direction; the point generates the line.

What we at first conceive to be a straight line of definite direction we soon perceive to be a curve, the directing force being outside of the life-sphere of that unit.

We discern that it has an orbit, and is responding to a gravitational pull. So that what was generated within the circle answers to the circle.

Further, we see that none of these units pursues a perfect or circular orbit, but that its course is marked by a certain eccentricity which entails that at certain stages of its career it wanders further from its gravitational centre than at others, and then we observe that its progress is slower.

Also, we observe that none of them keeps to a uniform plane, but shows a certain inclination or list of its own—sometimes being above and again below the normal plane. Moreover, it is seen to have an obliquity or deviation from the upright, and an oscillation on its own line of obliquity. It is, in fact, an average human being or a planet, as you please. It is a little world in itself, a microcosm.

Now get back to the point, which is merely position. The point is put in direct motion and the line is generated. This line, when put in direct motion, generates the superficies ; and this, again, the solid. Given a line in motion, we may derive the circle or the square, the symbol of the Spirit or that of Matter. From the motion of the circle we may derive the cylinder or pillar, and the sphere. But if one limb or semicircle remains fixed, its complement will by its motion describe an ellipse, and at two points lying in the same plane the centre of the circle will coincide with the foci. Beyond these three motions we cannot proceed. It is similar in the case of the square, and its resultant cube, cylinder, and cone.

Therefore our thought, which is three-dimensional, is capable of generating from the evolutions of a point these figures—the sphere, the cone, and the cube; and their superficial equivalents—the circle, the triangle, and the square; with their perverts—the oblong and the ellipse. These figures have always been used in symbolical thought to represent states of consciousness. But we are only concerned with them as related to the numbers 1, 3, 4, which denote God, Humanity, and Nature—Osiris, Horus, Isis. For we answer to the universal paradigm of the One Being, compounded of spirit, soul, and body.

Therefore we consent in our very being to this necessary geometrical relation of thought, and since all geometrical relations are expressions of numerical ratios, we give natural assent to the power of numbers on which, in the Pythagorean concept, the universe is founded. That this is truth the great Kepler has demonstrated, and also Newton. When, therefore, we ascribe certain qualities or properties to a number, it is on account of a particular connotation or association of ideas impressed upon us by reference to universal standards, principles, and laws. Thus, the circle, with its centre, represents to us the sun; and by correspondence of the natural with the spiritual, it also conveys the idea of the Deity. For, as all bodies within the system are illumined and warmed by the rays of the sun, which is their gravitational centre, so all souls are enlightened and quickened by the wisdom and love of God, who is their universal attractor. And as there is but one Sun who is supreme in the system, so there is but one God who is the universal Lord. It answers to the number 1.

So the triangle represents to us and connotes the idea of humanity, in its threefold aspect of spirit, soul, and body, its three-dimensional world of relativity and thought, and its threefold concept of time. It answers to the number 3.

The cross represents matter, but the cross is only the cube unfolded. Its number is 4.

What we have said of certain numbers we hold to be true only by reason of the correspondence existing between the higher and lower worlds, the sphere of causes and that of effects, the noumenal and phenomenal worlds. Not that numbers have any qualities or virtues of their own, but that they acquire such by reason of their quantitive relations to the causative world, which is the world of thought. A number is a seal or impress of natural law as surely as is the shape of a flower, the sound of an atmospheric vibration, the colour of an etheric wave. The orbit of a planet has relation to its mass, bulk, and velocity ; and similarly the significance of a number answers to definite archetypal or noumenal relations.

By all of which we mean no more than this : that

there is a system of interpretation in numerology which is supported by experience, but has its origin beyond the realm of the phenomenal world. If no such system existed, it would be impossible to prove the geometrical relations of thought. But this is done daily by those who make use of numbers for purposes of divination.

Divination may be regarded as both a science and an art. It assumes the properties of a science when there is a conscious process of discrimination, calculation, and interpretation involved. It may be called an art when it is conducted by subconscious and automatic means. This distinction is necessarily only a crude one, and open to many objections. I think I am right in saying that the activity of what we call the subconscious mind, in contradistinction to the attentive mind, and the related functioning of the automatic faculty, are facts admitted by science. But, however that may be, it is nevertheless a fact that there is a certain submerged area of the mind-sphere which is linked up with the World-Soul and is capable of automatically reflecting the things contained in the *memoria mundi*. This we see in the phenomena of psychometry, telepathy, and spontaneous clairvoyance. I regard astrology as in the nature of a science, as much so as astronomy, on which it is based, but inclusive also of the higher chemistry of nature, which has regard to the properties and reactions of the celestial bodies. The man who affirms the solidarity of the solar system and denies interplanetary action is an illogical fool. If he affirms interplanetary action and denies the possibility of planetary influence in human life, without inquiring whether such is a fact or not, he is a mere impostor.

The whole universe is linked up by such correspondence as is affirmed by astrologers to exist between the macrocosm and man. I cannot tell you why the sign Aries is related to the encephalon. I can only assert it as a fact in nature brought home to me by repeated experience of the effects of planets in that sign. We know that there is a force in nature which we call the attraction of gravitation. Science recognises the fact while yet unable to demonstrate the attraction. What has been hitherto regarded as a " pull " will later be more successfully demonstrated as a "push." Professor Hinton has said: " We know a great deal about the How of things ; it is the Why we do not understand." I totally disagree with him. We are deplorably ignorant of the first principles of existence. Our science is a mere record of observed phenomena and experimentation. It must always be so while we are ignorant of the nature of Life itself.

On the other hand, we leave our science behind, and make appeal to philosophical and religious principles when answering to the Why of existence. In such circumstance as this it will be convenient to regard the whole universe merely as a symbol of mind. The laws of thought imposed upon us by nature are as fully satisfied here—

⊙	☽	⊕
O	△	+
1	3	4

as by the most complex demonstration of the *Principia* of Newton or the three laws of Kepler. It is merely a matter of interpretation if we regard the universe as a symbol ; and what else it, or any part of it, may be I have not yet discovered.

All symbols, *i.e.* ideographs, are geometrical expressions of thought. So figures are expressions of numbers, as numbers are of quantitive relations. When the astronomer affirms that the planets move in elliptical orbits, he is employing a symbol and expressing a quantitive relationship. He is not expressing a fact, for he knows that no body could describe an ellipse about a moving focus and not be left behind in space. Yet he affirms the elliptical orbit and the proper motion of the sun through space at one and the same time. When affirming the elliptical orbit, he finds it convenient to posit a symbolical or fixed focus in the sun and a kenofocus in space. The demonstration is elaborate. It answers to observed phenomena. But so did the epicycle of Ptolemy. The ancient Chinese formulated a theory of eclipses which was found to be workable and in line with the events, but they had no conception of the earth as a spheroid. So, whether it be epicycle, ellipse, or cycloidal curve, it is pure symbolism ; an expression of quantitive relationship, not necessarily of fact.

Similarly, when the chemist uses the symbol H^2O or $H^2O2 =$ water, he expresses a quantitive relationship which does not inform us in any way concerning the process by which nature derives the fluid from the two gaseous volumes. You are left to discover the nature of oxygen and that of hydrogen, and whether the compound is mechanical or chemical. In this case it is mechanical, as if one should take two apples and one orange, and say, " Here is fruit."

If we admit the symbolism of the astronomer and that of the chemist, recognising it as an empiricism, we may not be accused of being unreasonable in asking that ours also may be recognised on the same grounds.

Whatever science we may study we shall find that it has its own terminology, its symbolism, and its empirical methods. Mathematics, as the basis of all science, is itself a universal symbolism, a language into which all knowledge is eventually translated and rendered communicable. The key to all knowledge is in the science of numbers.

CHAPTER III

NUMEROLOGY

HAVING cleared the ground by a general considera
tion of the principles involved in the science of
numerology, we may now proceed to an exposition
of the subject both from a traditional and empirical
point of view. I trust I have made it clear that no
claim is made for any occult power or mystic virtue
inhering in numbers as such. If they possess any
such power, it is solely by reason of associated ideas
in the human mind. I regard numbers only in the
light of symbols, and in this light I conceive it
quite possible, nay, even probable, that the higher
Intelligences who guide the destinies of mankind
may employ them as an universal language in order
to signal to our minds something concerning the
trend of things which is essential to our welfare. If
minds may be instructed by visions, dreams, and
oracles, they may also, and more generally, be so
by means of the mute language—I might say indeed
the mute eloquence—of numbers. If, as Pythagoras
said : "The world is built upon the power of
numbers," then numbers must be the key to the
understanding of the world. That many remarkable

C

prophecies have been, and can be, made by means of numbers is certain, and both Nostradamus and l'Abbé Goachim made use of them for this purpose. It was the recognition of the numerical value of letters that caused a change of name whenever a change of vocation or destiny was intended. The change of Abram's name to Abraham, that of Jacob to Israel, and similar occurrences recorded in the Hebrew Scriptures, have a definite pointing in this direction.

Some systems proceed by literal values, *i.e.* the numerical power of letters, and others by the sound or phonetic values. I may give an instance of the two methods for the purpose of distinction :—

```
N  a  p  o  l  e  o  n  e
5  1  8  6  3  1  6  5  1     = 36 = 9, Mars.
B  u  o  n  a  p  a  r  t  e
2  6  6  5  1  8  1  2  4  1 = 36 = 9, Mars.
```

Total, 36 + 36 = 72 = 9, Mars.

Here the phonetic value of the letters of both Christian and surnames amounts to a unit value of 9, which is the number of Mars, of fire, and the sword, of incision, direction, force, violence, and strife. It is a name that is " painted red all over." The key used is that of Haydon.

The literal enumeration, using the Hebraic values for the same name, yields Napoleone = 361 = 10 = 1, Sun ; Buonaparte = 815 = 5, Jupiter, which, according to the ancient Hebrew interpretation, would denote dignity, power, egotism, rulership, increase, and expansion. A highly fortunate combination of names.

At various stages in his remarkable career, he changed his signature from Napoleone Buonaparte (the original Corsican form) to Napoleon Buonaparte, Napoleon Bonaparte, Napoleon, and finally N——.

Many interpreters have used, with great success, the values attached to numbers by the Tarot,[1] especially the Twenty-two Major Keys, which, as I have elsewhere shown, represent the three stages of initiation into the Mysteries, consisting of the ten, seven, and three steps respectively, and ending in 21, " The Crown of the Magi," or 22, " The Fool." [2]

In the Tarotic enumeration, in its present form at least, the Twenty-two Keys are thus briefly defined :—

I. The Magician. Symbol of the Creator, who produces the universe apparently by the magical power of thought. The adept.

Symbol of the creative will, volition, desire, mastery of physical forces.

II. The Priestess. Symbol of the divine Sophia, creative imagination (allied to the creative will), Isis or Maya.

Symbolises the Gnosis, the creative power, attraction and repulsion, the law of the sexes, chemical affinity, imagination.

III. The Empress. The first product of the divine will and imagination, Urania.

---

[1] *The Key to the Tarot*, A. E. Waite. London : Wm. Rider & Son, Ltd.

[2] *A Manual of Occultism.* Wm. Rider & Son, Ltd., 1911.

Symbolises ideation, production, expansion, growth, riches, plenty.

IV. The Cube, or the Emperor.

Realisation of the virtues, affirmation and negation, discussion and solution. Happiness by attainment. Material effects. The concrete. Establishment, foundation.

V. The Hierophant or Master. Denotes the universal law, religion, discipline, precept and teaching. Liberty, regulation.

VI. The Two Ways, or the Lovers. Denotes discrimination, knowledge of good and evil, conscience. Privilege and duty, instinct, sex relations.

VII. The Chariot of Osiris. The knowledge of the seven principles, magnetic power, intellection, sensation, fulfilment of ambitions.

VIII. Justice. The sword and balance. Denotes retribution, judgment, reason, moderation, temperance, impartiality.

IX. The Hermit or Veiled Lamp. Denotes incarnation, prudence, circumspection, classification, selection, science, discovery, carefulness.

X. The Sphinx, or Wheel of Fortune. Cause and effect, the moral law, periodicity, revolution, circulation.

XI. The Muzzled Lion. Denotes power, force, determination, conquest, direction of force, determination, mastery, vitality.

XII. The Sacrifice. Spiritual debasement, reversal, overthrow, inversion, madness, depolarisation, loss, undoing.

XIII. Death the Reaper. Change, reaction, disappointment, denial, catalepsy, collapse, ruin and death.

XIV. The Two Urns. The vital forces, friendship, social obligations, reciprocal affection, chemistry.

XV. Typhon or Satan. Evil, wilfulness, mystery, controversy, fatality, passion, malice, riot and lawlessness.

XVI. The Stricken Tower. Sudden calamity, pride of intellect, ostentation, cataclysms, earthquakes, storms, overthrow, accidents.

XVII. The Star. Faith, assurance, hope, illumination, intuition, birth, success, expectations.

XVIII. The Twilight or Moon. Darkness, doubt, hesitation, negation, imbecility, lunacy, an adverse change.

XIX. The Great Light or Sun. Vital energy, magnetism, joy, happiness, strength, success, honours, elevation, attainment.

XX. The Resurrection. Spiritual awakening, genius, aspiration, activity, new regime, utility, work, occupation.

XXI. The Crown. Long life, power, adeptship, steadfastness, endurance, position, honours, distinction, wealth, inheritance.

XXII. Folly. Necessity, privation, egotism, credulity, error, vanity, blindness, ruin, insanity.

As in the enumeration of name values, it is the unit value which is finally significant, though the gross value is of some consideration. It may be convenient to reduce one or two of the alphabets to their numerical equivalents. The following are the unit values of the letters standing against them in the two enumerations, viz. :—

Hebraic.	Pythagorean.
1—A I Y Q J	1—A K T
2—B C K R	2—B L U
3—G L S	3—C M X
4—D M T	4—D N Y
5—E N	5—E O Z W
6—U V W X	6—F P J
7—O Z	7—G Q V
8—F Ph P H	8—H R Hi
9—Th Tz	9—I S Hu

The phonetic values, which have relation to the planetary enumeration, are as follows :—

1—A E Y or I (long)
2—B, K, R, PP, G (hard), O (short), Q, X
3—J, G (soft), Sh, L
4—D, T, M
5—N
6—U, OO, V, W, S
7—Z, O (initial)
8—P, Ph, F, H (aspirate), Ch (hard)
9—Th, Tz

Now each of these systems has to be employed in relation to its own method of interpretation.

The Hebrew method is employed for the kabalistic interpretation of the Scripture as in the *Zohar*. It is especially suited to the Tarotic interpretation by the Twenty-two Major Keys.

The ancient writers veiled their secrets by employing one of three methods :—

(a) The *Tem* which the letters of a word were replaced rs after a definite method. They first wr alphabet in three lines, representing the tens, and hundreds. These lines, each of ers, were again divided into three groups, nine in all. Any letter falling in the roup could be interchanged with another me group. Thus—

9	8		5	4	3	2	1
ט	ח		ה	ד	ג	ב	א

90	80		50	40	30	20	10
צ	פ		נ	מ	ל	כ	י

900	800		500	400	300	200	100
ץ	ף		ך	ת	ש	ר	ק

(b) *Gime* is was an arithmetical method by which rd was replaced by another having the merical value.

(c) *Nota* lection was made of certain letters acc he rules of the art, these letters being take e beginning, middle, or end of the words nce, so as to produce a single word from t ination.

Finally, th a secret writing, which was based upon murah. Thus the sentence, "God said : L ere be light," appears in this glyph as follows :

ꝉ ꙅ ᖍ ꙅ ᖍ ᑯ ꙅ ᖍ ᑯ ꙅ ᖍ ᑯ :

The Pythagorean alphabet is used in connection with the interpretation employed in that system.

In this system, every number up to 50, rising thence by tens to 100, has a definite signification ; and every succeeding hundred has a separate meaning. To these original interpretations others of a fanciful nature have since been added, as 365 = " astronomy and astrology," no doubt on account of the division of the year into 365 days ; and 666 = " enmity, secret plots, maliciousness," because of its use in the Apocalypse as the number or name of The Beast, which some took to be the devil incarnate, while others fitted it to the names of several illustrious persons in history, imputing to them an evil character ; when in fact, as Mr James Pryse has shown, it meant no more than the animal mind—*i.e.* the natural or lower intelligence of the average man, called in the Greek 'H φρήν.

The value or signification of the numbers, according to the Pythagorean scheme, is as follows :—

1. Impulse, passion, ambition.
2. Death, fatality, destruction.
3. Religion, faith, destiny.
4. Solidity, strength, power.
5. Marriage, pleasure, joy.
6. Perfection of work.
7. Rest, happiness, equilibrium.
8. Protection, justice.
9. Grief, anxiety, maiming.
10. Reason, success, aspiration.
11. Discord, offence, deceit.
12. A fortunate writing—a town or city.
13. Wickedness, wrong.
14. Sacrifice, loss.

15. Virtue, culture, integrity.
16. Luxury, sensuality, good-fortune.
17. Misfortune, disregard, oblivion.
18. Miserliness, hardness, tyranny.
19. Foolishness, insanity.
20. Wisdom, rigour, melancholy.
21. Mystery, fecundity, production.
22. Chastisement, penalty, hurt.
23. Revolt, bigotry, prejudice.
24. Travelling, exile, inconstancy.
25. Intelligence, progeny.
26. Benevolence, charity.
27. Bravery, heroism, daring.
28. Gifts, tokens, omens.
29. News, a chronicle.
30. Marriage, celebrity, celebration.
31. Goodness, aspiration, publicity.
32. Marriage nuptials, consummation.
33. Gentleness, virtue, grace.
34. Suffering, retribution, penalties.
35. Health, peace, competence.
36. Intuition, genius.
37. Fidelity, marital joys.
38. Malice, greed, deformity.
39. Laudation, honours.
40. Wedding, feasting, holiday.
41. Disgrace, scandal, abuse.
42. Short life, misery.
43. Worship, religion, sanctuary.
44. Elevation, kingship, ovation, magnificence.
45. Progeny, population.
46. Fecundity, fruitfulness.

47. Long life, happiness.
48. Justice, judgment, a court.
49. Avarice, cupidity.
50. Freedom, release, easiness.

60. Marital bereavement.
70. Initiation, science, integrity, virtue.
80. Protection, recovery, convalescence.
90. Affliction, disfavour, error, blindness.
100. Divine favour, ministry of angels.

200. Hesitation, fear, uncertainty.
300. Philosophy, knowledge, protection.
400. Long journeys, pilgrimage, exile.
500. Holiness, sanctity, selection.
600. Perfection, perfect performance.
700. Might, dominion, authority.
800. Conquest, empire, power.
900. Strife, war, feuds, eruptions.
1000. Mercy, charity, sympathy.

In the calculation of a name the values given above in the Pythagorean alphabet are set down in place of the letters. The total is then made, and the number is dissected by hundreds, tens, and units.

Thus, by taking out the unit values in the name of the great Liberal Minister of State, William Ewart Gladstone, we have—

William = 4922913 = 30 = 3
Ewart = 54181 = 19 = 1
Gladstone = 721491545 = 38 = 2

Then, from the total 312 we derive—

> 300 = philosophy, knowledge,
> 12 = a fortunate writing, a city,

and from the unit value of the sum 312 we get 6 = " Perfection of work," the very characteristic of the man.

The phonetic alphabet is used in connection with the planetary significations as given in Chapter I. I consider these values as altogether the most reliable and uniformly satisfactory. It should be observed that only those letters which contribute to the sounding of the word or name are to be employed. I have already given an instance in the case of Napoleone Buonaparte, the sum and unit values of which name = 9, the number of the sword, strife, etc. Tested by the same code, we have—

$$
\begin{aligned}
\text{Gladstone} &= 23146465 = 31 = 4 \\
\text{William} &= \quad\quad 6314 = 14 = 5 \\
\text{Ewart} &= \quad\quad 16124 = 14 = 5 \\
\hline
\text{Sum,} &\quad\quad\quad\quad\quad 14 = 5
\end{aligned}
$$

Here the number 5 dominates the characteristic signature, being inherent in the personal names of the great statesman, displaced in the family name and appearing in the sum of the whole appellation. It denotes reason, logic, ethics, travelling, commerce, utility.

It will be seen that logic, ethics, and utility are outside the sphere of party politics, universally

ascribed to this character, and are dominant in the
enumeration of the name. A glance at his most
successful opponent in the political world will be
of interest—

$$\text{Benjamin} = 2153145 = 21 = 3$$
$$\text{Disraeli} = 472131 = 18 = 9$$

$$\text{Sum,}   12 = 3$$

Here we have expansion, increase, capacity, riches,
and success repeated in the forename and the sum,
while in the surname 9 contributes that element
of strife, energy, enterprise, and keenness which is
associated with the political career and policy of
this striking and successful personality.

The conjunction of Jupiter $= 3$ and Mars $= 9$ in the
name denotes a tendency to extravagance, while it
also contributes an index of tremendous enthusiasm.
In the combination of Mercury $= 5$ and the Sun $= 4$
in Gladstone's name, on the other hand, we have a
more careful, orderly, and practical disposition indicated, the predominance of the number 5 giving
logic and rhetoric in a marked degree.

In the name of John Milton we have the Sun and
Moon combined, showing genius, change, travelling,
distinction ; but the sum of the name is 8, which
closes the life in tribulation and deprivation.

The illustrious name of William Shakespeare is
compounded of a double Mercury, which confers
reason and logic, and yields the sum of $10 = 1$, the
Sun, denoting honours, distinction, individuality.

His eminent contemporary, Francis Bacon, Lord

Verulam and Viscount St Albans, yields the values—

$$Francis = 821566 = 28 = 1$$
$$Bacon = 21225 = 12 = 3$$

Sum, 4

the numbers showing individuality, distinction, ambition, riches, increase, expansion, pride, realisation, and materiality ; a fortunate combination in many respects.

There is another kabala of great interest and instruction which has respect to the date of birth, and brings out successive periods of good and evil fortune in the life, when interpreted by the Tarotic alphabet from which it is derived ; but this I must deal with in another chapter.

CHAPTER IV

VARIOUS METHODS OF KABALISM

It has already been shown that the Hebrews, Aryans, and Greeks had each their methods of kabalism—that is, of using numbers in place of letters, and of giving to numbers a specific significance. It will now be my object to illustrate some of the more generally approved methods of kabalism, so that others may apply their own tests and gain advantage of personal experience in this study.

The Hebrew alphabet has special reference to the Tarot—which is obviously of Semitic origin, although it has received a more catholic interpretation. The method of applying the Tarot to the resolution of a person's signature is as follows :—

The values of the letters are set down against a person's name and multiplied successively by the number answering to the converse position of the letter in the name. The Christian and surnames being thus dealt with, the totals of each name are extended and added together, to which also the place of the Sun at his birth is added. The sum of

all is the key number of the name, and this, added
to the year in which the person is born, yields the
sum of the nativity, which, when extended and
added, gives the Tarotic signature of the person.
Thus—

John Milton, 9th December 1608 (O. S.) =19th
December (N. S.).   Sun in 9th sign, 28th degree.

							Sign	Degree
J	$1+4=$	4	M	$4\times6=$	24			
o	$7\times3=$	21	i	$1\times5=$	5			
h	$8\times2=$	16	l	$3\times4=$	12			
n	$5\times1=$	5	t	$4\times3=$	12			
			o	$7\times2=$	14			
			n	$5\times1=$	5			
		46			72		9	28

Then $4+6+7+2+9+2+8=38$ Key

1608   Year

1646   Sum

Here the key number, $38=11$, answers to the
Tarotic Key called *The Muzzled Lion*, which
denotes force, determination, mastery, vitality;
while the sum of the nativity, $1646=17$, answers
to *The Star of the Magi*, denoting hope, illumination, intuition, success.   This interpretation is
certainly apposite to the character and work of
the epic poet.

The key number, when thus obtained from the
Sun's position and the enumeration of the name,

is further applied to the current year in order to obtain the signature of that year.   Thus—

$$\begin{array}{r} \text{Key number}\quad 38 \\ \text{Year}\quad 1674 \\ \hline 1712 = 13 \end{array}$$

Then 13 is the signature of the year 1674 in regard to John Milton, native of the 28th degree of Sagittarius.

The 13th Major Key of the Tarot is *The Reaping Skeleton*, change, collapse, reaction, death; and in the year 1674 John Milton died.

Other examples of an equally striking nature will be found in my *Kabalistic Astrology*.

Another method of using the Tarot Keys consists in adding together the year and the age a person attains in that year, making a sum which answers, when reduced, to one of the Tarot Keys.   Thus, Napoleon was born in 1769.   He became First Consul for life in 1801, aged 32. $1801 + 32 = 1833 = 15$, an evil portent.   *Typhon* seated upon the iron cube in the Inferno.

Emperor in 1804, aged 35. $1804 + 35 = 1839 = 21$. *The Crown* = position, power, honour, distinction.

Divorced Josephine in 1809, aged 40. $1809 + 40 = 1849 = 22$.   *The Blind Fool* = selfishness, vanity, inconsequence, blindness, detachment, conspicuous folly, etc.

Defeated at Waterloo, 1815, aged 46. $1815 + 46 = 1861 = 16$.   *The Stricken Tower* = the descent of Typhon, pride of intellect and its consequences, humbling of the autocrat, overthrow, reversal, ruin, catastrophe.

It is not necessary to multiply instances.   These will occur to every reader, and considerable interest will be found to attach to the calculation and interpretation of the numerical values of personal instances.   It will hardly be necessary to point out that only great import attaches to the names and dates of great men.   Where one literally gains a crown under the 21st Key of the Tarot, another, of less ambitious life and smaller powers, should be well pleased with a commensurate fulfilment such as a rise in position or some passing honours.   The measure of one's soul in the universe is an equation not easily solved, and I know of no means—outside of direct revelation—other than astrology which can aid in that direction.   Yet it is well to know in what sphere of activity the powers may be most profitably employed, and to this end the Kabalists have devised a key based upon the square of three, which is the Table of Saturn or Fulfilment.   The square of 3 is 9, and if we arrange the digits 1 to 9 in such form that they make a magic square, i.e. so that it counts to the same total in any direction, we shall have this figure :—

4	9	2
3	5	7
8	1	6

Here it will be seen that the sum of any three figures, in any direction, =15, which number has already been mentioned as one of the sacred numbers, as it embodies the name of the Deity.

These numbers, 1 to 9, are divided into three groups, namely, the spiritual, the intellectual, and the material. Thus, the Sun 1, Jupiter 3, and Mars 9, are the *spiritual* numbers. The Moon 7, Mercury 5, and Venus 6, are the *mental* numbers; while Saturn 8, Sun 4, and Moon 2, are the *physical* numbers. We have, therefore, a second arrangement of these nine figures, which now stand as follows :—

3	1	9
6	7	5
2	8	4

On the base line we find the vital or solar principle, the astral or lunar, and the principle of mortality involved in their association, represented by Saturn.

In the middle region we have the emotional principle of Venus and the intellectual or Mercurial principle, united as Hermes-Aphrodite, to form the psychic or soul principle proper to the human being in process of evolution, represented by the positive lunar principle.

In the superior region there are represented the principles of freedom, that of expansion, and that of individuality, denoted by Mars, Jupiter, and the Sun respectively.

The next step is to take the date on which a person was born, employing always the date at noon preceding the hour of birth, for this is the true solar date, being 12 hours behind the secular date. Thus, 26th June, at 5.40 p.m. = 26th, while 26th June, at 9.0 a.m. = 25th, the 26th day not being complete until noon of the 26th. Let us suppose, for instance, a person born on 26th June at 10 a.m., in the year 1899. This gives us the date 25 − 6 − 99. The century figures are not employed. From this we derive the following table :—

		9'
6		5
2		

The first point that strikes us is the double 9; but as this is common to the year, it must not be taken as specially applicable to the person, but to the generation. He comes, then, of a stock making for spiritual enfranchisement, zealous and enthusiastic. Next we observe the 6 as peculiar to the month of the birth. This gives artistic faculty and intellection, tending to expression in art. Next we have the 2 as still more closely related to the individual. It shows material changes, flexibility, unstable fortunes, no strong bias, but much sensibility.

Lastly, the number 5 claims our attention, and this is the number which gives the final and personal touch to the direction of character and fortunes. It shows a capable intellect allied (through 6) to the artistic and ornamental ; some accomplishments.

Next we take the sum of the figures 25699 =31 =4, which shows a practical tendency to the whole character, a disposition to realise.

Finally, we take the combinations represented by the planets.

Moon (2), conjunction Venus (6).

Mars (9), conjunction Mercury (5).

The first of these shows art, music, poetry; the social accomplishments ; refinement. The other denotes keenness, alertness, acumen, with some degree of cupidity, cunning, and opportunism.

Having observed that the sum of the nativity is 4, it will be seen that any date whose figures add to the unit value of 4 will be fortunate to this person ; while those which have the unit value of 8 will be unfortunate. The key to this effect being that the Sun (4) is opposed by Saturn (8), Saturn tending to destroy both ☽ and ☉. For, on the material plane, Saturn (8) is the element of corruption involved by the relations of the Sun (male) and Moon (female) elements of Nature, as here shown :—

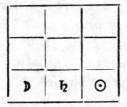

But, in its relation to the higher union of the Sun (spirit) and Moon (soul), it subserves the purposes of development and evolution, being, as it were, the corruptible husk whence spring the spiritual germ and its envelope or sheath. Wherefore, it is said : " It is sown in corruption ; it is raised in incorruption," which has reference to the soul of man. For which reason we posit the numerical analogue—

It will be seen that the planetary numbers are employed throughout, and also the planetary interpretations as already set forth. In this scheme—

1 stands for individuality, domination, egotism.

2. Flexibility, change, instability, travelling.

3. Expansion, increase, growth, opulence, congestion, riches.

4. Realisation, materiality, practical results, pride, ostentation.

5. Intellection, learning, activity, commerce, language, science.

6. Art, poetry, music, the social accomplishments, affection, love, sympathy.

7. Psychic force, influence, popularity, voyages adaptability, versatility, progress.

8. Corruption, disease, death, decay, loss, hurt imperfection, obstruction, privation.

9. Freedom, energy, keenness, acumen, zeal penetration, fire, fever.

The following synoptical charts will prove of interest :—

Napoleon I.
14/8/69.

Cecil Rhodes.
5/7/52.

Sum, 28 = 1.

Sum, 19 = 1.

Conjunctions.
Sun and Mars.
Sun and Saturn.

Conjunctions.
Moon and Mercury 2.

Shakespeare.
3/5/64.

3		
6	5	
		4

Sum, 18 = 9.

Conjunctions.

Jupiter and Venus.
Mercury and Sun.

Milton.
19/12/08.

	1'	9
2	8	

Sum, 21 = 3.

Conjunctions.

Sun and Mars.
Moon and Saturn.

The most amusing parallelism, and one that I think will conjure an answering smile to the lips of my readers, is to be found in the following :—

Cagliostro.
19/6/43.

3	1	9
6		
		4

Sum, 23 = 5.

Conjunctions.

Sun and Jupiter.
Sun and Mars.
Venus and Jupiter.

Sepharial.
19/3/64.

3	1	9
6		
		4

Sum, 23 = 5.

Conjunctions.

Sun and Jupiter.
Sun and Mars.
Venus and Jupiter.

This clearly shows some constitutional affinity, and the same may be traced in the famous parallelism of St Louis of France and King Louis XVI., thus—

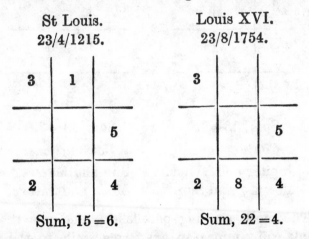

St Louis.
23/4/1215.

Louis XVI.
23/8/1754.

Sum, 15 = 6.

Sum, 22 = 4.

Wherein we see that in the chart of St Louis the Sun is dominant and conjoined with Jupiter, while in the case of Louis XVI. the superior Sun is in obscuration, and Saturn involved by a conjunction with the inferior Sun and the Moon. In the one case we have the Christian saint who was anxious to give up his throne and become a monk; and in the other an unfortunate monarch who was deposed and executed, his son being consigned to prison, where he died.

Now, by the numerical values of the names Louis IX. and Louis XVI., we obtain—

Louis IX. = 3619 = 19 = 1, Sun,
Louis XVI. = 36116 = 17 = 8, Saturn,

clearly showing the difference of their fortunes. Those who would pursue the subject, however, may find some interest in the remarkable kabala of the two kings of France set forth in my *Manual of Occultism.*

The chart of Oliver Cromwell shows a remarkable feature.   He was born 4/5/1599, or, old style, 25th April of the same year :—

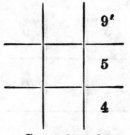

9'

5

4

Sum, 27 = 9.

Here the zeal, fire, and sword of Mars is most conspicuous, as it comes twice in the year number and also in the sum of the nativity ; the conjunctions being Mars and Mercury, Mercury and Sun.

The unfortunate exile, Napoleon III., has a chart quite in line with his known character and destiny. He was born on the 20th April 1808, of which the chart is—

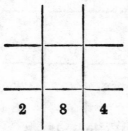

2 | 8 | 4

Sum, 14 = 5 ;   conjunctions, Moon and Saturn, Sun and Saturn ; a fairly rotten basis on which to effect a restoration.

It would be possible to adduce an indefinite number of instances in which the character and fortunes are clearly denoted. I may here cite an illustrious example or two before concluding :—

Queen Victoria, 23/5/19—

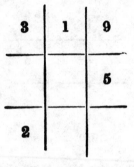

Sum, 20 = 2.

In which the conjunctions are : Sun and Jupiter, Sun and Mars, Mars and Mercury.

Horatio Nelson, 29/9/58—

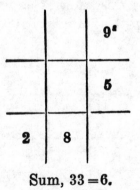

Sum, 33 = 6.

The deprivation of the right eye and right arm are shown by the conjunction of Moon and Saturn ;

the dominant double Mars, the zeal and fighting genius of the great admiral; while Mars and Mercury conjoined point to his astuteness, acumen, and alertness of mind. The sum 6 gives that Venusian touch to the character which is in line with the best traditions of the naval profession.

It should be carefully observed that the old style dates must be converted to new style before dealing with them; and, further, that the astronomical date must be taken in all cases, the observation being that, when the birth took place in the afternoon, the date is the *same* as the secular or civil date; while if it took place in the morning, the astronomical date will be that of the previous day in the civil calendar.

Emperor William II. has a characteristic chart—

27/1/59.

1	9
7	5
2	

Sum, 24 = 6.

The conjunctions are those of Sun and Mars, denoting the spiritual zeal and tireless energy of an enthusiastic nature, with Moon and Mercury, showing learning, activity, commerce, etc. The sum of the nativity gives just that touch of art and sociability which rounds off the corners of a naturally intense and keen nature.

The chart of the Empire, proclaimed 18th (morning) of January 1871 = 17/1/71, is very remarkable—

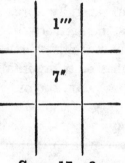

Sum, 17 = 8.
Conjunctions, Sun and Moon.

It shows a triple Sun and double Moon, which surely ought to make it shine ; but the sum of the chart is unfortunate.

The chart of the Union of Ireland and Great Britain does not show elements of stability—

2nd January 1801.

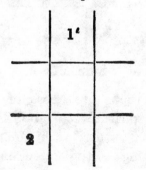

But, if it was effected in the forenoon, then a double Sun presides over its destiny, to the greater advantage of the kingdom.

On the whole, I think, it will be seen that the chart of the Square of Three, when properly dealt with, is capable of yielding some very striking results, both in regard to character and fortune. The Chinese use this chart in their divinations, and it is, perhaps, the oldest form of which we have any record.

CHAPTER V

NUMBER, FORM, COLOUR, SOUND

THE system of numerical kabalism I am here unfolding is linked up with other subjects through an astrological tradition. Once we admit the possibility that numbers may have an othic or symbolical value in human affairs, we have to seek for a key to this relationship.

But, before doing so, it should be made clear what it is we are affirming. It is this : Numbers have a signification or symbolical value irrespective of (a) our recognition of their symbolism, and (b) what we are led to recognise as natural causation. Let us look at these two theorems for a moment. If I posit the formula of the law of permutations $(2^n - 1)$ I am putting up a symbol which is intended to signify or signal something to the mind, as, for instance, that the possible combinations of any three principles, sounds, or colours, $= 2 \times 2 \times 2 - 1 = 7$. You may or may not read the signal, but that does not in any way alter either the law expressed by the formula or the truth of the expression. I say, therefore, that numbers have a symbolical value irrespective of our recognition of their symbolism. I have already affirmed the universe as a symbol. It exists, and has existed, for immense ages as a symbol, quite outside of our recognition as such. We are only now beginning to read its meaning. God [1] has been signalling us from our infancy. We have been ages learning the code; but we have it, and now we are engaged in reading the message.

The ancients displayed their knowledge of the symbolism of nature when, after the Triune Deity, they placed the seven great powers or archangels. " The One produced the Three, the Three produced the seven. These ten are all things."

There is no natural sequence between the number 8 and the things that number signifies to us. We find it attaching to all that is sinister and unfortunate. It is the chief terminal number, as we have seen, as it denotes death, decay, ruin, privation, loss, imperfection, and corruption. The idea is universal. The eighth division of the heavens is astrologically held to signify death and loss. The 8th sign of the zodiac is Scorpio, with its associated symbols Serpentarius and Draconis, nocturnal, poisonful, and death-dealing. After the 7th day of creation or unfoldment, death makes its appearance in the world. That is to say, after the universe has attained its fulness of evolution, it will begin to devolve, as a tree that has put forth leaf and flower and fruit begins to die down to its root. In our kabalism also we find this number in evidence wherever there is maiming, physical or

[1] The Lord Creator of our universe, not the inscrutable Absolute and Unmanifest.

mental imperfection, as in the case of Nelson, injured in sight and limb ; Milton, blind of both eyes ; Louis XVI., decapitated ; and an unfortunate host of others. I cite only an instance. If we can trace this covert agreement between the symbolism of nature and events of human life, or expressions of individual character, we may surely affirm that it exists apart from natural causation, for there is no causative relation between the occurrence of a number in a man's name or the date of his birth, and any event or characteristic we may associate with such a number.

A number, then, is merely a quantitative relationship, and a figure is that by which we symbolise it. The human personality is only a symbol by which a man expresses himself to his fellows. The physical universe is the personality of the universal Soul.

Accepting numbers as symbolical, therefore, we are led to seek for the key to this relationship. It exists, and can be traced to the ascriptions of the ancient astrologers. They affirmed planetary action in human life, and traced a connection of a symbolical nature between the domination of a particular planet and the repetition of a certain number in the life of an individual. Had they been the ignorant instead of the most enlightened of their time, they would have given to numbers something more than a symbolical signification. As it was, they regarded them as part of the system by which the gods signalled us, and in this light also they regarded the whole cosmos, the sun, moon, the planets, comets, and stars, as portents carrying to us not an influence in a natural or causative sense, but a significance in a symbolical sense. They learned to interpret the language of nature, and hence arose their systems of astrology and numerology, which latter they afterwards used to hide their secrets from the uninitiated.   Hence arose kabalism.

In this system they had a conception of the relations of man to the universe, calling him, in fact, the microcosm.

They divided the microcosm into four principles, the imperishable soul which reflected the Trinity of Deific Powers, the rational soul, the animal soul, and the gross body.   These they related to the cosmic bodies, conceiving them to be enveloped by an aura which defined their sphere of action and maintained their relationship, just as they held that the solar system was limited by a crystalline sphere.   They placed them in this order :—

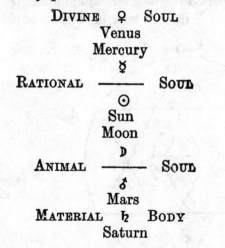

DIVINE ♀ SOUL
Venus
Mercury
☿
RATIONAL ——— SOUL
☉
Sun
Moon
☽
ANIMAL ——— SOUL
♂
Mars
MATERIAL ♄ BODY
Saturn

The cosmos was thus completed, the surrounding

E

and enfolding sphere of Jupiter, which they called
the auric body, being thus represented—

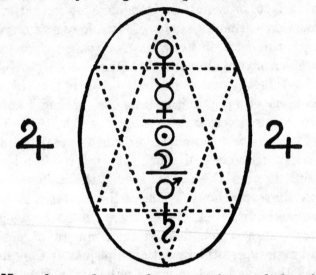

Now, by replacing these cosmic symbols with
their corresponding numerical symbols, the basis of
this system of numerology is at once apparent—

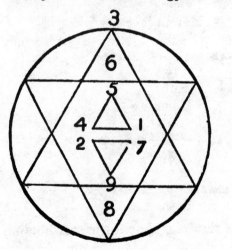

3

6

5

4 + 1

2 + 7

9

8

The total of these figures is $45 = 15 \times 3$, the triple name יה, in the understanding of which we are exhorted to praise.

Having shown the basis of the planetary enumeration, which will better appeal to students of esoteric philosophy than to others, I may now proceed to a consideration of planetary forms.

Observe, then, that 9 is associated with all sharp, keen, and pointed things, such as are made of steel and iron, spears, lances, scalpels, swords, knives, flints, tongues of flame, etc.

8 is a symbol of involution, and represents all serpentine and scroll forms, the convolute ⑥ and double convolute ⑧, the letter s, and all sibilant sounds, as in hissing.

7 represented by crescent forms, dexter curves, and horned shapes.

6 is associated with symmetrical and well-formed bodies, graceful curves and rounded figures, in which symmetry and balance are the prevailing feature.

5 is related to sharp but disjointed forms, articulations, links, and jointed bodies.

4 is connected with square bodies, rectangles, crosses, and horizontal lines.

3 with triangles, tripods, and bodies having three divisions ; also with integumenta, envelopes, and spheroids, ovals, and bodies capable of expansion and contraction.

2 is a number associated with sinister curves, forms having round bases, as bowls, vases, etc., parallels and pairs of things, such as pillars, etc.

1 represents upright columns, monoliths, spheres, circles, perpendicular lines, and orifices.

The colours associated with the planets, **numbers,** and forms, are—

> 9   Red or crimson.
> 8   Black or deep brown.
> 7   Silver or opalescence.
> 6   Pale blue or turquoise.
> 5   Indigo or dark blue.
> 4   Orange or ruddy gold.
> 3   Violet.
> 2   Yellow or cream.
> 1   White.

The notes or sounds answering to the planetary and therefore also to the numerical powers, and their appropriate colours, are as follows :—

C	D	E	F	G	A	B
☉	♄	☿	☽	♂	♀	♃
$\frac{4}{1}$	8	5	$\frac{7}{2}$	9	6	3

Those of my readers who have a faculty for interpretation will do well to consult the 1623 folio of Shakespeare's *Taming of the Shrew,* in which the key to this " gamouth," or gamut of the spheres, is set forth to some extent under a glyph of names and words. I am very certain that Shakespeare was neither Kabalist nor Rosicrucian, but he employs knowledge of both faculties. The astrologer will observe that the poet was born with Neptune in the mid-heaven, a position of no little significance.

Some mystics consider that Uranus falls into the system of numerology by regarding it as the first of a new gamut, corresponding to the Sun, then $1+9=10$ Uranus, while Neptune, "the superior Venus," will have to wait realisation until we have evolved up to $6+9=15$, which is a deific height to which, for the moment, we need not aspire, contenting ourselves by "filling up the spaces in between."

CHAPTER VI

NAMES, NUMBERS, AND INCIDENTS

ONE of the most interesting forms of the kabalism of numbers is that which relates names to incidents by means of the numerical value of letters.

To each letter of the alphabet a unit value is given, the valuation following the Hebrew code, as already given. These values are then multiplied by the inverse order of the letters, the products being finally added together. The unit value of the sum of these products constitutes the kabalistic key number. This key number being referred to the Tarot, an interpretation is obtained.

Each of the Tarotic numbers has a fourfold interpretation, namely, a spiritual, intellectual, psychic, and physical, the correspondence running through from the world of principles to that of causes, thence to the world of effects, terminating in the world of ultimates, which is the concrete world of physical phenomena.

The full interpretation of the Twenty-two Major Keys of the Tarot will be found in my *Manual of Occultism*, but I have thought it wise to give a brief rendering of the keys in these pages, as the reader is constantly referred to them. The method

followed in this kabalism will easily be understood
by the following example :—

Francis Bacon, which is
8215213 21275 =39.

Francis has 7 letters, therefore the highest multi-
plier will be 7.   Then

$$
\begin{array}{rrr}
7 \text{ times } 8 & = & 56 \\
6 & 2 & 12 \\
5 & 1 & 5 \\
4 & 5 & 20 \\
3 & 2 & 6 \\
2 & 1 & 2 \\
1 & 3 & 3 \\
\hline
& 104 & =5
\end{array}
$$

Bacon has 5 letters, and the multiplication begins
with that number and falls to unity—

$$
\begin{array}{rrr}
5 \text{ times } 2 & = & 10 \\
4 & 1 & 4 \\
3 & 2 & 6 \\
2 & 7 & 14 \\
1 & 5 & 5 \\
\hline
& 39 & =12
\end{array}
$$

The interpretation of the whole name is therefore
as follows :—

5. *The Hierophant* or Master of the Secrets =
universal law, discipline, religion, liberty within
the limits of the law.

12. *The Sacrifice* = repression, inversion, overthrow, downfall, the debasement of that which is
superior to the ends of the inferior.

For the sum of the name we have $5 + 12 = 17$,

The Star of the Magi. This denotes revelation, knowledge, illumination, success.

" The star " presiding over the destiny indicates a remarkable birth, a brilliant career, but danger of untimely dissolution or obscuration.

In connection with this kabala I am glad to be able to cite an instance of Bacon's mastery of kabalism which was published in the *Associated Accountants' Journal* recently. It employs an anagram, cryptogram, and a numerical kabala. In the 1623 folio edition of *Love's Labours Lost*, Act iv. Sc. i., occurs the concatenabolic word " honorificabilitudinitatibus," which is found to be the key word of the anagram : *Hi ludi orbi tuiti F. Baconis nati*, which is rendered : These plays entrusted to the world were created by F. Bacon. The numerical value of the letters follows the order of the alphabet, the letters I and J being identical. Then the word is enumerated thus—

H O N O R I F I C A B I L I T U D I N I T A T I B U S
8, 14, 13, 14, 17, 9, 6, 9, 3, 1, 2, 9, 11, 9, 19, 20, 4, 9, 13, 9, 19, 1, 19, 9, 2, 20, 18

The first and last letters in each part of the anagram are used for the kabala, thus—

8	H	I	9
11	LUD	I	9
14	ORB	I	9
19	TUIT	I	9
6	F.		
2	BACONI	S	18
13	NAT	I	9
73	+	63	= 136

This is the first key.

The second key is obtained by adding together the value of all the letters included between the first and last in each word :—

U D R B U I T A C O N I A T
20, 4, 17, 2, 20, 9, 19, 1, 3, 14, 13, 9, 1, 19 = 151

The last key is found in the number of letters in the word : Honorificabilitudinitatibus, which is 27, and also in the cryptogram, *Hi ludi orbi tuiti F. Baconis nati,* which also is 27.

Reference to the folio under these numbers—

Page 136
Line   27
Word 151

disregarding all words in parenthesis, brings us to the remarkable word (honorific., etc.) from which we set out in this most remarkable kabalistic enumeration. Bacon was a Rosicrucian, and would be familiar with the employment of the kabala in all its forms. Can we say the same of Shakespeare ? If not, we must conclude on the evidence before us that a man of immeasurably greater erudition and faculty set his seal and signature upon his own work and committed it to the play-actor for production, casting his bread upon the waters in certain knowledge that it would return to him after many days.

An interesting kabala may be derived from the use of the following values :—

A	B	C	D	E	F	G	H	I
J	K	L	M	N	O	P	Q	R
S	T	U	V	W	X	Y	Z	
1	2	3	4	5	6	7	8	9

It has been used to show the affinity or connected-
ness between names used in conjunction, and
those also that are used in substitution or become
welded by association and the force of circumstance. By this code

> William $=34=7.$
> Gladstone $=34=7.$
> Napoleon $=38=2.$
> Bonaparte $=38=2.$
> Jack $= 7$ for John $=7.$
> Flo $= 7$ for Florence $=7.$
> Harry $= 7$ for Henry $=7.$

This observation is by " Numerary " $=7$, whose
Christian names are William $=7$, and Henry $=7$.
He gives the following instance of associated
names :—

> Crippen $=9$.   Le Neve $=9$.

As casual observations they are useful and interesting, but the code does not lend itself to a symbolical interpretation. The Hebrew code in connection with the Tarot, and the planetary code in
connection with astrology, do, on the other hand,
lend themselves to a very consistent symbolism.
Thus, it has been shown that the name of a warship
has a numerical value which, when reduced within
the limit of the 22 keys or letters of the Hebrew
alphabet, answers to the ascription of the Point of

the Tarot, to which it is directly referred by that number.

Among American ships there stands out in tragic relief the ill-fated *Maine*, $=41155=16$, and Point 16 of the Tarot is *The Stricken Tower*, the citadel overthrown, catastrophe, etc.

Among our British vessels there are three which bear the sinister names of

$$Serpent = 3528554 = 32 = 5$$
$$Viper = 61852 = 22$$
$$Cobra = 27221 = 14$$

Point 22 is *Blind Folly*, unforeseen danger, error. Point 14 is *The Two Urns*. The vessel broken in two.

The significance of the number 8, which is the serpentine or reptile number, and its associations with death and loss, has already been mentioned. Among vessels whose value is 8 there is the troopship *Birkenhead* $=2122558514=35=8$.

The *Royal George*, another ill-fated vessel, has the value of 12, *The Sacrifice*, the victim, reversal, overthrow, etc.

In the *Manual of Occultism*, I published a kabala called the "Secret Progression." It is there applied to the solution of a somewhat complex problem, which was this :—

The number of births which took place in 36 large towns in Great Britain in a particular week of the year were given from the published reports of the

Registrar-General. It was required to find the number which would take place in the same towns in a corresponding week in the ensuing year. This problem was successfully resolved by the kabala of the Secret Progression.

This kabala, when perfected, answers four tests, viz.: the minor additive, the major additive, the minor differential, and the major differential. The whole process having been displayed in the instance cited, I will only, in this place, give an illustration of the two additive keys. This case concerned a lottery result submitted to me by a correspondent. The past five winning numbers in the first thousand were—

$$342, \quad 651, \quad 298, \quad 542, \quad 631,$$

and I had to find the next.

Minor Additive.

1. $342 = 9 = 9$
2. $651 = 12 = 3$ $\quad = 12 = 3$
3. $298 = 19 = 1$ $\quad = 4 = 4 \quad = 7$ $\quad = 14$
4. $542 = 11 = 2$ $\quad = 3 = 3 \quad = 7$ $\quad = 13$
5. $631 = 10 = 1$ $\quad = 3 = 3 \quad = 6$ $\quad = 12$
   ——— $\quad = 3 = 3 \quad = 6$
6. ? 2

There is a numerical series of 14, 13, 12, which requires that the number shall be one whose integers add up to 2, 11, or 20.

Major Additive.

$$
\begin{array}{l}
342 \\
651 = 993 = 21 \\
298 = 949 = 22 \\
542 = 840 = 12 \\
631 = 1173 = 12
\end{array}
\quad
\begin{array}{l}
= 43 \\
= 34 \\
= 24 \\
= 15
\end{array}
\quad
\begin{array}{l}
= 77 \\
= 58 \\
= 39
\end{array}
$$

$$\;?\qquad\qquad 3$$

This yields a number which, added to 631, gives a sum the integers of which have a unit value of 3. From these two numerical series 14, 13, 12—77, 58, 39, which show equal intervals, we have obtained some notion of the constituents of the number required. The Major Additive Key gives us a closer inspection, but there are yet too many numbers answering to the requirements of the process. These are rapidly disposed of by the Differential Methods (minor and major), and in effect we have the number 497, which answers all the tests. Its integers $= 2$ as required by the Minor Additive process, thus, $4 + 9 + 7 = 20 = 2$. When added to 631, the last winning number, the sum of $1128 = 1 + 1 + 2 + 8 = 12 = 3$, as required by the Major Additive. The number of the winning ticket in the first thousand of the 6th series was 497.

A correspondent sends me the following case of a successful divination by this kabala. The figures are taken from the actual results of a public lottery held at stated intervals. The numbers used are from 1 to 90, and out of these only one number is drawn. The previous five winning numbers were 30, 46, 77, 30, and 79. The 6th is required to be known. Then,

By the Minor Differential.

$$
\begin{array}{llllll}
30 = 3 \\
 & = 7 \\
46 = 10 & & = 4 & = 11 = 2 \\
 & & & & = 8 \\
77 = 14 & & = 11 & = 15 = 6 \\
 & & & & = 12 \\
30 = 3 & & = 13 & = 24 = 6 \\
 & & & & = 16 \\
79 = 16 & & = 13 & = 19 = 10 \\
 & & 6 \\
? \quad 10
\end{array}
$$

The intervals being equal, the number required will be one whose integers add to 10.

By the Major Differential.

$$
\begin{array}{llllll}
30 \\
46 & 16 & 7 \ldots 7 & 11 & 2 \\
77 & 31 & 4 \ldots 4 & 6 & 6 & 8 \\
30 & 47 & 11 \ldots 2 & 6 & 6 & 12 \\
79 & 49 & 13 \ldots 4 & 10 & 10 & 16 \\
 & ? & 6 \ldots 6
\end{array}
$$

The intervals being equal, the number required is one whose difference of 79 yields a number whose integers add to 6.

There is no need to proceed further, as there is only one number fulfilling the requirements of both tests, viz. 19, whose integers add to 10 and whose difference of 79 yields 60, whose integers add to 6. Number 19 was the winning number.

These numerical progressions appear to have been successfully used by that much-abused initiate who called himself Count Cagliostro. They have been found to have a connection with the sequence of events when derived from a radical epoch. Thus the House of Brunswick began with George I. in

1714, which is therefore a radical epoch.   Then by progression—

George I. ascends	1714
1+7+1+4	13
George II. ascends	1727
1+7+2+7	17
Stuart Rebellion	1744
1+7+4+4	16
George III. ascends	1760
1+7+6+0	14
American Rebellion	1774
1+7+7+4	19
French Revolution	1793
1+7+9+3	20
The Grand Alliance	1813
Prince George Regent.	

The fall of Robespierre the Incorruptible, in 1794, affords an epoch in the history of France.   Thus—

Robespierre fell	1794
1+7+9+4	21
Napoleon fell	1815
1+8+1+5	15
Charles X. fell	1830
1+8+3+0	12
Death of Duc d'Orleans	1842

(Eldest son of Louis Philippe and heir to the throne of France.)

Thus history reveals to us this correlated successiveness or law of numerical sequence which we find to have representation also in the lives of individuals. Those who diligently apply themselves to the study of numerology will continually find confirmation of this law, which is observed by nature in cosmic relations, as in the common expression of Kepler's law, by which we know that a projectile force varies inversely as the square of the distance, the application of which to the solar system gave rise to Bode's law, which is thus represented :

☿	♀	⊕	♂	*	♃	♄	♅
0	3	6	12	24	48	96	192
4	4	4	4	4	4	4	4
4	7	10	16	28	52	100	196

these figures being an approximation to the proportional distance of the planets from the Sun, where R.V. Earth = 10. The actual figures in these terms are—

☿	♀	⊕	♂	*	♃	♄	♅
3·9	7·2	10	15·2	—	52	95·4	191·8

If the planets had no influence on one another, and their motions were consequently uniform, then their distances would not display the proportional differences noted.

The whole groundwork of astronomical science points to the regard which nature has to quantitive relations—that is to say, to numbers—and consequently the study of numbers, their properties and combinations, serves to educate the mind to an anticipation of the greater problems of celestial laws by the operation of which the universe is what it is and the destiny of man such as we find it, both racial and individual.

Nothing could be more convincing in regard to the integrity of Nature and her conservancy of the established relationships of her components than the astronomical fact that, in a system of mutual interaction—where everything is in a condition of unstable equilibrium—the ratios of the distances and motions of the planetary bodies remain undisturbed. Thus, while constantly maintaining the invariable laws of her constitution, Nature affords opportunity of change, development and evolution to every living product.

CHAPTER VII

CHANCE EVENTS

WHEN we speak of a chance event, we really express our ignorance of the law governing the occurrence. We do not seriously assume to mean that Nature has not provided for such event, or that it had no natural causation. We speak of coincidences, as when an astrologer makes a singularly pointed prediction which afterwards proves to be in line with the facts. But we must not think that in the use of that word we have disposed of the scientific possibility of prediction. We may take comfort in it as did the old lady in the blessed word " Mesopotamia," but that is all that it can do for us. The use of the expression " coincidence " is a scientific statement of a fact. We assert thereby that the time and circumstance prescribed in the prophecy *coincide* with the event in fulfilment—that the prediction, in short, is true to time and nature of event.

But many coincidences make a law. If some apples fell off the trees into space, some obliquely into our neighbour's garden, and others directly to the earth, the law of gravity would never have been discovered. Ages ago things were supposed to fall because they were heavier than air, and a good deal of suffering would have been spared the pioneers of scientific thought had this belief been maintained. The fact, however, that all the apples fell in lines perpendicular to the tangent of the earth's circumference, *i.e.* in a straight line towards the earth's centre, and that one of them coincided with the thinking-box of a scientific man, set the whole world wondering. The attraction of gravitation had been discovered. Modern science has said much which is contrary to the *Principia* of Newton. To-day it has stumbled up against certain phenomena which seem to indicate that, after all, it may not be the attraction of gravitation that does these things. The facts do not answer to the theory of attraction. When it is seen that intermolecular ether is negative to spatial ether it may be found convenient to look at the obverse side of the door, and, instead of reading " pull," the scientist may find " push " as an answer to his question. In other words, bodies may be impelled towards the earth by the " push " of spatial ether, instead of being drawn to the earth by the " pull " of the earth's mass. So much, then, for the argument from coincidence. Suppose that, instead of relegating everything we do not understand to the domain of chance, we endeavour to seek a law which shall not only include the facts but render the prediction of others of a similar nature possible. I will hazard a suggestion which may form a working basis for an intelligible theory of prediction.

We have already viewed the universe as the personality or embodiment of a Creative Power. We have seen that it is a symbol, and that it answers to a system of physiognomy by which we have learned something concerning the character of the Creator whose forces ensoul it. Let us, then, regard the universe as man. The Rosicrucians so regarded it, and called it Adam Kadmon; Swedenborg called it the Grand Man, the Macroprosopus.

The astrologers have for many ages related the encircling zodiac to the zones or divisions of the human body. Aries they found to correspond to the head, Taurus to the neck, Gemini to the arms, and so down to the feet, which correspond to Pisces. "As above, so below"; the great is reflected in the small. The circle of the zodiac has its mundane relations. An empiricism continued through many centuries determined the signs corresponding to various areas of the earth, to territories, kingdoms, cities, and towns.

The method employed was that of the scientific experimentalist. Here is a toxine, let us see what effect it will have when injected. The experiment yields certain results, and research is made for an antidote, something that will neutralise the action of the poison. Or, a bacteriologist makes a culture of germs and studies their effects upon animal bodies. He also experiments on the culture itself to ascertain what medium favours the development of the germs, and what tends to sterilise the medium and render it fatal to the development of the germs. Then, by empirical means, he has two great facts before him : (a) that certain germ cultures produce certain morbid conditions in animal bodies, and (b) that certain media neutralise the action of these germs.

The astrologers followed the same method. They observed the effects following immediately upon the ingress of the various planets into the signs of the zodiac, and what happened during the stay of the planet in each sign. They determined the specific natures of the planets and their modifications by a careful and patient empiricism. Then the deductive method was more extensively employed, and, from like causes, like effects were anticipated. A retrospective calculation gave them the means of ascertaining the past effects of planetary positions, while a prospective calculation enabled them to predict what might reasonably be expected from identical causes in the future.

When two clouds are electrified, one becomes negative to the other, they rush together, and their impact produces thunder ; while the discharge of electricity produces lightning, as if the terminals of a battery were brought together. The lightning flash is only a big spark.

Now, the astrologers had already discovered that Mars was a positive planet and a heat producer, while Saturn was a negative planet and a cold producer. They were naturally curious to observe what effects would transpire when these planets were in conjunction, i.e. in the same part of the heavens as seen from the Earth's centre.

There were two means open to them, one being

to " wait and see," the other retrospection. By a combination of the known orbital motions of the two bodies, they were able to construct a table of the past conjunctions of these planets through the entire circle of the zodiac. Astronomy, chronology, and history conspired to the result, and the effects of the conjunctions of Mars and Saturn in the successive signs of the zodiac were predicable in a general manner for all time. Needless to say they were of an adverse, and most frequently of a violent, nature.

There is a conjunction of these planets every alternate year, the conjunction falling in the next sign on each occasion ; so that in 265 years it performs nine revolutions, and comes nearly to the same place in the zodiac.

If we trace the conjunction through recent years, we find a singular uniformity of ill effects attending upon the countries ruled by the sign of conjunction.

Sagittarius rules Spain and Italy, the opposition Gemini ruling the United States ; Capricorn rules India, Aquarius rules Russia, Pisces rules Portugal, Aries rules England, Taurus rules Ireland, Cancer rules Scotland and Holland, Leo rules France, according to ancient observations. Let us trace some recent events :—

1897. November, Mars and Saturn conjoined in
        Sagittarius.
        Hispano-American War, 1898.
1899. December, conjunction in the same sign.
        King Humbert of Italy assassinated, 1900.

1901. December, conjunction in Capricorn.
    Bande-Mataram Agitation, 1902.
1903. December, conjunction in Aquarius.
    Russo-Japanese War, 1904.
1905. December, again in Aquarius.
    Russian Revolt, 1906.
    " Red Sunday," 1906.
1907. December, conjunction in Pisces.
    Assassination of King and Crown Prince
        of Portugal, 1908; Followed by Re-
        volution.
1909. December, conjunction in Aries.
    Death of King Edward VII., 1910.
    Democratic Ascendancy, 1910.
1911. August, conjunction in Taurus.
1913. August, conjunction in Gemini.

What we may expect to follow will best be
defined by reference to the past effects of similar
positions. The last conjunction in Taurus was
1881. This was the year of the Agrarian outrage
in Ireland, and the murder of Burke and Cavendish
in Phœnix Park.

Using our greater period of 265 years, we find
the following parallel :—

1644. Saturn and Mars in Aries.
+265 Marston Moor. Overthrow of the Royalists,
    1644.

1909. Democratic Ascendancy, 1910.
    Death of King Edward, 1910.

1646.   Saturn and Mars in Taurus.
+265   The Irish Rebellion, 1646.
———
1911.   The Irish Protest, 1911.

1648.   Saturn and Mars in Gemini.
+265   London invested by Cromwell, 1648.
       King Charles in flight.
       The House of Lords abolished, 1648.
       King Charles beheaded, 1649.
———
1913.

1650.   Saturn and Mars in Cancer.
+265   Great Floods in Holland, 1650.
       Scotland invaded and reduced by Cromwell,
         1650.
———
1915.

The question now arises, what connection have planetary periods with numerology ? In a general sense they tend to establish the physiognomy of Nature as a scientific study. If the powers that be elect to signal us by means of celestial phenomena, why not by numerical figures ? If by planetary periods we may trace the periodicity of events, why not by numerical sequences ?

What we have to remember is that there is no such thing as chance in a universe controlled by law. We have to reduce all our observations to a statement which, if not conformable to any known law, is at least not in conflict with such laws as we know. A law should include all the facts. A theory should be sufficiently elastic to admit new observations. An intelligent theory of the universe leaves room for variety of interpretation.

The Hindus say that the period of 120 years is the sum of a human life. Ptolemy, who had no associations with Hindu thought, ascribed the periods of the planets as follows :—

Moon 4 years, Mercury 10, Venus 8, Mars 15, Jupiter 12, and Saturn 30, and all these periods are comprehended in 120, which is their least common measure.

From this we derive a very interesting kabala as follows :—

Moon   4 years into 120 = 30
Saturn 30 ,,   ,,   ,, = 4

The Moon and Saturn are opposed to one another in nature, and rule opposite signs.

Mercury 10 years into 120 = 12
Jupiter 12 ,,   ,,   ,, = 10

Jupiter and Mercury are opposed to one another, and rule opposite signs.

Venus   8 years into 120 = 15
Mars   15 ,,   ,,   ,, = 8

Venus and Mars are opposed to one another, and rule opposite signs ; the whole scheme being thus symbolically expressed :—

Plan.	Signs.	Per.	Per.	Signs.	Plan.
♂	♈ ♏	15	8	♎ ♉	♀
♃	♐ ♓	12	10	♊ ♍	☿
♄	♑	30	4	♋	☽

Outside of this scheme is the Sun, ruler of ♌,
with a period = 1 year = 360°, embracing 3 times 120,
the symbol of divinity, or the Trinity in Unity.

The period of Mars multiplied by that of Venus
= 120 years.

The period of Jupiter by that of Mercury = 120
years.

The period of Saturn by that of the Moon = 120
years.

In one day the Sun completes its apparent circuit
of the heavens, and advances 1°, making 361°.
This quantity is 19 × 19, and Ptolemy gives the
period of the Sun as 19 years. It is also to be
observed that the Sun and Moon are conjoined in
the same point of the zodiac every 19 years. Thus
we see that there is a connection between periodicity
and the symbolism of the heavens, and between
symbolism and numerology.

CHAPTER VIII

REDUCTION TO LAW

WE have now come to the point where it will be advisable to attempt the task of reducing these detached or chance experiences to law.

In this process I shall make use of three keys already referred to in this work, but not yet clearly set forth.

The first is the astral key, the second the name key, and the third the number key. The last two may conveniently be dealt with together in a separate chapter. I will take the astral key first as being the foundation of the system of symbolism I am about to use.

The circle of 24 hours is a natural symbol corresponding to the zodiacal circle of the year. Every day the Sun rises, passes the meridian of a place, and sets upon the west horizon, completing a day of mean value 12 hours, the night being of value 24 − D.

At the equinoxes, March 21 and September 23, the Sun rises at 6 and sets at 6, the day being at the mean value. During the summer the day is longer and in winter shorter than the mean, according to the latitude of the place.

The circle of 24 hours is divided into day and

night. The day of 12 hours (+ or −) is divided into 12 equal parts called planetary hours, which are each of equal length, but more or less than 60 minutes according to the season of the year.

The planetary enumeration of the hours begins at local sunrise, the first hour being ruled by the planet which gives its name to the day, thus—

☉	Sun	rules	Sunday.
☽	Moon	,,	Monday.
♂	Mars	,,	Tuesday.
☿	Mercury	,,	Wednesday.
♃	Jupiter	,,	Thursday.
♀	Venus	,,	Friday.
♄	Saturn	,,	Saturday.

Then the Sun will rule the first hour on Sunday, the Moon the first hour after sunrise on Monday, and so on. The other planets rule in rotation, as shown in the following table of Planetary Hours:—

HORARY SPECULUM

DAYS.	PLANETARY HOURS.											
	1	2	3	4	5	6	7	8	9	10	11	12
Sunday	☉	♀	☿	☽	♄	♃	♂	☉	♀	☿	☽	♄
Monday	☽	♄	♃	♂	☉	♀	☿	☽	♄	♃	♂	☉
Tuesday	♂	☉	♀	☿	☽	♄	♃	♂	☉	♀	☿	☽
Wednesday	☿	☽	♄	♃	♂	☉	♀	☿	☽	♄	♃	♂
Thursday	♃	♂	☉	♀	☿	☽	♄	♃	♂	☉	♀	☿
Friday	♀	☿	☽	♄	♃	♂	☉	♀	☿	☽	♄	♃
Saturday	♄	♃	♂	☉	♀	☿	☽	♄	♃	♂	☉	♀

The night hours begin at 13 in continuation of this table, which only gives the 12 diurnal hours. If the nocturnal of Sunday are continued on after ♄ 12, it will be found that they terminate at 24 ☿, and the next hour, being the first hour after sunrise on Monday, is ruled by the Moon.

The next thing to determine is the hour of local sunrise. A very slipshod and wholly erroneous method in common use—through the agency of a would-be Kabalist, who should be astronomer also but is not—consists in adding the longitude west of Greenwich to the time of sunrise at Greenwich. This would be a correct procedure for the time of the Sun's meridian passage if applied to the right ascension of the Sun or the time of its apparent transit at Greenwich; but, in regard to sunrise, it leaves out of consideration the important factor of ascensional difference due to latitude of the place.

The calculation is not difficult, so that I do not hesitate to inflict it upon my readers, especially as they are presumed to have a *penchant* for figures :—

Formula.—To the log. tan. of the *latitude* of the place, add the log. tan. of the Sun's *declination* = the log. sine of the Sun's *ascensional difference* under the said latitude.

Add this ascensional difference to 90° when the Sun's declination is south, and subtract it when the declination is north. Multiply the result by 4, and call the degrees *minutes*, and the minutes call *seconds*. The result will be the time before noon at which sunrise occurred locally. There is, of course, a small second difference due to the variation of declination, but this is quite inconsiderable if the declination be taken for 6 a.m. every day.

Example.—Time of sunrise, 30th April 1911, at Greenwich. Sun's declination from Ephemeris at

$$
\begin{array}{lll}
\text{6 a.m.} & \quad . \quad \quad . \quad \quad . & 14° \ 26' \text{ N.} \\
\text{Lat. of Greenwich} & 51° \ 28' \text{ N.} \\
\text{Then tan. log. } 14° \ 26' & 9\cdot41057 \\
+ \quad \text{,,} \quad \quad \text{,,} \quad 51° \ 28' & 0\cdot09888 \\
\hline
= \text{sine} \quad \text{,,} \quad 18° \ 51' & 9\cdot50945 \\
\text{Add} \quad \quad 90\cdot0 \\
\hline
108°\cdot51' \\
\text{Multiply by} \quad \quad 4 \\
\hline
\end{array}
$$

$$435^{m} \ 24^{s} = 7^{h} \ 15^{m} \ 24^{s}$$

Take from 12   0   0

Mean time of sunrise   4   44   36

But, on reference to the almanac, it will be seen that the Sun is before the clock by $2^{m} \ 44^{s}$, *i.e.* the Sun passed the meridian nearly 3 minutes before the clock indicated noon. Therefore, from

$$
\begin{array}{r}
4 \cdot 44 \cdot 36 \\
\text{Take} \quad \quad 2 \cdot 44 \\
\hline
4 \cdot 41 \cdot 52 \\
\end{array}
$$

remains the Greenwich mean time of sunrise.

Astronomers further correct this quantity by aberration, parallax, and nutation; but with these we are not concerned in the present instance.

Now, let us find sunrise at Liverpool on the same

day, the latitude of the place being 53° 25′, and the
declination of Sun as before.

$$
\begin{array}{llll}
\text{Log. tan.} & 53°\ 25′ & 0\cdot12947 \\
\text{"} \quad \text{"} & 14\ \ 26 & 9\cdot41057 \\
\hline
\text{"} \ \ \text{sine} & 20°\ 17′ & 9\cdot54004 \\
\text{To} & 90°\ 0′ \\
\text{Add} & 20\cdot17 \\
\hline
& 110\cdot17 \\
\text{Mult.} & \quad 4 \\
\hline
& 441^{m}\ 8^{s} =7^{h}\ 21^{m}\ 8^{s}
\end{array}
$$

We have already found that the ascensional
difference for London was on 30th April, 18° 51′,
and for Liverpool it is 20° 17′. The difference of
1° 26′ multiplied by 4 gives $5^{m}\ 44^{s}$ as the difference
due to latitude only, so that, if the place were in the
same meridian as London, the Sun would rise on
it nearly 6^{m} earlier than London. But Liverpool
is $12^{m}\ 16^{s}$ W. of London, and thus we have:

$$
\begin{array}{rr}
+\ 12^{m} & 16^{s} \\
-\ \ 5 & 44 \\
\hline
+\ \ 6 & 32
\end{array}
$$

to be added to the Greenwich mean time of sunrise,
which is found, in its corrected value given in the
almanac, to be = 4·37 a.m.

Then to—

Sunrise, London . . .	$4^{h}\ 37^{m}$ a.m.
Add Liverpool equation . .	+7
Time of sunrise at Liverpool .	4 44

which is a very different thing from merely adding the W. long. to the time of Greenwich sunrise, as given by the author of *The Mysteries of Sound and Number*, thus :

By the almanac, 4^h 37^m a.m.
Liverpool West,   12
                        ————
                        4 49

It naturally follows that a system which requires that the time of an event be known within 4 mins. must in these circumstances prove an egregious failure, and require any amount of juggling with the phonetic values in order to accommodate itself (after the event) to the facts.

The view of the Kabalist is that the divisions of time should be natural and not artificial, and that the phonetic values should be constant.

We have found the beginning of our natural day at sunrise.   Let us now find the length of the day :—

The time of sunrise 4^h 39^m 52^s
Taken from   12   0   0
                      ————————————
                       7 20   8
Multiplied by   2
                      ————————————
= Length of day   14 40 16

An easy rule is to multiply the time of sunrise by 2, and it will give the length of the night, which, taken from 24 hours, gives the length of the day, which is double the time of sunset.   Thus—

Sunrise at   4^h 39^m 52^s

                       2

Length of night = 9   19   44

      From   24   0   0

Length of day   14   40   16

And 7^h 20^m 8^s, the time of sunset, $\times 2 = 14^h\ 40^m$ 16^s, as before.

Divide the length of day by 12 to obtain the duration of each planetary hour of that day. As

$$14^h\ 40^m\ 16^s \div 12 = 1^h\ 13^m\ 21\tfrac{1}{3}^s.$$

This quantity, being added successively to the time of sunrise, will give the beginning of the 12 planetary hours.

Thus, for the given day we have—

BEGINNINGS OF HOURS
Sunday, 30 April 1911

1.	☉	4 · 39 · 52 a.m.	8.	☉	1 · 13 · 21 p.m.
2.	♀	5 · 53 · 13 ,,	9.	♀	2 · 26 · 42 ,,
3.	☿	7 · 6 · 34 ,,	10.	☿	3 · 40 · 3 ,,
4.	☽	8 · 19 · 56 ,,	11.	☽	4 · 53 · 25 ,,
5.	♄	9 · 33 · 17 ,,	12.	♄	6 · 6 · 46 ,,
6.	♃	10 · 46 · 38 ,,	13.	♃	7 · 20 · 8 ,,
7.	♂	12 · 0 · 0 ,,			Night begins.

It will be seen that there are 6 planetary hours from sunrise to noon, and 6 from noon to sunset. The former are *positive*, and the latter *negative*. In the present demonstration, we are concerned with the latter part of the day during the negative hours.

The planetary numbers have already been given, and on the Sunday in question they rule as follows:—

SUNDAY

Morning		*Afternoon*	
☉	1 positive.	♂	5 negative.
♀	6 ,,	☉	4 ,,
☿	5 ,,	♀	3 ,,
☽	7 ,,	☿	9 ,,
♄	8 ,,	☽	2 ,,
♃	3 ,,	♄	1 ,,

This means that during the afternoon of Sunday the first hour is ruled by ♂, whose number is 9, but as it is a negative hour it is represented by 5, which is the negative of 9. Thus—

	+	−	
☉	1	4	= 5
☽	7	2	= 9
♄	8	1	= 9
♃	3	6	= 9
♂	9	5	= 5
♀	6	3	= 9
☿	5	9	= 5

We thus see that the positive and negative values of all the planets add to a sum whose unit value is 5 or 9, whence we have the kabalistic value $5 + 9 = 14$, *i.e.* the two aspects (male and female, positive and negative) of the Sevenfold Powers.

SUBDIVISIONS

We have obtained the length of the natural day, and also that of the planetary hours. We now have to subdivide the hour into 7 equal parts as nearly as may be, giving to each part a successional rule, and therefore a numerical value. It will then be seen that each section yields an event which is in harmony with its nature.

For this purpose take the negative hours in the afternoon of Tuesday, the 26th April 1910. The time from noon to sunset is 7ʰ 11ᵐ. Divide this by 6 and obtain 1ʰ 11ᵐ 50ˢ for the length of each planetary hour of the afternoon.

This quantity has now to be divided by 7 in order to obtain the planetary subdivision of the hour. This amounts to 10ᵐ 16ˢ nearly.

We are now able to construct a table as follows :—

Hours Negative

♂ 1. 11.50 p.m.		Commencement of
☉ 2. 23.40 „		hours on Tuesday,
♀ 3. 35.30 „		26th April 1910.
☿ 4. 47.20 „		

Tuesday, 26th April 1910.
Sunset 7ʰ 11ᵐ. Hor. 1ʰ 11ᵐ 50ˢ. Div. 10ᵐ 16ˢ.

H. M. S.	H. M. S.	H. M. S.	H. M. S.
♂ 1·11·50	☉ 2·23·40	♀ 3·35·30	☿ 4·47·20
☉ 1·22· 6	♀ 2·33·56	☿ 3·45·46	☽ 4·57·36
♀ 1·32·22	☿ 2·44·12	☽ 3·56· 2	♄ 5· 7·52
☿ 1·42·38	☽ 2·54·28	♄ 4· 6·18	♃ 5·18· 8
☽ 1·52·54	♄ 3· 4·44	♃ 4·16·34	♂ 5·28·24
♄ 2· 3·10	♃ 3·15· 0	♂ 4·26·50	☉ 5·38·40
♃ 2·13·26	♂ 3·25·16	☉ 4·37· 6	♀ 5·48·56
Hor. ♂	Hor. ☉	Hor. ♀	Hor. ☿

In bringing this matter of numerical values to the test, we must have recourse to names. On the above date there was racing at Newmarket, and the following were the names of the winners of the several races :—

>2.0   Boabdil.
>2.30 Brillante.
>3.0   Castellane.
>3.30 Ulster King.
>4.0   Paltry.
>4.30 Grain.
>5.0   Glacier.

The period from 1.53 to 2.3 p.m. is ruled by the ☽. The hour being negative, we consult the sign in which the Moon is placed on this day, and find by the almanac that it is ♏ Scorpio, ruled by Mars, whose number is 9.

$$\text{Boabdil} = 261243 = 18 = 9.$$

The period from 2.24 to 2.34 is ruled by the Sun, whose negative number is 8.

$$\text{Brillante} = 223154 = 17 = 8.$$

The period from 2.54 to 3.5 is ruled by the ☽ in Scorpio = 9, or negative 5.

$$\text{Castellane} = 21641315 = 23 = 5.$$

The period from 3.25 to 3.35 is ruled by Mars, positive 9.

$$\text{Ulster King} = 236412252 = 27 = 9.$$

The period from 3.56 to 4.6 is ruled by ☽, negative 2.

$$\text{Paltry} = 823421 = 20 = 2.$$

The period from 4.27 to 4.37 is ruled by ♂.

$$\text{Grain} = 2215 = 10 = 1.$$

This is a first exception. The period from 4.58 to 5.8 is ruled by the Moon in ♏ = 9, or negative 5. .

$$\text{Glacier} = 23162 = 14 = 5.$$

But this may be thought fortuitous or possibly

forced. Let us therefore look at the next day, 27th April, when the winners were as follows :—

2.0 Betsy Jane Period ♂
2.30 Desespoir „ ☽
3.10 Neil Gow „ ☉
3.45 Lady Frivoles „ ♄
4.15 Orné „ ☉
4.45 Acunha „ ☽

The ☽ was now in Sagittarius = Jupiter = 3 positive, 6 negative.

Betsy Jane = 21461315 = 23 = 5, won in negative Mars 5.

Desespoir = 41616822 = 30 = 3, won in Moon period with Moon in Jupiter's sign = 3.

Neil Gow = 51322 = 13 = 4, won in period of Sun negative.

Lady Frivoles = 314182637 = 35 = 8, won in period of Saturn.

Orné = 2251 = 10 = 1, won in period of Sun.

Acunha = 12651 = 15 = 6, won in period of Moon in 3 or negative 6.

It is not my purpose in this place to formulate a racing system, but merely to demonstrate the value of sounds, their relationship to numbers, and the connection of both with symbolical planetary periods, which links the whole matter together into a single concept, namely—

The circle = infinity or zero, since all circles are equal to one another and converge in the point at the centre.

We can now pass on to a consideration of other kabalas.

CHAPTER IX

NUMBER AND AUTOMATISM

THERE is a great variety of kabalas in existence; but most of them have fallen into disuse, owing, no doubt, to the general disposition to rely wholly upon the rational faculty, or what is called the common-sense judgment of things. This doubtless is all that is left to the average man, since the intuition has been dulled by constant dependence on external phenomena, and the instinctive or automatic faculty has been left behind in the process of evolution. But, as we have seen in the course of our demonstration, the soul of man (the luni-solar principle) gravitates between the animal and the divine, between instinct and intuition. The automatic faculty at play in the domain of sense is called instinct, while its operations in the domain of the intellect are recognised as intuition. Divination, which depends so largely upon this faculty, is universally associated with the symbolism of numbers.

One such system may here be cited. Everybody knows the magical formula called Abracadabra, which some derive from $\alpha\beta\rho\alpha\chi\iota s$, the limitless or

eternal, but which I think may be with greater
reason defined as the creative word. The form
it takes is that of an inverted triangle, a rectangle,
or a double equilateral.

The two forms are here displayed :—

ABRACADABRA	ABRACADABRA
ABRACADABR	BRACADABR
ABRACADAB	RACADAB
ABRACADA	ACADA
ABRACAD	CAD
ABRACA	A
ABRAC	CAD
ABRA	ACADA
ABR	RACADAB
AB	BRACADABR
A	ABRACADABRA

From this paradigm the numerologists invented
a scheme of divination which takes this form :—

A question being put in so many words as is
convenient for its expression, the number of the
words is counted and set down ; and this figure is
followed by the number of letters in each of the
words.

The figures in this line are then successively
added together, the first with the second, the second
with the third, the third with the fourth, and so on
until they have been paired and added, the one to
the other. The sum, abated by 9 whenever it
exceeds that amount, is set down beneath, so as
to form a second line of figures. These are then
treated in the same manner, by successive pairing

and addition, and a third line is produced. Each successive line being one figure less than the one above it, it follows that the process eventually brings out a single figure. It is this figure that is dealt with in the divination. The number is referred to its planetary equivalent and the interpretation made thence in accord with the nature of the question.

A single illustration will doubtless suffice.

A person asks : "Shall I gain my desire ? "

There are 5 words in this sentence, so the figure 5 is set down. "Shall " contains 5 letters, " I " 1, " gain " 4, " my " 2, "desire" 6. Then the first line will stand thus : 551426, and the kabala, when completed, will be as follows :—

$$551426$$
$$16568$$
$$7225$$
$$947$$
$$42$$
$$6$$

Here the resultant figure is 6, which is the number of Venus, and in reference to the question it reads :—

" There will be a peaceful and satisfactory conclusion resulting in pleasure."

Had the number 8 been the resultant, it would import delay or probable disappointment, for 8 is the number of Saturn = privation.

Had 3 resulted, then Jupiter would augur acquisition, and that readily ; for Jupiter denotes increase, acquisition, expansion, good fortune.

6 brings peaceful solutions and pleasures ; 5

travelling, activity, worry, and anxiety, restlessness, etc. ; 2 or 7 bring changes, uncertainty and vacillation. But 7 is powerful with the influence of women or the public, and 2 shows a faint heart and a change of intention or desire. As 7 is the number of " completion " and the Moon denotes women, we may understand the cryptic utterance :

" The stone that the builders rejected, the same shall become the head of the corner " (corner-stone or capital), an interpretation that should gratify the vanity of those who clamour for women's *rights*, but will be realised only by those who wisely recognise and use their *privileges*.

A variant of this kabala is as follows :—

The resultant digit being an even number, the triangle is searched along the right side and the top line for three other even numbers, which are extracted in order as they occur. But if the resultant be odd, then the left side and tops are searched for three other odd numbers.

These, when found, are set down together with the resultant first obtained, and the whole are then added together. The sum is then divided by 9, and the remainder is the number from which the augury is taken.

Thus, in the example given, the resultant being 9, an odd number, the left side of the triangle of figures yields three others, viz. : 771, all being odd. Then $9+7+7+1=24=6$, from which the augury would be taken and an interpretation made in terms of Venus in relation to the question.

Here it should be remarked that the divination is to be effected always by a method which has previously been determined upon, for the numbers signify nothing of themselves. They gain their significance by the associations we attach to them in our thought, and in this sense only are they symbolical, *i.e.* by association or by employment. If, therefore, Nature employs a numerical symbolism, we may conformably employ certain numbers as symbols, and indeed all numbers, by reference to their components or their unit values. The method employed is therefore of importance, for it would be unreasonable to use one method for deriving our symbol, and another for its interpretation. Decide, therefore, what method of divination you intend to employ, and use that method both in enumeration and interpretation of your question.

Nature uses a symbolism which is wholly unintelligible to the great majority of people, and this fact appears to sustain the argument that numbers have a significance apart from our recognition of it. This, at first sight, may appear contradictory to what I have just said regarding the significance of numbers; but I spoke of them as symbols, and they appear as symbols only when we have learned their true significance and begin to employ them as expressions of quantitive relations. Nature exists quite apart from our individual consciousness, as natural history will inform us, but we cannot exist as individuals apart from the consciousness of Nature. Consequently, nothing of our thought or experience is outside of natural expression. It is, therefore, entirely symbolical, and our best divinations are those which are derived from a strict regard to the language and figuring of Nature.

When I said that Nature uses a symbolism, and that it has consciousness of us as individuals, I regarded it mediately as the expression of Divine Intelligence. It is in reality the Deity, who is conscious in and through Nature, as man is conscious in and through his body.

The celestial motions are part of the symbolism we are considering; each of the planets is a symbol of some special focal centre of deific force. The Moons are symbols, and so are comets. The Sun has been used by us as a symbol of the deific Power for ages. It is probably so used throughout the humanities of all its satellites. It is the first and greatest revelation of God to man.

But Saturn and Jupiter and all of the bodies of the system exist and perform their functions, and symbolise the different aspects and quantities of the One, altogether apart from the consciousness and understanding of the average clodpole. Therefore, we say Nature is a symbol, and that it attains signification for us only when we understand it. Its language being understood, we may employ it, interpreting its dark passages by aid of the few sentences of which we are sure.

If cosmos had no laws, if the planets moved in mixed orbits as they listed and at varying velocities irrespective of their mutual distances, their numbers would cease to have any basis or significance and $2 \times 2 = 9$ would be as true as that $2 + 2 = 4$. It has been suggested that probably the decimal system of enumeration was universally adopted because when a man had counted up to ten he had no more " digits " on which to count. This may be true, probably is ; but it does not solve for us the problem as to why man had ten digits, or, although a freak may be furnished with twelve, Nature gets back to the decimal basis as speedily as possible, as if anxious to correct an error. And it is said, too, that there cannot be more than ten ciphers, because unity, 1, and zero, 0, begin and end the expression of the Deity; and when combined they are ϕ *phi*, the source of all things and the end of all, the alpha, A, and omega, Ω, united as $\mathcal{R}$, the symbol of the palingenesis. But so also do all the other pairs, as 2 and 8 = 10, 3 and 7 = 10, 4 and 6 = 10, for 1 and 9 are the same as 1 and 0. In effect, we find only 5 is left behind, unpaired and unrelated; and 5 is the symbol of Mercury, the intelligent principle in man which stands in the midst of the universe and cognises that which is above and that which is below. The secret of numbers is open to every one who *uses* his five senses, and reflects upon the quantitive relations of the things sensed.

We are as much subject to the laws of sense as to those of thought. Our enumeration is no more arbitrary than our perceptions of colour or sound. Certain combinations of colour and of sound satisfy the sense, while others, on the contrary, offend it. But what of the barbarian standards ? Do they not point the fact that ours is a cultivated sense ? They do ; and by this culture we intend nothing

but the bringing of our own senses into harmonious
relations with a higher standard of perception—that
is to say, into closer relations with the soul of things.
If we have finer perceptions of harmony, it is because
we have finer mental perceptions of the harmonies
of Nature. Before figures were invented to express
quantities, there was a mental perception of quantitive relations. The idea of Venus de Milo existed
in the sculptor's mind before it received material
expression in stone. The idea will persist after the
figure has perished by the hand of Time. Number,
as a universal concept, is variously expressed by
figures of different forms. These forms are in-
constant, as also are those by which we express
sound, but number and sound as mental phenomena
persist after we have ceased to see and hear.

CHAPTER X

THOUGHT-READING BY NUMBERS

WHAT I have previously said in regard to the geometrical relations of thought will have prepared the reader for the following illustration of the process of thought-reading by means of numbers. Thought is of two orders, conscious thought elaborated by the functions of the attentive mind, and unconscious, or what is now called subconscious, thought. This latter function of the mind is abundantly illustrated by the phenomenon of spontaneous telepathy. At any given moment a person's mind is negative to some others and positive to the rest. Every brain, while functioning, creates definite vibrations or waves in the etheric ambient.

These waves impinge upon the brains of others, and, if in syntonic relations with them, will cause an apperception of personality, so that the individuals affected will immediately create a mental image of the person whose thought is projected, and whose presence is shortly made apparent to the senses. There is then the proverbial "talk of angels." Yet it will be found upon inquiry not only that the transmitter is unconscious of any effort towards self-projection, but wholly oblivious of the vicinity of the percipient. The conclusion, based upon a close study of this familiar but little understood phenomenon, is that the subconscious, or subliminal, mind of the projector is not only aware of the presence of other minds, but is capable of projecting itself into immediate relations with them. This projection is received by the percipient as a subconscious impression which presently wells

up into the region of the attentive mind in such way as to create a subject of thought. Extremely sensitive persons not only have an apperception of a presence, but also a vision. By the same or similar functioning of the subconscious mind, we are made aware that certain people are inimical to our interests. We smother the impression in deference to our good taste, or "the proprieties," admit them to our confidence, and everlastingly regret the fact that we did not act upon our "first impressions."

There is, as I have said in a former chapter, a part of us which is in touch with the world-soul, and capable of sharing in the universal experiences of that universal principle. We may express this relationship as in the diagram on the preceding page.

The world-soul is again in its turn linked to the universal soul. The world-soul is the planetary or earth consciousness; the universal consciousness is centred in the solar sphere, which is the co-ordinating centre of the system, spiritually, psychically, and physically. That is why the seers and prophets call the Lord of the Universe the " Day Star " and the " Sun of Righteousness."

But to get back to our position. The geometrical relations of thought are such that every idea is capable of numerical expression, and this fact appears to have been known to the Orientals, for it was from one of them that I had first illustration of it. It was the occasion of a meeting of friends interested in spiritual and psychic matters. I was invited by a Swami to take in hand or think of any object I might select. I immediately complied, taking special precautions that sight of the object was not obtained by him. In his absence from my room I took a postage-stamp, of value one anna, and placed it in a rather large box, holding this latter in my hand. I then recalled the Swami and bent my thought upon the stamp within the box. The Swami asked me to give him a number, the first that came into my mind, and I gave him one. He then immediately described the subject of my thought. It was of "square" form, but longer than it was broad; very thin, it had two colours on one side only, its edges were like a saw, and the value of it was one anna. Needless to say, I was much impressed by the experiment, but said at once that the number asked for was only a blind, and that it was a feat of direct thought-reading without contact. The event proved that I was quite wrong, for he presently described things spoken about in letters as yet unopened, and further made prediction of certain events which afterwards transpired. On each occasion he required that I should give him a number. Finally, he convinced me most forcibly by revealing the process to me so that I was myself able to repeat the experiments quite successfully, and have since used the method on many occasions for describing people's thoughts, answering questions, predicting events, and finding lost things. It is a feat for which one may claim no merit, being wholly dependent on the working of the subconscious mind in the consultant himself. The argument is that the subliminal mind knows that concerning which the supraliminal mind exercises itself, but it lacks the means, while the attentive mind is functioning, of impressing itself. In the use of numbers, however, it finds an automatic means of expression.

It is my intention to give the reader a partial knowledge of the process, sufficient, in fact, to enable him to make experiment of the numerical relations of thought. I remember that one of the earliest opportunities I had of testing my proficiency in this method was when, on a certain evening, I

H

was suddenly surprised to see my *vis-à-vis* at the dinner-table put her hand to her throat with an expression of alarm. I gave her instant attention, and was relieved in some measure when she exclaimed : " I have lost my coral necklace, with all my keepsake pendants on it ! " I immediately undertook to trace the lost article, and, having got a number from her, I announced that the article would be found near an iron railing or partition, and close to where a horse was standing. So much I learned from the number given to me. What followed was merely diplomatic resource, or, as a dramatic artist would say, " business." I knew that the lady had just been walking by the riverside, and I also knew that kine and horses were at grass in the fields beyond the hawthorn hedge which ran along one side of the tow-path. I did not, however, recollect any iron gate or railing. The suggestion of a hunt was quickly followed up, and I led the way, keeping an eye open in the gathering gloom for indications of some iron. We had gone about half a mile when the whinny of a horse was heard, and I laughingly remarked that that was half the necklace. Coming up to the place where the horse stood, we found to our immense satisfaction that its nose was resting on a length of iron railing which had been introduced to repair a gap in the hedge. We stopped at that, and on striking a light, found the broken necklace on the towpath where, in another step, we should have crushed it under-foot. This was the beginning of a career of usefulness in numerology, which has now been under cultivation

for many years. We never talk of things being lost
nowadays. We say they are " unnumbered," or
that " the ticket has come unstuck " ! We find them
by the aid of numbers. Other incidents connected
with the power of thought-reading by numbers will
be found in my *Manual of Occultism.* And now, to
dispense with the undesirable personal element, let
us see how much of the method can be discreetly
communicated.

On a question arising in the mind of a nature
which cannot be answered by reference to the
ordinary channels or means of information, let
9 numbers be set down spontaneously as they
occur, and to these let there be added always the
figure 3, whether that figure has been previously
employed or not. Make a sum of the 10 figures,
and observe the nature of the figures which are
represented in the sum. For the interpretation of
the numbers I must refer the reader to succeeding
chapters, as the matter is of some length.

The process employed is based upon the occult
fact that, if the mind is concerned about any matter,
the figures that are then automatically delivered
by the mind bear a direct relationship to the nature
of the thought, and in themselves afford the means
of a solution. An instance of this may be cited
from the Scripture, which the Kabalists have
revealed. In the prophecy of Jacob concerning
the future of his sons, Judah is referred to as a
lion's whelp. " The sceptre shall not depart from
Judah, nor the law-giver from between his feet,
until Shiloh shall come." The sceptre is Regulus,

the law-giver is Cepheus, and Shiloh or Shuleh is
Cor Scorpio, whose rising is the signal for Regulus
to depart from the mid-heaven with its opposition
point of Cepheus from the nadir. The last two
words of this sentence in the Hebrew are : יבא שילה.
Reference to the Hebrew alphabet will give the
numerical values :—

י	Iod	=	10	מ	Mem	=	40
ב	Beth	=	2	ש	Shin	=	300
א	Aleph	=	1	י	Iod	=	10
ש	Shin	=	300	ח	Heth	=	8
י	Iod	=	10				——
ל	Lamed	=	30		Total	=	358
ה	Hé	=	5				
	Total	=	358				

From this we learn that the spontaneous utterance of the dying patriarch, "Shiloh shall come!"
contained the numerical revelation of the Messiah :
משיח.

When, therefore, we speak of thought-reading
by numbers, we do not refer to the conscious
thought of the transmitter, nor to any special
psychic faculty in the percipient, but to the subconscious thought, or knowledge rather, of the
transmitter, whose external or attentive mind is
seeking a solution ; and to the system of numerology which enables that solution to be found
either by oneself or another.

In the East, but more especially in India, the
science of numbers has been continuously studied,

not only with a view to the higher mathem.
but for purposes of cryptic expression and divinati.

Thus, they number the years according to a
certain sequence, from 1 to 60. The year of the
cycle is then multiplied by 2. From the product 3 is
subtracted. The result is then divided by 7, and
the remainder will indicate the crop conditions of
the year according to the following sequence :—

The remainder being

1. Dearness and scarcity.
2. Plenitude and cheapness.
3. Average yield and steadiness.
4. Dearness and poverty.
5. Plenty and cheap.
5. Adequate at steady value.
0. Scarcity and famine prices.

From this we learn that there is an expectancy
of similar conditions every 4th year, with an intervening period of famine every 7th year.

They have also a numerical system of *Arudha*
by which lost things are found. The number of
the asterism occupied by the Moon, the age of the
Moon and quarter are added together, and from
these, 3 is subtracted. The sum is multiplied by
8 and divided by 7, when, if

1 remains, the article is underground.
2. It is in a pot or kumbha.
3. The article is in water.
4. In the open air.
5. In a shell or husk.
6. In manure or soil.
7. In ashes.

I have not made experiment of this method, as the losing habit is not upon me, and the Victorian code conduces to honesty among menials; but it appears to me that the possibilities in regard to the whereabouts of a lost article are by no means exhausted in this category of seven places.

I have, however, seen hidden things exactly located by means of a system of *sulyāna* based upon similar factors, but it was confined to the house in which the divination was made.

CHAPTER XI

THE SIGNIFICANCE OF NUMBERS

In the preceding chapter I have given the rule for the automatic resolution of questions by means of numbers. The mind having been fixed upon the question to be asked or the matter upon which information is sought, nine numbers are set down, to which 3 is added, and the total is then referred to the nature of the question.

EXAMPLE

What am I thinking of ?

$$985627142 = 44$$
$$\text{Add} \quad 3$$
$$\overline{\quad 47}$$

The answer : "You are thinking of a value, measure, or weight, a matter of proportion, and of yourself in certain relations."

THINGS THOUGHT OF

The sum of 10 numbers being :

1. You think of position, of elevation, things above you, a master or progenitor, a pinnacle, head, or prominence, and its levelling or downfall.

2. Of distance, things remote, a journey or a foreign land.

3. You think of a personal event, an ailment, probably a fever, heat, or anger.

4. Of a domestic affair. The family circle. Love and pleasure; of the heart, or something greatly desired.

5. Of marriage; an understanding or agreement; of things in union or harmony.

6. Of news, things related, a brother, means of communication, journeys.

7. Of a house, of things underground, of land or water in expanse, of the ocean, change, or removal.

8. Of antique things or foreign products, a foreign country, of the Orient.

9. Of a death or loss, of defective contracts, of means of restitution.

10. Of an unfortunate alliance, troublesome agreement, or disputation.

11. Of the value of property, a mine, or matter relating to real estate.

12. Of pleasant surroundings, some festivity, gala, convivial meeting, fine clothes and personal comforts.

13. Of money, speculative matters, gain.

14. Of a short journey, a cruise, or matters connected with messages across the water; a female relation.

15. Of a bereavement or death; funereal vestments, mourning; a loss or misfortune.

16. Of a fortunate and happy alliance, a wife. a good understanding or agreement.

17. Of a servant; or nearer to yourself, of some discomfort, disease, or ailment.

18. Of a pleasant journey; a thing of gold; love, domesticity, or joy; a brother, or a message desired.

19. Of some restraint, confinement, imprisonment, seclusion; a child.

20. Of a journey or letter; something carried; yourself in communication with another; a roadway.

21. Of gain, money, some financial advantage, things in possession, of something white and silvery, a rupee.

22. Of an unfortunate marriage or a sick partner, a bad contract, difficulties, an enemy or rival.

23. Of good living, rich clothes, plentiful food, faithful servants, good health, creature comforts, position.

24. Of uncertain position; a family dispute; children; an unfortunate venture; illicit love affairs.

25. Of much gain, great wealth, gold, the sun, something shining or brilliant.

26. Of peaceful possession, good property, the house, of level ground, foundations.

27. A closed place or room, a short journey by boat; of a brother, or person in relation to yourself; a letter or a messenger.

28. Of yourself in imagination; of white linen; a bowl or silver pot; a new moon.

29. Of ill-health; a blood disorder; poor fare; a time of poverty and trial.

30. Of happy children, a pleasant experience, union, a fortunate dowry or legacy.

31. Of something underground, a snake in the house, a scorpion or reptile, a foreign land.

32. Of a king or rajah, a golden vestment, the sun, your own individuality and character.

33. Of a pleasant message, a good position, a brother, some distinction.

34. Of financial benefit, a purchase of food or other necessaries, grain, etc., some corporeal benefit.

35. Of a female, a birth, a plot or scheme, something secret to yourself; a confinement.

36. Of a loss by speculation, a sick child, an unhappy family, misery and trouble.

37. Of an unfortunate contract, an unhappy marriage, a house or property, a stable.

38. Of a death by malaria or enteric fever; of a journey, a message; of a sister; a neighbouring tank or pool.

39. Of a closed place or temple; a gilded chamber, a king's sequestration or exile.

40. Of money, things of value, jewels or apparel, the price of grain.

41. Of yourself or your figure, your apparel, investiture, food, position, credit.

42. Of a friend, a woman of quality, a patroness or her favour, a gathering of people, a convention.

43. Of ancestral property, an old man, an old building, the value of minerals, a cemetery.

44. Of a brother, a letter from across the seas or from a great distance, a book of theology, a *sástra*, of good health, of personal comforts, a luxury.

45. Of a marriage, of gain or loss, a thing of small value, an anna, tilt, bias, inequality, fraud.

46. Of a friend, a man of position and honour ; something of gold, of value, a jewel, a ring of gold.

47. Of yourself, of justice, of equity, of value, measure, weight, proportion, peace, satisfaction, rest, a death.

48. Of a robing-room, a private place, a servant in hiding, a woman's health, of news from a distance.

49. Of a change of position, your own mother, a thing of distinction, a capitol, a woman in power, a queen or râni.

50. Of a painful journey, a sister in distress, a doleful message, a call to office.

51. Of gain and affluence, a stake or bet, of children, money from afar, a profession.

52. Of personal disease or death, things lost, hidden, or occult, of a manservant ; a red cloth ; hot food ; a doctor ; *yama* ; a reptile.

53. Of high office, the rajah or king, a man in power, loss of gold, a dead lion.

54. Of a dangerous illness, a woman in distress, of a wife, a girl, a contract or agreement, four walls.

55. Of a death, a lost paper, a message gone astray, a young girl, a gathering, a friend.

56. Of a foreign country beyond the seas, of a sea voyage, a *s'akti*, a religious gathering, a publication, a ship, a ghost.

57. Of acquired wealth, a hoard or store, a pension or inheritance, a male relative.

58. Of acquisition, personal influence, a grandee,

vakil or lawyer, a judge, *guru* or *prohita*, instruction, the *Vedas*, a Brahmin; personal property,
estate.

59. Of a death-chamber, a hospital or sick-room,
a male child; the household fire, a venture or
hazard.

60. Of a Parsee; a religious ceremony; a foreign
king; a Rishi; *samādhi*; Brahma; the sun of
heaven; I'shvara; time.

61. Of food; trading; fine apparel; a male
friend; a market-place or exchange; a manservant;
a Vaishnavite Brahmin.

62. Of a writing or agreement; an undertaking
or contract; a legal process; position; master-
ship; a father.

63. Of a dead woman; some lost property; a
winding-sheet or death-cloth; a waning moon; the
wife's dowry; an ablution.

64. Of yourself in regard to position; of acquired property; an inheritance; an old man;
duration; a bargain or exchange.

65. Of a short journey and return; going and
coming; a foot journey; a closed room; a fortunate confinement; a sister; a *mantram*.

66. A *smashâna* or burning ground; a rocky
place; minerals; a medical adviser; a dead friend;
a burning house; dry ground or sand.

67. A dead rajah; the loss of gold; the wife's
dowry; a girdle; a sick child.

68. Of a female child; the home circle; a
position of trust; security.

69. Of clothing; a servant; a ship; merchan-

dise ; food stuffs ; trade ; a thing of science ; a *vedanga.*

70. Of a wife ; an agreement ; a public gathering ; a full moon.

71. A waterpot or *kumbha* ; an old association ; a friend ; yourself with others in company ; a private place or room ; a warder.

72. Of wealth ; a princely friend ; a Brahmin ; a religious meeting ; of sandals and things in pairs.

73. Of a brother ; a position ; the death of a ruler ; a quick journey ; an angry message ; honours ; succession ; a writing.

74. Of a brilliant sun ; a great shining ; eyesight ; a proud wife ; a powerful enemy ; hunting.

75. Of a pleasant place ; a rich estate ; *moksha* ; buried treasure ; cattle.

76. Of a son ; a place of learning ; a school-house ; a bride ; a *Bramhāchāri.*

77. Of a white turban or *dhoti* ; a serving-maid ; medicine ; water ; drinking.

78. Of an aged friend ; an institution ; an old alliance ; a hospital ; a man in prison.

79. Of oneself ; of increase and prosperity, position, power, and affluence ; of extremities, the feet ; a pair of sandals ; an understanding ; a judge or advocate.

80. Of gain ; a risk of loss ; a loss by fire ; of a foreign land ; a far-off death ; a *pralaya* ; a voyage.

81. Of a rich relative ; fine apparel ; golden ornaments ; personal health ; ripe fruit.

82. Of a peaceful death ; a rich dowry ; a

pleasant message ; an elephant ride ; a journey for profit ; a sister.

83. Of trading ; a treaty or agreement ; a lease of property ; a gateway or passage ; a bride or betrothal.

84. Of a daughter ; a tank or bathing-place ; a public festival ; *Durga* ; a holiday ; clean linen ; of one beloved.

At this point the enumerations cease, since there are numbers employed and none can be more than 9, so that $9^2 + 3 = 84$ will complete the resolutions. There are, it will be observed, several interpretations to each resultant number, but when the kabala is worked out to its finality, there is little doubt as to which interpretation to use. Thus, from the resultant figures 36 I obtain, by change of components, the number 156 ; and $36 = 9$, while $156 - 3 = 153 = 9$. From $57 = 12$, I get the permutation 123, and $123 - 3 = 120 = 12$. Then, by a process of selection, a particular signification is derived. The property of the figures employed is of some interest, and, in fact, of eventual importance.

RESULTANT, $36 = 9$

Permutations

$156 - 3 = 153 = 9$
$165 - 3 = 162 = 9$
$516 - 3 = 513 = 9$
$561 - 3 = 558 = 9$
$615 - 3 = 612 = 9$
$651 - 3 = 648 = 9$

RESULTANT, $57 = 12$ or 3

Permutations

$$123 - 3 = 120 = 12 \text{ or } 3$$
$$132 - 3 = 129 = 12 \text{ or } 3$$
$$213 - 3 = 210 = 3$$
$$231 - 3 = 228 = 12 \text{ or } 3$$
$$312 - 3 = 309 = 12 \text{ or } 3$$
$$321 - 3 = 318 = 12 \text{ or } 3$$

I may now proceed to another aspect of the same kabala.

CHAPTER XII

OF THINGS LOST

As will probably be understood when the basis of this kabala is known, the divination may extend to a practically unlimited variety of affairs. Questions concerning the diagnosis of disease, concerning investments, finance, property, position, occupation, domestic and social affairs, can be readily resolved by an extension of the first part of the divination, *i.e.* what is thought of. For if, in this system, the number does not answer to the thing or matter in mind, then no resolution can be made, and the consultant must free his mind of all other matters, concentrate on the simple question or object, and then deliver another series of numbers. It generally transpires, however, that the number reveals the matter in question at once, and the number is then dealt with according to rule.

To deliver a resolution in regard to all the affairs of life would of itself fill a large volume. I shall therefore content myself by a single resolution of things lost. The number being given as before and resolved, if the resultant be

1. The object must be looked for in a principal

room near white linen. A fair child should be questioned.

2. It will be found in the house by aid of a serving maid, in or close to a vase or bowl.

3. In a passage or between papers.

4. The article is in your possession, and is not lost.

5. You will get it back yourself with very little seeking. Look under a hat, turban, or other head-gear.

6. Where sandals or boots are kept, probably on a shelf, stand, or rack.

7. Ask your servant, a maid especially connected with the wardrobe.

8. On a shelf or horizontal ledge. A servant or workman will find it.

9. A child has it among some clothing.

10. You get it back. It is in the chief room.

11. You must take a short journey to a tank, pool, or stretch of water.

12. You have not lost it, but mislaid it near your work, in your office, or by books and papers. It is safe.

13. Look where you keep your cloak, shawl, or shoulder wraps. It is near neck-gear.

14. Under a turban or hat. If outside, try a lavatory, sewer, or drain. Doubtful recovery.

15. Ask the wife (or husband), and, failing that source, look through the stables or where horses are kept.

16. The cook will enlighten you. You will re-cover it.

17. On a shelf or section of a cabinet, where works of art or valuables are kept.

18. The thing is lost in the house, and will be recovered from among clothes.

19. A short distance off in a dry, arid spot or sandy lane.

20. The article is not lost, but mislaid only. It will be found by water, or close to fine linen.

21. You have the article yourself. It is in a box or case which folds in two parts.

22. The thing is on a shelf in the house, and will be speedily found.

23. A short distance away; try another room where clothes are kept.

24. You hold the article. It is not lost in any sense.

25. A speedy finding among your personal effects. Find something white and round. It is there.

26. Ask the oldest man in the house. He will have placed it in safety.

27. Search the stables and question the ghariwān or coachman.

28. A dead loss. Spare yourself the trouble of seeking it.

29. An old servant or syce will give you a hint. The article is returned.

30. You will get it back by inquiry among the children or students. Lost in play.

31. In a closet or drain of the house. By good fortune you get it back again.

32. On a near verandah or ledge; something oblong.

33. You have it, and will find it among your effects, probably in a dhoti or clothes.

34. Near a fire, or in a principal room by a fireplace. It is quite close, and will be soon recovered.

35. In a secret spot near water. Your wife's (or husband's) private room. Try a washing-stand.

36. Will be returned by an ayah or a guardian of children.

37. In a shrine-room or private apartment. Will be found on the premises.

38. You will get it back by a short journey to a place of ablution used by you.

39. The article is not lost, but put aside upon a shelf.

40. You will find it in your own dhoti or other article of apparel; rolled in a turban, loin-cloth, etc.

41. Where the wife's or husband's shoes are kept. In the house.

42. In the house of the bawarchi or cook. Near some water or a kumbha.

43. Not far away. Try the pandal of the ghariwān and the stables. You get it back.

44. You have it. Look among the oil-pots or lamps. It will need purifying.

45. It is as good as found. Put your hand on a shelf and take it.

46. Your partner has it in safe custody.

47. Two servants are working together; question them. The one who is uneasy on his feet could inform you.

48. Where you keep the drinking-water.

49. As good as lost for ever. If found, will be badly damaged.

50. Not lost, but in a box or receptacle of two parts. You have it.

51. You will immediately recover it from a place of ablution.

52. Ask your partner or the chief woman of the house ; her relatives may help you. It has changed hands.

53. A manservant has it in possession now. He will restore it.

54. It is in the family circle. Try the children's quarter.

55. It is on the premises near a rain-pipe, or where water is.

56. A short distance away. A communication with your last halting-place will discover it.

57. You have the article ; it is in a saddle-bag, a hip-pocket, or where your sporting tackle is kept.

58. It is in two persons' hands, and may, with difficulty, be recovered. It has been treated for.

57. An old servant has it. It will be found among bread or in a cake, or in flour.

60. It appears to be lost beyond recovery.

61. In the lower part of the house, near sandals or boots, socks or hose.

62. A journey off. You will not recover it.

63. You have the article. It is in an old, dark place, or among old effects.

64. The article is in your possession. It has been mislaid and forgotten, and will be recovered in due course. Look in dark corners and high places.

65. It has gone out of your possession and will be recovered if at all by employing an agent.

66. It is lost by conspiracy of two servants. It can hardly be recovered. The man with the maimed hand is the one to interrogate.

67. You will recover it by the aid of a young person or child.

68. It is at the top of the house. A servant will fetch it.

69. A distance away. Your last halting-place. Near to a pyal or entrance to a house of a relative.

70. You have the article. It is where water is kept.

71. The article is not lost, but is in your possession. Begin at your feet and you will soon have it in view.

72. It is in your personal possession, close to a kumbha or water-pot.

73. You will recover it by official inquiry.

74. A faithful servant will restore it to you.

75. The article has gone into the hands of young fellows. It will be restored but in a damaged condition or depreciated in value.

76. It is in the house, where bread and cereals are kept.

77. A short distance off. It will be brought to the house by a servant.

78. Some little way off, near oxen. Will hardly be recovered.

79. You have the article. It is close to some steel or iron.

80. The article is in your possession. In a thing

of two parts, a box or case ; footgear is close at hand.

81. Look among clothes, and you may be fortunate enough to find it.

82. Where the cooking is done, in a kitchen. Test the khānsāmah.

83. A young girl will recover it for you. It is near a tank or pool.

84. It is in the house, in a double receptacle, box, or case.

It will be seen that many of the foregoing divinations are particularly pointed and explicit. If true and dependable they are undoubtedly very remarkable. They are true in my personal experience, and I have used them for years and on various occasions, so that I am in a position to speak for them. It is remarkable how completely successful they may prove in the hands of a person possessing the power of divination. This, of course, lies at the root of any divination, whether it has a numerical basis or any other form of symbolical foundation. If the divinatory faculty is there, any form or system may be used, but some are capable of yielding a closer result than others, and for this reason are to be preferred. If the divinatory faculty is not present in a person, he must, when consulting another, make use of a proxy or agent in whom such faculty has been proved by experiment to exist. If a person void of the faculty shuffles a pack of cards, or uses figures as a means of divination, the most expert Cartomante or

Kabalist will prove ineffectual, since they can only interpret what lies before them. It is better that they should conduct the divination from first to last. The faculty does not necessarily lie with the Kabalist. His work begins and ends with the interpretation of the numbers submitted to him. Consequently, we frequently find that a person who is in no way a " sensitive," nor even possessed of ordinary intuitive powers, but who is nevertheless a good Kabalist, knowing how to interpret the symbolism of numbers, gets credit for being a most remarkable " medium," as if nothing in the world that is to be talked about can be accomplished without the aid of disembodied spirits. Let me say at once that one who is an occultist is the very last to be regarded as a medium. Save in the ultimate sense that we are all from archangel to microbe, " fulfilling the Word " in some capacity or other, it cannot be said that we are played upon by the larvæ of a morbid and earth-bound humanity. The occultist does not get his information "through," as spiritualists and psychic phenomenalists are wont to say, but he gets it direct from Nature, whose symbolism he has learned to read.

If the " spirits " whom the *gobe-mouches* listen to with such rapt attention were capable of demonstrating their superior condition by the revelation of knowledge transcending that of the average embodied human, they would make such demonstration in such form and at such times as that the whole world would benefit from it. The fact that we have not added one syllable to the sum total of human knowledge by this means since the dawn of modern spiritualism, ought to prove the futility of the whole pursuit. There are phenomena without doubt, which prove the existence in Nature of certain unfamiliar forces, but they prove nothing that is spiritual, are most frequently grossly material, and in no instance are they to be compared with the daylight performances of the Indian Yogi. The spiritualist séance has only succeeded in perpetuating the fact of post-mortem existence, of which the world at no time has been seriously in doubt, but it has failed to prove to us immortality. Indeed, it presents only a doubtful case for spirit identity. If its claims were not so foolishly preposterous, its contribution to modern speculative problems would be received with greater respect and consideration. The results of years of patient study and research having recently been described by a certain ignoramus as due to the exercise of a special psychic faculty or to spirit communications, compels this discrimination, in which I trust I have done no hurt to the feelings of any sincere investigator into what are called spiritual phenomena.

CHAPTER XIII

THE KABALISM OF CYCLES

IT would appear that the origination of the decimal system of enumeration, which proceeds from one to nine and recommences the series at a higher power, increasing successively by tens, was an implicit recognition of the law of cyclic recurrence. There is no reason why units should not have gone from 1 to 13. The Hebrews may be said to think in twelves but count in tens, and this counting by tens is universal. Thus, while we have twelve months answering to the twelve signs, the seven days answering to the seven anciently recognised bodies of the solar system, there is in all Oriental nations a predilection for the method of counting by tens. This cyclic law has been recognised not only in science, but also in commerce, finance, and even agriculture. The suggestion, therefore, that events are in terms of nine, is not in itself a very exceptional statement. The fact that its application to specific cases yields results of a surprisingly exact nature, tends rather to confirm the view of the Kabalists, who regard the number 9 much as the Alchemists regarded their " Red Dragon "—as a species of general solvent. Thus, any number being reduced to its unit value, as $1911 = 12 = 3$, the addition of the number 9 will produce the same unit value successively as $1920 = 12 = 3$, $1929 = 21 = 3$. $1938 = 21 = 3$, etc. Hence, in the conception of those who see significance in numbers, the application of any factor to this cyclic series must have some special pointing.

Such a factor is to be found in the numerical value of a person's name, as we have already seen, and this, when applied to the year in which that person was born, or in which any great crisis was reached, is found to have a kabalistic significance when reduced to terms of the Tarot—a favourite but by no means the only method of interpretation.

One such kabala occurs to me as worthy of citation in regard to this law of cycles.

According to this kabala it was seen that the year 1815 was destined to be one of great significance to the " Little Corporal Violet."

Napoleon was born in 1769, and attained his 46th year in 1815. If now we add together 1815 and 46 we obtain $1861 = 1 + 8 + 6 + 1 = 16$. Referring this number to the Tarot keys we find No. $16 =$ " The Stricken Tower," a man falling headlong from an eminence, his crown falling in advance of him. It denotes the judgment of Heaven, reversal, danger of ruin, disaster, catastrophe.

Cecil Rhodes, the " Colossus " of South Africa, was born in 1853 and attained his 49th year in 1902.

Then 1902 + 49 = 1951 = 16, again " The Stricken Tower ! " Miss Sophia Hickman, of the Royal Free Hospital, was found poisoned in Richmond Park in August 1903. She was born on 22nd June 1874, and entered her 30th year in 1903. If to 1903 we add 30, the sum 1933 = 16.

M. Carnot, the French President, was born in 1837, and in 1894 attained 57 years of age. Then 1894 + 57 = 1951 = 16.

The poet Shelley was born in 1792, and entered his 30th year in 1822. The year 1822 + 30 = 1852 = 16.

It will be seen, therefore, that this number 16, and also 13, which is the " Reaper " or " The Reaping Skeleton," *i.e.* Death, are the most singularly fatal in the whole of the 22 keys of the Tarot.

This cyclic recurrence of certain like incidents observed in several cases appears to have led to the construction of what are called " Alfridaries." By these tables it is presumed that the life is subject to successive combinations of planetary influence during its entire course. The starting-point is from the Sun or Moon according to the time of day at which the birth took place. If in the afternoon from the Sun, and in the morning from the Moon. For those who were born after noon were held to be generated under solar influence, while those born after midnight were regarded as Moon-born. An example of an alfridary is appended :—

ALFRIDARY

AFTN. .	☽	☿	♀	☉	♂	♃	♄	☽	☿	♀	MORN
Sun .	1	8	15	22	29	36	43	50	57	64	Moon
Venus .	2	9	16	23	30	37	44	51	58	65	Mercury
Mercury.	3	10	17	24	31	38	45	52	59	66	Venus
Moon .	4	11	18	25	32	39	46	53	60	67	Sun
Saturn .	5	12	19	26	33	40	47	54	61	68	Mars
Jupiter .	6	13	20	27	34	41	48	55	62	69	Jupiter
Mars .	7	14	21	28	35	42	49	56	63	70	Saturn

By this alfridary we see that a person born at 4 p.m. would commence life under the joint influence of the Sun and Moon, the second year being under the Moon and Venus, the third under Moon and Mercury, and so on; the 8th year being under Mercury and the Sun; and the dangerous periods would be those under the influence of Mars from 29 to 35, and Saturn from 43 to 49; the grand climacteric at threescore years and ten, and falling under the influence of Saturn and Mars conjoined, the 33rd and 49th years being similarly prone to ill effects. But I think it will be conceded that any such cut-and-dried method of prognostication as is here imposed, is agreeable neither to experience nor reason. In the numerical system, however, it is different, inasmuch as the progression is made not by years only, but by reference to the age attained in successive years, and as the Tarot extends only to 22 points, which is not a multiple of 9, there is not that degree of repetition which characterises the alfridaric prognostics. Thus, a person born in 1864 =19, *Illumination*, attains the age of 1 year in 1865, the sum being 1866 =21 ; the age of 2 in 1866, the sum 1868 =23 ; but, as there are only 22 points or keys, 23 will be equal to 1.

Then follows the series :—

1867,	age	3,	sum	1870 =16
1868,	,,	4,	,,	1872 =18
1869,	,,	5,	,,	1874 =20
1870,	,,	6,	,,	1876 =22
1871,	,,	7,	,,	1878 = 2
1872,	,,	8,	,,	1880 =17
1873,	,,	9,	,,	1882 =19
1874,	,,	10,	,,	1884 =21
1875,	,,	11,	,,	1886 = 1
1876,	,,	12,	,,	1888 = 3
1877,	,,	13,	,,	1890 =18
1878,	,,	14,	,,	1892 =20
1879,	,,	15,	,,	1894 =22
1880,	,,	16,	,,	1896 = 2
	etc.			etc.

This idea of the cyclic law, or law of periodicity, has arrested the attention of scientists, among whom we may cite Mendelieff, who has shown that the atomic weights of the elements follow the natural octave ; and Sir William Crookes, whose *Genesis of the Elements* develops the same idea in regard to the differentiation of protyle via the hydrogen base by a graduation of the vibration-frequency and a proportionate diminishing of the mean free path or play-space of the various atoms. Then, again, the researches of Prof. Ray Lancaster in regard to sunspots has shown that the solar disturbances come sporadically, *i.e.* in groups, at definite and well-defined periods. It has been shown, too, that these periods correspond to periods of famine, etc.

Periodicity is, of course, at the base of planetary motions, and therefore also of cosmic changes.

In human life we observe that there is a tendency of any action to automatically repeat itself, so that what was primarily a voluntary act tends to fall into the region of the automatic, and so become a habit. Let us suppose that nature has a habit of procedure peculiar to its constitution, then it will, in effect, observe a course which reveals a periodic law, another name for numerical sequence. We call it a law because it responds to a numerical sequence, not because we pretend to an understanding of its causation.

But we really have no need to cite a supposititious case, for we well know that nature has such a habitual course as that suggested, and this is at the root of the vaticinations of the astrologers. Lunations and eclipses run in cycles, as also do the conjunctions and oppositions of the planets of the system. There is the 19-year cycle of the lunation, at the end of which they recur in the same part of the zodiac—that is to say, at the same distance from the equinox on the same day of the year. If any effects of a physical nature can be rightly attributed to the combined action of the luminaries, then such effects will follow a cyclic repetition every nineteen years. The phenomenon of the tides is, I think, sufficiently obvious to be accepted as a basis of our argument without dissent. But we have no reason to suppose that Nature ceases to exist where we cease to perceive her; indeed, the revelations of modern science during the past twenty years sufficiently attest the folly of accepting the ordinary sense perception as the criterion of evidence. That being so, we are entitled, by a philosophical consideration of the relations of noumena and phenomena, to posit a possible extension of tidal influence into the domain of phreno-psychic functions.

And if the luminaries so act to produce visible effects in the physical world, and appreciable effects also in the super-physical world, we may argue similarly in regard to the conjunctions and oppositions of other bodies of our system, since we are well assured of its solidarity. Then the conjunctions of Mars and Mercury, of Jupiter and Saturn, of Saturn and Mars, etc., will have their specific effects in the economy of the system; and this brings us immediately to the fact of periodicity in natural phenomena. For if a conjunction of Mars and Mercury takes place in a particular part of the zodiac to-day, it will again have place in the same celestial region at the end of every successive **period** of 79 years ; and similarly with the other planets, as Saturn and Mars in 30 years, Jupiter and Saturn in 60 years, and so of the rest, some being of greater frequency and less effect, others of less frequency and proportionately greater effect, according to their distances from the Sun and their consequent velocities.

Now, since the periodic times of the planets bear a definite known ratio to their distances from the centre, Nature is seen to observe quantitive relations; which is actually what we look for in, and define as, cosmic law. Without this regard to numbers, the cosmos would be chaotic and unintelligible to us. But it is so well sustained by its laws, and so thoroughly harmonious in its relations, that we are able to say to within a minute of space where any celestial body will be found hundreds or thousands of years hence, and where it was as many years ago.

But what of those radiant bodies which occasionally make incursion to our system, the comets and the star showers ? Although their density is exceedingly small, and their action upon the planetary bodies practically nil from a gravitational point of view, their presence and great velocity must produce terrific perturbations in spatial ether, and that these visitants affect our atmosphere is evident from their luminosity, since etheric vibration becomes light only within our atmosphere. Similarly, they may produce great heat and consequent drought and famine, and also they may affect men's minds by the dependence of our thought and feeling on physical conditions.

Finally, they may be symbols or signs by which something we do not quite understand is signalled to us by the Great Intelligence. If we study them we may find out their meaning. When the hieroglyphics of Egypt were first discovered they formed an entirely unknown language. But by great patience the symbolical writings of the ancient priests of Isis and Osiris and Amen Ra have been deciphered by the Egyptologists, and the language reconstructed so far as to be quite intelligible.

If Nature is the book of God and the revelation of God to man, then, by the deciphering of natural symbols, we may arrive at an understanding of the divine language, the will and intention it expresses, and the purpose of creation with which God has been trying to impress us throughout the ages.

Eventually we may find that in the study of the universal language we are realising ourselves, entering into the history and future of our own evolution, and then it will appear that cosmic laws are human laws, as well economic and social as moral and spiritual, and that the universe is man, the embodiment of divine thought, the expression of a perfect geometry, a complex mathematical formula which, when resolved, will be found to follow the numerical resolution—

$$\frac{1}{7} = \cdot142857 \qquad \frac{5}{7} = \cdot714285$$
$$\frac{2}{7} = \cdot285714 \qquad \frac{6}{7} = \cdot857142$$
$$\frac{3}{7} = \cdot428571 \qquad 1 = \cdot9 \text{ to infinity}$$
$$\frac{4}{7} = \cdot571428$$

—that is to say, a recurring decimal in terms of unity.

K

CHAPTER XIV

SUCCESS AND FAILURE

WHEN we look round upon life, we are constantly struck by the inequalities existing between faculty and its material efficiency. The market value of any kind of ability is, of course, determined by the economic law of supply and demand, and a man of exceptional ability in some particular field of work will find little call for his labours. It is not so much that they are not wanted, but that he lacks the faculty of creating a demand by impressing others of their need for his work. The man who discovered the process of making magnesia by the ton ought to have been worth a million pounds at least. The fact that he died a poor man does not detract from his chemical ability; it only shows that he lacked the commercial instinct, a common defect of the real student in any department of knowledge. There are, however, other and more subtle causes at work to produce failure of this sort where success of another sort is conspicuous. Every man is, in fine, a Number. He is embodied number. That is to say, the mass-chord of his whole constitution is in terms of a single digit, to which he answers in the gamut of life. If, for instance, his number is 3, then he is in sympathetic vibratory relations with all others whose number is 6, and in syntonic relations with those whose number is 3. But he would be in discordant relations with all men whose number is 5. Now let us suppose, as our kabala indeed suggests, that the number 3 answers to the theological, and that 5, in terms of the same kabala, answers to the commercial. We can understand at once the fundamental difference existing between these natures. Again, let 9 respond to and represent the executive faculty, then we may expect an affinity or sympathetic relationship with 5, the commercial faculty. Our kabala informs us that 9 and 5 are in such relations.

Similarly, in regard to 3, which denotes increase, expansion, optimism, and growth, and 8, which denotes decrease, privation, destruction, loss, and pessimism, they are in opposition, and are mutually destructive.

Consequently, we may derive some benefit of a practical nature from the measure of our own selves, and an understanding of the faculty we are designed to represent in the economy of life. If the name of a person should appear too slender an argument for differences of faculty and function, differences of fortune and of character, then let the date of birth stand as symbol of the man—without reference to his potential or measure of power, but merely in regard to his dominant characteristic and faculty.

If we find it answers, as must be the case where the kabalism is truly made, then it will afford an immediate key, not only to the character of the man, but also to the means by which he can most effectively pursue the line of least resistance, and so make the greatest progress.

For it will be seen at once that he is not likely to prosper or effectively work out his destiny in association with persons whose key number is opposed to his own; and on the contrary, he will improve his fortunes and reinforce his powers by uniting his efforts to those of others whose key number is the same, or at least of a sympathetic nature. Thus, a man born under the signature of Mars and the number 9, would blight his prospects by alliance with one born under Mercury and the number 5.

But it is perhaps a waste of words to argue each case on its own merits, and the ground can be covered by a single tabular statement of the sympathies and antipathies represented by the key number of an individual. This number, I need hardly add, is the result of adding together the day, month, and year of birth. In this scheme the year is generic, the month specific, and the day individualistic. For there are many thousands born every year, about one-twelfth being born in each month; while a comparative few come out under the particular day, still fewer in any hour, and less still in any minute. Thus, in London the population of 4,758,218 in 1907, with a birth-rate for the year of 25·6 per thousand of the population, gives 121,810 births in the 12 months. Then we have, in round figures,

Per year,	121,810
„ month,	10,150
„ day,	338
„ hour,	14

We see how busy a place London is from a psychic point of view, and how souls come tumbling into existence at the rate of 14 per hour on account of the enormous vortex of attraction which is set up by the whirl of its great activity and desire force.

It has already been shown how the smaller periods of time are calculated from the planetary days and hours, and hence we may say that the line of demarcation is fairly well defined in every case.

Thus, a person born on Tuesday, 26th April 1910, at 4·5 in the afternoon, would be primarily under the dominance of the planet ♂ Tuesday; in a more intimate sense under the planet ♀ Venus, governing the hour, and specifically under the influence of ☽, which governs the exact minute of the birth.

From these elements we have the figures 532, all being negative, and the sum of these is 10 = 1, which is the key number of that individual. This method will be found more exact and representative even than the kabala of the Table of Three already dealt with in these pages.

Now, having the key number of an individual,

we can apply it in a variety of ways to the ordinary affairs of daily life. Knowing his number, a man may choose a house by the agreement of its number or name-value with his own, may make choice of a wife, select a fortunate day on which to transact important business, and otherwise variously dispose himself in regard to an environment which by numerical selection is calculated to reinforce and uphold his effectiveness.

The choice of a day must be made by its number, and likewise the hour and subdivision of the hour ; while association with any other person should be controlled by regard to his key number of birth, or if this be not known, by comparison of the two dates from the Table of Three. For it frequently happens that a person does not know the hour of his birth, still less the exact time, and in these cases the Table of Three may conveniently be used. But in every case comparison must be made from the same basis and by the same method, whether by the Table of Three, the enumeration of the name, the Tarot, or any other means.

CHAPTER XV

THE LAW OF VALUES

WE have already seen, when considering the principle of enumeration, that numbers express only
quantitive relations unless we elect to regard them
symbolically, when they assume a significance of an
entirely different nature. We have seen that
unity $=1$ can be expressed in terms of an indefinite
state of eternal becoming, as when $1 = \cdot \dot{9}$ to infinity.
It is also possible to say $1 = 1 + x$, where x is an
infinite potential. For aught we know, the amœba
is potential man. Natural history seems to lend
colour to the conception of a continual progression
in the scale of evolution. We do not know how
inorganic matter becomes organic, how the mineral
becomes translated into the vegetable and the
vegetable into the animal, but here and there we
find examples of the transition. We cover the whole
ground of manifold creation by a single word when
we speak of differentiation, and the whole process
of infinite progression of the forms of life when we
define evolution. At root of all is the one Life, the
one Substance, the one Great Intelligence, from
which all proceeds and to which all aspires.

Quantitive relations have no fixed value. Before we can say $2+2=4$ we have to posit a qualitative value which has regard to the nature of the things thus put together. Here we are giving to numbers something more than the power to express quantitive relations, we are giving them a qualitative value. We exercise this discrimination when we seek to form a cricket team or an eight-oar crew. It is not merely a question of 11 men or 8 men, but of 11 cricketers and 8 oarsmen. Hence it is not the fact that 11 men make a cricket team. They must first learn to play cricket.

Moral values attach to numbers quite as much as do exchange values. Shakespeare expressed this fact in the saying : " He is well paid who is well satisfied." One can give a small boy a penny and a workman a shilling and get more work in exchange from the boy while giving equal satisfaction to both. Yet the needs of the man in a given time are not eleven times greater than those of the boy in the same time. Hence the penny and the shilling obtain a moral value in addition to their exchange value. Each is a token, and intrinsically of equal value in certain circumstances, so that $1=1+11$ is a possible expression of fact.

Nature has more regard to potentiality than to potency, to future possibilities than to present circumstance. Consequently, we find that her expressions of value are not fixed, but have always a cumulative adjunct represented by $+x^n$, which we understand to mean indefinite evolution—as, for example, $Adam = 1+4+4 = 9+x^n$. When the poet speaks of " the diapason closing strong in man," we apprehend his meaning but disagree as to his values. He leaves out of sight the fact that Nature as instrument is not affected by the limitations that are imposed upon ourselves, and that the divine harmony is not realised in man as we know him, because he is not a plenary expression of the soul of the Great Performer. The theme, if pursued to its logical conclusion, will bring us again to the fact that all values are relative, and since we are mainly concerned in this place with numbers as expressions of human relations—that is, with their symbolical values—we may pursue the study along these lines to greater advantage.

That perspicuous thinker and fine poet, George Macdonald, LL.D., in his *Phantastes*, has this pertinent passage :—

" They who believe in the influence of the stars over the fates of men, are, in feeling at least, nearer the truth than they who regard the heavenly bodies as related to them merely by a common obedience to an external law. All that man sees has to do with man. Worlds cannot be without an intermundane relationship. The community of the centre of all creation suggests an inter-radiating connection and dependence of the parts. Else a grander idea is conceivable than that which is already embodied. The blank, which is only a forgotten life, lying behind the consciousness, and the misty splendour, which is an undeveloped life, lying before it, may be full of mysterious revelation of other connections with the worlds around us than

those of science and poetry. No shining belt or
gleaming moon, no red and green glory in self-
encircling twin-stars, but has a relation to the
hidden things of a man's soul, and, it may be, with
the secret history of his body as well. They are
portions of the living house wherein he abides."

This thought is a very vital one. It suggests the
concept of the idealist that nothing exists for us
save in our consciousness, all things being related
to us through our senses and our thoughts. Whatever affects the consciousness affects the man, and
in an intimate sense *is* man, as Henry Sutton has so
well expressed it—

> " Man doth usurp all space,
> Stares thee in rock, bush, river, in the face;
> Never yet thine eyes beheld a tree;
> 'Tis no sea thou seest in the sea—
> 'Tis but a disguised humanity.
> To avoid thy fellow, vain thy plan;
> All that interests a man *is* man."

These lines have the endorsement of George
Macdonald, who quotes them in his *Fairie Romance*
with evident appreciation. The idea of all Nature
being a " disguised humanity " is excellent, the
phrase unique, and we, as students of the book of
God's revelation, have to find the story of man's
origin, history, and development in the world about
us, as well distant as near.

In the sense that Henry Sutton has so well put it,
we may infer by human relations all of his powers,
needs, hopes, joys, and aspirations that can find
sublunary expression ; and that which presses him

most closely in daily life is his need.   It is not what
a man has, but what he wants, that shapes his
course and determines his efforts.   It is man's need
that gives to things their market value and makes
opportunity for faculty and capital.

Thus we get a new value for the number 8 and the
planet Saturn, which stand as symbols of privation.
We see them as the cause of all striving, and, in
effect, $8 =$ evolution ; and since evolution involves
growth, expansion, development, the expression
and realisation of potential faculty, we find that
8 is potentially 3.

In a universe where everything is in a state of
flux, where the *status quo* is an unstable equilibrium,
we find that reaction is the law.   For every rise
there is a fall, for every flow an ebb, for every
perihelion an aphelion, for every flood a drought.
The experience is universal, and so fully recognised
by the man in the street as to have given rise to
the following jingle, which probably had its origin
with some unfortunate speculator on the Stock
Exchange :—

> " After the rise, the fall;
> After the boom, the slump;
> After the fizz and the big cigar,
> The cigarette and the hump ! "

It expresses a recognition of the law of action
and reaction, which is responsible for the stability
of the universe.

We have already found that $8 =$ privation.   We
have connoted death, decay, ruin, injury, maiming,
with this unfortunate number.   It has been ascribed

to Saturn, the planet whose mass-chord of vibration is most inimical to us of the earth sphere whose number is 4 (materiality), and our satellite the Moon whose numbers are 7 (increscent) and 2 (decrescent). Let us trace this influence in terms of cosmical law. The planet Saturn was in the sign Sagittarius in the year 1898. For many centuries prior to this date it had been known by observation that this sign of the zodiac " governed " Spain. Not that any disrespect was intended to the king, or even to Don Cæsar de Bazan, but that the fortunes of that country were found to answer to the affections of that sign by the successive incursions of the various planets—as was noted by Kepler, who found it not beneath him to confess that " A most unfailing experience of the course of human events in harmony with the changes occurring in the heavens has instructed and compelled my unwilling belief."

In 1898, therefore, we find Spain, in strict agreement with this dictum, suddenly plunged into a most unexpected and unfortunate war with the United States of America. " Spanish Fours " went down with a run on the Stock Exchange, and thousands of Spanish holders of the Government Stock were ruined. Spain lost her possessions in the West Indies and the Philippines, and a heavy indemnity was imposed when finally it capitulated. Altogether, some 100,000 men were killed during the hostilities. It was a black hour for Spain indeed. Since then the Spanish " Maine " has had a new meaning, for it has been officially ascertained by the salving of the American war-vessel that it was not blown up by any Spaniard, but exploded from its own magazines, the explosion taking place from within and not outside of the vessel. There was, therefore, no adequate *casus belli*, and if we could eliminate Saturn and the number 8 from the sign Sagittarius in the year $1898 = 1+8+9+8 = 26 = 8$, we should find no reason to suspect that there might be one. Yet it is significant that the present writer specifically predicted this great struggle between America and Spain, the concomitant rise in the price of wheat, the loss of life and territory sustained by Spain, and the reconstruction of its Government Stock in the following year.

The Russo-Japanese war took place in 1905, and was similarly attended by the transit of Saturn through Russia's ruling sign Aquarius. The prediction of its defeat was an easy matter to those instructed in natural symbolism, and the revolution, also specifically predicted, was the result of Saturn and Mars being conjoined in Aquarius.

When Saturn passed into Pisces, which rules Portugal, the unrest and dissatisfaction of the populace found signal expression in the assassination of the King and Crown Prince, and was shortly followed by the revolution, due to the conjunction of Saturn and Mars as before, which deposed the monarchy.

Now, if we look at the corresponding values of the chief securities of these countries, we shall find that they reflect the "depression" of the public mind due to the influence of Saturn.

Spanish Fours, prior to the war, were in the

region of 80. In 1898 they fell to something under 30. Russias show the following remarkable fluctuations :—

5 per cent. Loan (1822)
1897 = 154   1906 = 90

4 per cent. Bonds
1896 = 105   1906 = 71

3 per cent. Bonds
1898 = 96   1907 = 61

3½ per cent. Gold Loan (1894)
1897 = 103   1906 = 60

The figures given are the highest and lowest between the years 1895 and 1907 for the several securities. We thus see that the lowest for the period of 12 years is touched at the time of Saturn's influence.

Portuguese 3 per cent. stock stood at 72 in 1906, and the influence of Saturn was such as to bring the value down to 58 in 1908.

Japan, ruled by Libra, shows no corresponding depreciation as did Russia from influence of Saturn, for in 1906 the 4½ per cent. (1905) bonds stood at the highest point of over 97 since the date of issue, and in 1910, when $4 = 3$ (increase and expansion) was in Libra, the price went up to over 102.

The evidence is sufficiently marked to dispel all doubt as to the action of the planets upon human affairs, and we may consider the observation of Kepler to be justified.

Now we, as Kabalists, are chiefly concerned with the fact that the integrity of Nature is upheld by this coincidence of symbolism with " the course of mundane events." In these pages I have endeavoured to show that symbology extends far beyond the circle, the cross, or any other geometrical form which ordinarily is employed as such. I have brought in figures and numbers as symbols, and have linked them with sounds and colours. But this does not exhaust symbolism, nor does the application of the symbology of form, colour, sound, and number to individual character and fortune constitute the whole subject. We must extend our symbolism to the entire universe, and our interpretations must have regard to the evolution of the human race as a whole. The Kabalists, following the lines already instituted by the observations of astrologers, have attempted such an universal symbolism.

The twelve labours of Hercules, the feats of Samson, and the progress of Israel from the captivity to the partitioning of Palestine, are so many symbols or ideographs set up to signal the evolutional progress of the race. Each is capable of a zodiacal interpretation (*vide* Drummond's *Œdipus Judaicus*). Those who would pursue the subject of zodiacal symbolism in relation to the great epochs of human history should endeavour to obtain the works of C. Massey, E. V. Kenealy, J. Mackay, and Capt. Drayton, in each of which some glimpses of the system of interpretation are to be found.

In the present instance, we are concerned chiefly

with the kabalism of numbers in relation to the law of values. This cannot be effectively followed apart from a study of cosmic elements, the planets of the solar system, the cycles of the lunations and eclipses, and the divisions of the heavens called the signs of the zodiac. It is the recurrence of these planetary periods and luni-solar cycles that constitutes the ebb and flow of human affairs and the corresponding changes or fluctuations in values. The cycle of Saturn is 30 years, of Jupiter 12, of Mars 15, of the Sun 19, of Venus 8, of Mercury 10, and of the Moon 4. The saros or eclipse cycle is 18 years $10\frac{1}{2}$ days, which, in 3 cycles, amounts to 54 years 1 month, and in 36 cycles to 649 years, after which the eclipses begin again and recur on the same days of the year. Those who have studied the marked physical effects due to, and coincident with, central eclipse, especially when the Moon is in perigee, *i.e.* at nearest distance from the Earth, will be prepared to allow that such may also have an effect upon individuals. Tycho admitted the symbolism of eclipses, and has given us examples of his interpretations, while Kepler has argued for their causative relations with humanity. It is an ancient belief, much better sustained by observation than many of our modern scientific theories, and can be accepted on the authority of those who have made the matter a subject of study for many years. Applying this observed malefic influence of eclipses to the problem of values, let A be the place of the sun at the birth of a person, that of a ruler or president; let B be the place of the

Moon ; and CC' and DD' the meridian and horizon respectively :—

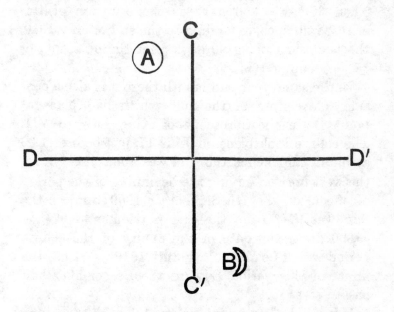

It will be found that whenever an eclipse of either luminary shall fall on any of these points, a period of sickness, depression of fortune, loss and disaster, will follow, such period commencing as many days from the date of eclipse as the luminary is degrees from the horizon it last crossed, whether E. or W., and the duration being equal to four times the number of days that the luminary is distant in degrees from the horizon to which it is proceeding. Thus, for example, there was a total eclipse of the Moon on the night of the 3rd June 1909, which accordingly fell on the point A in the horoscope of H.M. King George V., then Prince of Wales ; the

L

eclipsed Moon being then about 90° from the west
horizon and an equal distance from the east horizon.
Then $90 \times 4 = 360$ days as the duration of this
eclipse influence, extending to the end of May 1910,
the beginning being 90 days after the birthday, or
1st September 1909.

In the same year and month there was also a considerable eclipse of the Sun, which had place at
point D' in the horoscope of King Edward VII.
The eclipse took place on June 17, just before 11.30
at night, and hence the Sun was about $82\frac{1}{2}$° from
the west horizon, giving the beginning of the period
of effects on the 7th September 1909, and, as the
Sun was $97\frac{1}{2}$° from the east horizon, and $97\frac{1}{2} \times 4$
$=390$ days, the date of the expiry of the eclipse
period would be about 12th July 1910.   Within the
limits of this period Edward the Peacemaker had
passed away.

If instead of an individual we take the horoscope
of a nation, we shall find the same rule holds good,
but this statement is open to the objection that
whereas the individual horoscope is certainly known
from the moment of birth, that of a nation has to be
empirically determined by a long series of observations.   We do not certainly know by what method
Nature partitions the zodiac among the nations, or
how she determines the destiny of any country from
the affections of a particular sign, but we know from
experience that in some particular manner there is
a correspondence between the signs and the several
members of the human body, and between the signs
and various countries which are found to answer to

them. The facts cannot be disputed; the reasons
are perhaps obscure, and it is therefore convenient
to regard the whole scheme as having a human significance and, in a special sense, intelligible only in
terms of human consciousness and experience.

Then Saturn, as privation, threatens the life every
7 or 8 years by its quadrature, but more especially
every 15 years by its conjunction and opposition ;
while ♃ gives increase and expansion every 4th year,
and more especially every 12th year.

Events that characterised any particular month
are apt to find repetition every 19th year in the
same month of the year, because the lunations repeat themselves after 19 years about the same date,
and are therefore in the same horoscopical relations
as 19 years previously. This law of "correlated
successiveness," as it has been called, is the means
employed by nature to preserve the equilibrium of
things and regulate the law of values. It gives
rise to diversity of fortune, and thus fosters interdependence among the various sections of humanity.
For, while it is true that one governs and another
serves, one has wealth and another lack of means,
it is also true that nothing is effected save by the
consent of that which is below. We see this in
horoscopy, where the Sun promises some good by
its benefic aspect to some planet in the horoscope,
but is unable to bring it into effect until the Moon
comes to the same or a similar aspect in the horoscope. The gods will that there should be a beginning
of the millennium to-morrow if not to-day, but
humanity does not like it so, and the great day of

universal peace and goodwill is indefinitely post-
poned.   A king is ruler by the will of the people, for
none can be king without subjects, and therefore we
see that it is one of Nature's economic laws that the
superior depends upon that which is inferior, while
that which is beneath receives the sanction and
purpose of its existence from above.

A man whose signature is 3 can become rich by
expenditure and the free use of that which he
possesses ; while one whose signature is 8 can only
become so in course of time by frugality, patience,
self-denial, privation, and hard saving.   For Jupiter
demands expansion, liberty, *largesse,* and generosity
from those whom he endows, while Saturn demands
a " time contract " and much durance from his
subjects.   Mars, on the other hand, requires a risk, a
hazard, a speculation or daring exploit, something
that is " touch and go," as a fuse in a mine or a
match to gunpowder.   In every department of life
it is always the same mandate under a variety of
conditions.   " Take what thou wilt, but pay the
price," as Emerson has wisely said.

A man whose signature is Mars, whose number is
9, will have a positive and forceful nature.   He
may express it in lawlessness and open violence, and
bring himself under the penalty of the law; or he
may undertake some great pioneer work in which
concentrated energy, direction of force, intrepidity,
zeal and intensity are effective characteristics, and
so gain honours and emoluments for himself.   At
quite an early stage in the study of the law of values
we find that a number signifies a definite character-

istic, but does not indicate anything concerning the manner of its expression. The influence of 8 may operate to produce reservation, conservation, steadiness, or it may tend to deprivation, misfortune, and misanthropy. Character is the expression of individuality as seen through the coloured glass of personality and environment. Numbers are a key to this expression, but they do not inform us as to individual attributes or inherent powers. Nature, however, is jealous of her products, and observes the law of the conservation of energy in human destiny as in cosmic operations, and conceivably follows the lines of least resistance by adapting environment to aptitude, or, at all events, affording suitable birth-conditions to every evolving entity.

Similarly, Saturn = 8, may tend to a scarcity of an article by diminishing production or supplies; in such case the price of the commodity will be temporarily enhanced. On the other hand, it may operate to diminish the demand for the article, which consequently falls in value. The key to this interpretation of 8, or any other number or corresponding planet, is one of the arcana of kabalistic and astrological science which have been successfully applied to the question of values for many years past, not only as to the greater periodic movements of the various markets, but also the monthly and daily fluctuations, so that the whole matter is in evidence and in every way confirms the view of Kepler concerning the concurrence of mundane events with changes occurring in the heavens.

The introduction of this subject of the law of values, and the study of it from the point of view indicated at the outset of the present work, is the outcome of an admonition received many years ago from a man of known commercial ability and sufficient common sense to harbour a belief in the solidarity of the universe and the consequent probability of planetary influence in human life. "Make your science practical, and it will be recognised," he said, and in order to do so we must interpret the language of Nature into terms of everyday life. Neither astrology nor kabalism is a religion. They will never save a soul from self-destruction, but they can throw a welcome light upon the dark and narrow paths through which many a starved and belated soul has to push its way towards the place where humanity has set its camp. Where there was tyranny and servitude, oppression and slavery, opulence and indigence, happiness and misery in a world already made, the light of natural symbolism reveals an infinity of changing conditions and a universal service of indefinite opportunity occurring to each and every soul in a world that is for ever in the making. For the teaching of the universal symbolism is a scientific optimism for which we have the warrant of analogy. Whatever may be the sun to which a soul may be attracted, we know that it is answering to a gravitational pull and slowly but surely approaching the consummation of its purpose. At this period in its career it may be in aphelion, far away in the drear wilderness of life, with a minimum of light and heat to cheer it on its way. But the law of compensation is for ever at work, and, as surely as a soul is now in aphelion, it will some day be in perihelion, bathed in the sunshine of a perfect day and as near as the law of his being will permit to the object of his ambitions. Further, we know that at every successive revolution he will come to a place that is a little nearer to the heart of being. The law of evolution is cyclic or periodic, it is never retrogressive, but always progressive. The spiral course of a gravitating body has given rise to the idea among superficial observers that humanity retrogresses or continually pursues the same unchanging orbit. Closer observation will show that, whereas it appears to return to the same place, it is in reality a little nearer to its gravitating centre at every revolution. In a single revolution, the increment is inappreciable ; in a thousand or ten thousand it becomes considerable. To-day the Earth is nearer to the Sun than it was twenty centuries ago, and the Moon is further away from the Earth ; but also the velocity of both has changed, and the Earth turns upon its axis in a shorter interval of time. We are getting closer to the centre of gravity ; we are, as is our planet, answering to the inward pull. The best of men are deifying, most of us a-humanising, still ; but all are gradually, imperceptibly—yet surely—evolving. We need no other argument than that afforded by cosmic law to uphold the doctrine of optimism. The laws of periodicity, of cyclic progress and of gravitation, ensure the working out of the law of compensation, and this is the basis of our law of values which here has been partially considered. We learn from the law of values that rise and fall, increase and decrease, gain and loss, are only relative and at most but temporary terms, having no permanent value in a scheme that demands continual progress. But also it affords us that measure of opportunity which is required for the exercise of our faculties and powers, and the old adage, " Needs must when the devil drives," is only another expression of the fact that " Necessity is the mother of invention," and equally that " Suffering is the cause of evolution," for

> " Stronger than woe is will ;
> That which is good
> Doth pass to better, best."

Without restriction and pain, without need and suffering, there would be no sustained effort towards expansion, and without effort no development of power and faculty.

Thus we see how the study of the universe as symbol leads us to a more just conception of the Divine Economy, and how the law of values, when worked out to its last equation, speaks only of the beneficence of God. Incidentally it may serve us to improve our opportunities and make the best of life by timely effort in work that is agreeable to our natures and within the range of our faculties, as indicated to us by the kabala of numbers and other means of interpretation available to us. What I have here tried to show is the fact that $1 = 1 + x^n$, and $8 = 3$. To have succeeded, if only par-

tially, will be to have given to the kabalistic theory
a new value, lifting it to the position of a gospel of
optimism, at the same time inviting the philosophical consideration of a new law of values, which has
regard to the scientific fact of human evolution and
the moral incident of individual aspiration.

I have already said that neither kabalism nor
astrology is a religion, and I do not see cause to depart from this statement. I am inclined to think,
however, that both may contribute something to the
structure of a true religion which has regard to the
symbolical value of the universe as the revelation
of God to man. Emerson, in his essay on "Idealism,"
has seized upon this idea and embodied it in the
following fine phrase, which I venture to quote from
memory: "The idealist views the world in God.
He sees the whole circle of events, of persons and
things, not as painfully accumulated, atom by atom,
act after act, in an age creeping past, but as one
vast scene painted on the instant eternity by the
hand of God for the eternal contemplation of the
human soul."

The laws of thought imposed upon us by $2^2 = 4$
(materiality) may be changed by an altered relation
to the universe, and it may then appear that the
apparent changes taking place in the world about
are reflections answering to changes in our consciousness, and that the great picture of man in the
image and likeness of God, the "fulness of the
stature of Christ," has never undergone any change
since the world began.

CHAPTER XVI

BRUNO'S SYMBOLISM

THROUGHOUT this work we have been able to trace that unity in diversity and that diversity in unity which constitutes a canon of faith. We see throughout the manifest universe a unity as to essence and a diversity as to expression which was perhaps better understood by Bruno than by his inquisitors who formulated the doctrine.

Bruno was the originator of the Doctrine of Correspondences which was afterwards and perhaps more patiently illustrated by Swedenborg. The Nolan philosopher was an originator of the Hermetic doctrine "As above, so below," for he affirmed that the smallest thinkable body is a mirror of the universe.

As to the Doctrine of Correspondences, we have this formula from him: What harmony is to the universe, so is virtue to the individual and social law to the community. What light is to the stars, so is intelligence to the spirit and science to humanity. Here we have the correspondences of harmony, virtue, and social law. Also of the universe, the individual, and humanity. Bruno recognises that man as individual is an embodiment of the universe, and that the same quality and the same conditions as those which are required to uphold the universe are essential to humanity and each of its members. This clearly shows that he was a deductive philosopher, arguing from universals to particulars. He further shows that light in the physical world, intelligence in the spiritual world, and science in the social world are correspondences. Further, he shows that the mathematical point, the physical atom, and the spiritual monad are correspondences. This infers something more than a mere analogy or similitude. It argues a direct interaction or continuity the one with the other. It means, in fact, that the physical atom is the ultimate expression of the spiritual monad, and that without the latter there could be no physical existence whatsoever, since the physical universe is the bodying forth of the spiritual. Hence physically we have the atom, intellectually the point, and spiritually the monad. This monad is the divine spark or scintilla in the human being, the "light that lighteth every man when he cometh into the world."

Astronomically this monad is the Sun, the centre and source of life and light to our system of worlds. It is the ultimate manifestation of the Central Fact of Being, the manifestation to us of the divine Wisdom and Love. Without its continual radiation the worlds would be but barren wildernesses and lifeless orbs revolving in space. Indeed, they could hardly be said to exist as worlds. So without

the Wisdom and Love of God directing and vital-
ising the human soul it could produce nothing of
good and would be but the play of natural forces.
But inasmuch as this play of natural forces is
nothing but an expression of the Divine Will, even
they could not be said to exist apart from the Source
of their expression. Thus we see how Bruno
rightly apprehended the spiritual significance of
the physical facts of the universe, and how he
regarded the integrity of things to consist in their
divine dependence.

Because of this essential unity of all things the
number One has come to be invested in all
kabalistic systems with singular and even divine
attributes. Thus we see how in the universal system
1 symbolises manifestation from zero 0, the positive
and active principle in all forms of life. It stands
also for the Logos, which is the manifestation in
time and space to us of the Divine Unmanifest
Being. It represents also individuality; in a religious sense the Lord, and in a scientific sense the
underlying unity of things. A symbol of the Sun.

In the Tarot it indicates " the Magus," which is
a symbol of the Creator, who produces the
universe by the magical power of His ideation.
Even the Ephesians, punctilious in all the
externals of religion, erected an altar " to the
Unknown God," fearing lest in the construction of
their pantheon they had ignorantly omitted one to
whom recognition was due ; and it was the custom
among the ancients either to add or remit one from
the allotted number. Thus there came to be " luck

in odd numbers," of which one was the first and most significant.

These are ideas which, as Bruno said, "germinate like amputated roots, ancient truths which are again unfolded, occult verities that are now revealed, constituting a new light that during the long night has been hidden beneath the horizon of our consciousness, and now, little by little, makes its way towards the meridian of our intelligence." For these truths were expressions of the Soul of Things, in which the philosopher had implicit faith, for always beyond the thing of form he beheld the soul of it, which was its imperishable part.

Thus he speaks of the Soul of the World as "the formal constitutive principle of the world and of all that it contains ; for all things, although not animal, are animate." And this doctrine is again and again repeated in the various works of this intuitive thinker, as in the *Ceneri,* where it is said : " Everything participates in Life, there are innumerable lives not only in us but in all composite bodies, and when we regard a thing which is said to be dying, we should rather understand that it changes, and that there is an end to that accidental composition and configuration, whilst there yet remain those things that are incorrupt and for ever immortal. . . . Nothing is ever annihilated or lost to being save the accidental, exterior, and material form it holds." Concerning Matter itself, Bruno held that it was eternal and indestructible as to its essence, though evanescent and mutable as to form : " All the difference that we see in bodies is in regard to their form, complexion, constitution, and other properties and relationships, which is nothing more than a different mode of the same substance, the unchangeable and eternal essence in which are all forms, constitutions, and members, unmanifest and homogeneous."

From the Spirit, which is the life of the universe, proceed the life and soul of whatsoever is living and ensouled and understood to be immortal, as also are all the bodies as to their substance, being not otherwise dead save in that they are subject to dispersion and aggregation, which is clearly expressed in Ecclesiastes : " That which is to be hath already been, verily there is nothing new under the sun." For Bruno spoke of spontaneous generation, of the origin and transformation of the species, in a manner that was foreign to the thought of his times.

Bruno was enabled to anticipate much of modern scientific and philosophical thought solely because he had studied a pure Kabalism, which recognised Number as implicit in all the works of the Spirit. Consequently, he protests against " the foolish and unreasoning idolaters," meaning of course those who upheld the crass orthodoxy of his day in Europe, who, he affirmed, " have no cause to deride the magic and the divine cult of the Egyptians, which in all things and in all effects, according to the scope of each, contemplated the Divine. . . . They knew, did those sages, that God was in all things, and that divinity was latent in Nature."

It is from this point of view that we are able to

raise the study of Kabalism to its true and proper place among the sciences, and endow it with the virtue and quality of a system of thought. All that we know or can ever know of the Supreme Mind and Will is embodied and expressed in Nature, and the study of natural phenomena must therefore be our guide to true religion. For the reversion of man to the Divine is through Nature to Nature's God by means of contemplation. It is not then enough that we study to know the relations of things themselves to one another, but we must study the relations of things in themselves to the source of their existence.

As in music the tones bear a certain proportional relativity to one another without violating the sense of harmony, irrespective of the exact number of vibrations constituting the tonic, so the whole universe embodies a certain relativity of its parts, irrespective of the exact measurement of any one of its bodies.

Thus a stringed instrument may be raised or lowered to any pitch without in any way affecting its manipulation or the relative value of its notes. Similarly the distances of the planets from the Sun may be increased or reduced from what we now assume them to be, without in the least affecting our astronomy or altering in any way the relative distances of the various bodies from their common centre. In a manifest universe there is no such thing as an absolute standard, everything is relative. We see and know things only in relation to one another. It has been said, for instance, that " the distance from the Earth to the Sun is the measuring-rod by which we compute all other (astronomical) distances," and although we may concede that others may know better than the late J. R. Hind, F.R.S., their standard remains the same.

If two observers look at the same body in space from two widely sundered points of view, their lines of vision will intersect one another at an angle which is proportionate to the distance of the

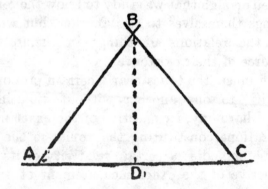

body—the nearer the body the greater the angle. This angle is called Parallax, and by knowing this angle and the distance between the observers we can find the length of the perpendicular which bisects it and the angle of Parallax, and this length will be the distance of the body from the Earth, as here shown.

Let A and C be the observers, and B the body in space. Then the angles at A and C are known by observation, and thence is derived the angle at B. Having the two angles and the base we can find the other sides and also the length of the perpendicular BD, which is the distance of the body B.

We have already seen that, as regards the solar system, the orbits of the several planets are what we hold them to be only in regard to a stationary Sun, whereas we are confidently assured that the Sun is itself in motion through space, which by no means interferes with the relative distances of the bodies themselves, but entirely dispels any idea of a fixed relationship such as that implied by the elliptical orbit. And if we take the physical fact that all bodies at 37 times their own diameters from the eye appear to the spectator as of equal size, then some of our notions about the distance of bodies in space will have to be revised. Relative truths are all that we can hope for in regard to anything in this universe, since everything is conditioned by our own consciousness and sense-limitations, but the relations of our perceptions should nevertheless be true.

This relativity of perception and apprehension of the universe about us puts us in the position of interpreters. We take the phenomenon as a signal, and from a series we establish a code which thereafter we apply to a variety of different sets of phenomena. This constitutes our science. Kabalism in the same manner establishes a certain relativity between numbers, which we regard as the quantitive relations of things, and thence arises a system of interpretation which is capable of a universal application.

But this does not give us an absolute value for

M

One. Thus it may stand for unity in the abstract as the principle of being or existence. On the other hand, it may symbolise Deity, the universe, ego, the atom, the monad, or aught else that in itself is a sole entity.

There is thus a relativity in Unity as well as essential identity, although in things of a kind relativity is usually regarded as beginning with Two. For we see that the atom is related to the individual, and the individual to the universe, and the universe to its Lord, who is in sole relations with the Unmanifest Deity, the Absolute or Zero, 0. There are what Swedenborg would call " discrete degrees " between each of these existences. But if we have two atoms or two egos, two monads, etc., the two are on the same plane of existence as one another, and are therefore continuous of each other, as to the plane of their existence, while remaining separate entities, which is what Swedenborg calls a " continuous degree."

Now as all planes are in continuity, as required by their existence as planes, we may say that matter is continuous of matter throughout the universe, that mind is continuous of mind, and spirit of spirit. Further, from what we have already argued about discrete degrees, we are able to say that matter is the substratum of mind, as mind is of spirit, and spirit of Deity. Moreover, the doctrine of the Immanence of God requires that He is present in all His creations, not immediately as oxygen in air, but mediately as the will and consciousness are in the body of man. Therefore, by a variety of dependencies, all existences upon all planes are linked together, and together constitute the body of God. Thus when we speak of the Living God we should understand that conscious Will which is the life of the universe and expressed in all its operations, relations, and conditions. But even so we are at liberty to reflect that this universe of ours is but an infinitesimal part of the existent, and ought therefore to be regarded rather as a molecule belonging to the Corpus Dei and not the entire body.

Here we come at once to the monadology of Leibnitz, which was so fully apprehended by Bruno as to constitute an essential part of his philosophy. In this system of thought we regard every part, every atom, as reflecting every other part of the body to which it belongs, and therefore every universe comes to be a reflex of the Divine, as if a light falling upon a crystal sphere should illuminate the entire sphere and therefore all of its parts or molecules, and thus there would be a myriad molecules, each consisting of millions of atoms, all illuminated from a single source of light ; and, *mirabile dictu*, every atom is a sphere in itself.

If now we take the idea of continuity in matter we shall find that it can only be worked out on the principle of the hexagon. No other form is capable of affording contact with an equal number of units of the same form and size as itself. There is a magic in the number Six which enters freely into all Nature. Water, for example, crystallises at an angle of 60 degrees, which is one-sixth of the circle.

Hence water was held among the Theurgists to be the prime base of all this world's evolutions. Six is the number of perfection of work, industry, occupation; and as Nature is regarded as the mother of all things, so the astrologers put the mother symbol as the sixth sign of the zodiac. The significance of the interlaced equilateral triangles is already well known. It illustrates the sacred nature of the number Six. Perhaps the better formula of water $= 2H_2O$ will appeal to the scientific mind in symbol.

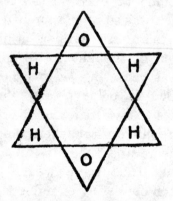

It may be convenient to regard all matter from the point of view that the atom is a hexahedron rather than a sphere. My faith in ancient creeds is by no means exhausted, for at all points I find them to be more imaginative and suggestive than the dry formularies of modern anomalistic science. To the extent that a theory of matter is universal and capable of spiritual interpretation it is to be preferred.

For the reason that Six was found to be a number
representing Creation, the number Seven attained
a dignity and significance which we can only
compare with the divine attributes. It was the
point within the triangles, the centre of the hexagon,
which by existence constituted a unifying factor and
gave it a particular virtue. It was at once seized
upon by the Hermetic philosophers to indicate the
totality of things. It became related to the
Sabbath, and was used to signify fulness and completion. So a week was made to consist of seven
days, and a great cycle of seven millenniums. The
Kabalists brought it out from the Oriental
mysteries to typify the seven creative forces, the
three lords with their *s'aktis*—Brahma, Vishnu, S'iva
—Saraswati, Lakshmi, Parvati. They symbolised
the solar system under a glyph, which employed
the seven bodies known at that time, thus:—

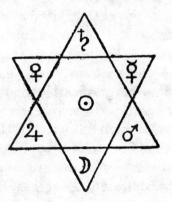

Here we see the symbol of the Sun holding the
central position, surrounded by a ternary of the

three major planets, Saturn, Jupiter, and Mars, and a complemental ternary of the three minor bodies, Venus, Mercury, and the Moon.

The symbols were repeated in the seven lamps and the branches of the golden candlestick. The septenary idea is indigenous to the Hebraic system, and is found in evidence at all stages of its development, from the Chaldean conception of the Creation to the establishing of the Covenant and the building of the Temple. There can be little doubt that the ceremonial of the Jews was based upon astronomical ideas then current, and St Paul bears testimony to this in speaking of the ordinances of Moses and the construction of the Tabernacle, which he says was ordained " after the pattern of things in the heavens." The leper was told by Elijah to wash himself seven times in the river Jordan—a cryptic symbol of the Gilgaluth or cyclic law of rebirth, the name Jordan signifying River of Knowledge. David the King prays that his soul may be " tried as silver is tried and seven times purified in the furnace of earth." For it appears that the Hebrews believed that incarnations were necessary until the seven stages of purification had been effected. The furnace of earth is of course the material body, and the silver thrown into it for the purpose of purification is the human soul, typified by the Moon, which rules silver. Similarly we have the perfection of things indicated by stages of seven times seven, which is the Hebrew jubilee—though for some reason unknown we have adopted the custom of celebrating the jubilee at the end of the fiftieth year, instead of the end of the forty-ninth or beginning of the fiftieth,—and we find that "seven times seven" and "seventy times seven" are numbers that indicate completeness and perfection, a Sabbath of Sabbaths. Thus the Israelites are represented as having passed around the walls of Jericho seven times each day for seven days, after which they celebrated the jubilee (hornblowing).

In connection with the subject of the Gilgaluth or cyclic revolutions of the human soul, we have to employ the symbols of the Sun and Moon as representing spirit and matter, or the natural elements of fire and water. "Except ye be born of water and the Spirit, ye cannot enter the kingdom of God," is in this sense apposite. The numbers of the Sun and Moon are respectively 36 and 28, which being multiplied into one another yield 1008, a number of considerable astronomical importance; and one-seventh of this is 144, which is, as we have seen, the number of the Man "of the fulness of the stature of Christ," and the original type Adam is enumerated thus in the Hebrew Kabala—A1, D4, M4, or 144, which is 12×12, the measure of the New Jerusalem.

Thus we see how the One is manifest in the Six, and how the One working in and through the Six produces the fulness of perfection and the "fulfilling of the law." The potentiality of all things is therefore in the One, the phenomenal manifestation in the Six.

CHAPTER XVII

COSMIC ANALOGIES

In a former chapter I have shown that the value of Pi = 3·14159 is contained in the sum of an age, a year, and a day of Brahma. I am not in a position to prove that the ancient Hindus, in instituting these periods, had any idea whatsoever of the mathematical ratio of the diameter to the circumference of a circle, but I should be quite prepared to find that all their great periods were but multiples of some that are commonly observed in astronomy.

It remains a singular fact that Kepler's law of the distance of the planets being regulated by their velocities so that they describe by their vectors equal areas in equal times, is in direct relations with the value πa^2, which represents the area of a circle. Here we employ the value of = 3·14159, and this, we have seen, is comprehended in the following periods :—

Brahmic Age	3,110,400,000,000	years.
Brahmic Year	31,104,000,000	,,
Brahmic Day	86,400,000	,,

3,141,590,400,000	,,

This seems to be directly related to the Hindu conception of the ages already referred to as the Gold, Silver, Copper, and Iron Ages or Yugas, known as the Satya, Treta, Dvapara, and Kali Yugas respectively. For we find upon enumeration that they are of value as follows :—

Satya Yuga . . . 1,728,000 years.
Treta Yuga . . . 1,296,000 ,,
Dvapara Yuga . . 864,000 ,,
Kali Yuga . . . 432,000 ,,

The total of these years is 4,320,000 solar years.

The Brahmic Day therefore bears a definite relationship to the Dvapara Yuga and to the Satya Yuga. Also we observe that the half of the Great Year of Plato (25,920 years) is 12,960 years, which is the one-hundredth part of the Treta Yuga. So that there can be very little doubt that these astronomical periods of the ancients are all linked up together in such manner as to form a complete system of astronomical chronology. The difficulty is to trace them to their source. It is of course observed that they are formed on a numerical progression of $1234=10$, and that the sum of the four ages is 10 times the value of the first, as 432,000 and 4,320,000. This would be the case with any numerical series in the ratio of 1234. I think, however, that the basis of the system is to be found in the multiple of 72, that being the number of years in which the precession of the equinoxes amounts to one degree of the ecliptic. There are 60 minutes in 1 degree and $60 \times 72 = 4320$, which

gives us the basis of the yugas.   Also 6 times 60 =
360, the number of degrees in the circle, and 6
times 4,320 = 25,920, which is the Great Year.
That which was known as the Naros of 600 years,
during which one of the twelve manifestations of
the Deity was presumed to rule on the Earth, gives
us the value 600 × 12 = 7200 years, and 60 times
this is 432,000 years, which is the length of the
Kali Yuga.   These inquiries are extremely interesting to pursue.

The ancients knew of a motion of the Earth's
axis which had reference to the obliquity of the
ecliptic, and they appear to have used these ages
in order to indicate the times during which the
pole of the Earth passed through a definite number
of degrees.

The belief is supported by the observations of
various astronomers such as Herschel, Maskelyne,
and others, who have shown that the diminution
amounts to half a second per year or fifty seconds
per century, and this is exactly one-hundredth of
the precession of the equinoxes.

If therefore we take the progression of 1, 2, 3
times the value of twelve revolutions of the circle =
360 × 12, we shall get the basic value of the cycle
4320 years × 1, 2, 3, thus :—

$$1 = 4,320 \text{ years}$$
$$2 = 8,640 \quad ,,$$
$$3 = 12,960 \quad ,,$$

Total   25,920 years

which is the Great Year, the entire precessional

revolution and the value of six cycles of 4320 years. Therefore it appears that the number of the degrees in the circle multiplied by the number of the signs of the zodiac is equivalent to the Precessional Year or Great Year divided by six.

There may possibly be other grounds for deriving the cycle first of all referred to, namely, the Brahmic Age, but the above appears to me to be the most likely, and the correspondences are too close to be overlooked even by those who have a scientifically educated dislike for "round figures." Nevertheless, so far as the precessional increment is concerned, there is nothing whatsoever to show that the present rate of precession is constant. It is estimated at 50·2453 seconds, but the records clearly show that it was formerly less than now. Probably a consideration of the true cause of precession will lead eventually to the fact that the variation is plus up to a certain point in the solar orbit and afterwards minus, and the mean will be fifty seconds exactly.

This would answer exactly to the theory of Kepler, in which the elliptical orbit requires that the Sun has an aphelion and perihelion of its own, and that its motion in space is therefore variable, being greatest at the perihelion and least at the aphelion, as is the case with the planets of this system and also of the satellites.

I do not consider that the ages of the ancients were the products of the imagination, but that they were invented from observation in the first place and afterwards augmented on speculative grounds.

For I have shown that there is a basis from which they could very well have originated, and this basis is an astronomical one.

If the theory of the continuous change in the obliquity of the ecliptic, due to the Earth's gradual change of axial inclination, be true, it will follow that at one time the axis must have been in the plane of the orbit, and the polar regions would have marked alternations of summer and winter, such as the planet Mars now undergoes from the same cause, and the equatorial belt of the Earth must then have been one perpetual ice-belt. At the present time, when the axis is assuming the perpendicular, we get a more uniform distribution of the Sun's rays throughout the year over the whole surface of the globe ; but the ideal condition from the point of view of habitability will be when the axis is quite vertical to the plane of the orbit, for then there will be no difference between summer and winter in any particular latitude.

Another point of considerable interest is left out of account in the earlier pages of this work when citing Bode's Law (p. 72). The discussion of the point did not seem apposite to the matter immediately in hand, but it may here be dealt with in connection with the cosmical facts we are considering.

The proportionate vectors of the planets, excepting Mercury, etc., are given on the basis of a progression of $3(2^{n-2})+4$, from which we see that the Earth equals 10. Neptune is omitted from this series, but it may be added by doubling the figures for Uranus and adding 4, thus $192 \times 2 = 384$, to which 4 being added we get 388 as the value for Neptune. The actual distance of the body is usually given as 2760 millions of miles from the Sun, and this would work out at 300 times the vector of the Earth. This clearly shows that Bode's Law is but an approximation which would work out if the sizes of the various bodies were proportionate to their velocities as these are to their distances from the centre. But Neptune is affected by Jupiter and Saturn as well as by Uranus, and the net result is that it is much nearer than is required by the law above cited.

When, however, we come to consider the planet itself we find that it is in a state of chaos, not far removed from nebulosity, and so remote from the Sun as to be in these conditions quite uninhabitable unless we presume, as we certainly have cause to do, that it has a dense atmosphere, and therefore is capable of retaining the heat generated from itself. It would then only require that the bodies upon it should be tenuous and of small gravity, and there would then be nothing against its habitability. Indeed, it seems part of Nature's economy to continue to open up in space new centres of activity in preparation for the advent of man in proportion as the planets nearest the Sun become, from their age and proximity to the Sun, gradually less suited to the habitation of man.

On these grounds we have every reason to regard with respect the ancient Puranic concept of the Laya Centres or vortices from which the worlds are evolved. The gamut of the solar system is raised a tone without the relativity of its parts being at all affected. It is even possible that the discarnate humanity of this system will find new habitations in the planets which are ex-Saturnian. Then Uranus will become the higher Mercury, or a repetition of Mercury's life an octave higher in the scale of things, and Neptune will thus be the higher Venus of our system and the habitat of the discarnate Venusians. The extra-Neptunian planet will, on this basis, become the future abiding place and seminary of the Earth's humanity, at a time when our planet is no longer habitable or fails to afford the requisite conditions for further evolution. The idea is not so fanciful as it looks. The seer of Patmos saw "a new heaven and a new earth" opened up before his exalted vision. We cannot otherwise regard these distant planets of our system than as latent centres of future activity and evolutional progress, and as, so far as we know, both light and heat are necessary for the continuance of life, it is only reasonable to assume that by the time these planets are capable of sustaining life upon them they will be considerably nearer the Sun than they are now. But we speak of times that are immensely remote, but with which, as evolving monads, we shall probably be intimately concerned. At all events we have to regard these distant planets either as inhabited by a humanity physically adapted to the peculiar conditions they afford, or as seed-grounds for a future humanity.

We cannot regard them as purposeless, for there is no analogy from which to argue.

Nature appears to indulge in these octaves. As a writer more than twenty years ago observed :— " When the first note of a new octave is evolved, man first begins to live." In the evolutional scale we have the several stages—igneous, gaseous, fluidic, mineral, vegetable, animal, and human. The eighth note is a repetition of the first, but on a higher gamut, and what in the primal stage of the Earth's evolution was the igneous life of the physical monad, here in the new scale is represented by the fusion of the spiritual monad with the higher forms of matter as comprised in the nervous organism of man. This union of the physical and spiritual monads constitutes that beginning of the new octave referred to above. What is known as the Uranian Age is now opening up in the world, and during its course of 2160 years the seeds of a higher humanity will be sown in soil that is already prepared for it in the great intellectual areas of the world. This is the age of the " pouring out of the Spirit upon all flesh," represented zodiacally by the sign Aquarius. Out of the celestial seeding-ground represented by the " Milky Way " new suns will be evolved. But not in two thousand years can these future worlds evolve further than to form nucleoli. In man, however, already prepared for the inception of the seeds of a higher and more abundant spiritual growth, it may well be that the subsidiary cycle of the present race of humanity can give rise to a tremendous output of extraordinary faculty and the realisation of social ideals and scientific attainments such as the world has not experienced at any time since the dawn of life upon this planet.

For whereas there have been previous Uranian Ages in the course of the great solar cycles, at every return humanity is found at a successively higher stage of evolution, and therefore capable of responding in a higher degree to the impulses of the Spirit. In all there are 100 cycles or Great Years, amounting to 2,592,000 years, during which a complete revolution is formed, and then a new direction is given to the axis of the Earth, bringing our globe into new relations with the circumambient stars. When we consider the fact that the furthest star in the confines of space is knit closely to our earth as to all other worlds throughout the vast empyrean, this new relativity of our world will be seen as the cause of a new evolution when " a new heaven and a new earth " may be said to be actually produced.

These dreams of the ancient seers and philosophers will be found on examination to be grounded in astronomical facts. So great is their significance and so ingenious their conception, we cannot but be struck with the various discoveries, astronomical and geographical, which conspire to uphold them. From another point of view, the theory of new centres opening up in space as the march of human evolution in connection with cosmic changes seems to require, we have collateral proof of this, so far as Uranus and Neptune are concerned, from the facts of astrology. In this system it is found that Uranus answers directly to intellectual genius of an inventive and original type, so that at times it appears that those who are affected by it are almost inspired. The planet is said to denote inventive genius, inspiration, inventive faculty, originality, eccentricity, a precocious and wayward mind. It answers to electrical energy in the physical world, and is typified by the lightning flash.

Neptune, on the other hand, appears to be indicative of the artistic genius, and has special relation to rhythmic vibration, sense of harmony. The planet is prominent in the horoscopes of those who are æsthetically disposed, and a study of the characters of those born under its direct influence will reveal the fact that they answer to the planet Venus on a higher gamut. Undoubtedly there are as yet inadequate means for the full expression of these higher vibrations in the human organism, but to the extent to which they manifest they are unmistabably abnormal and even supernormal in their effects.

Such being the case, we have every reason to regard these occult concepts with due respect, and to seek if possible a means of accommodating them to our scheme of thought in regard to human faculty. The effort of Nature to evolve special nervous conditions for the expression of these latent and higher faculties of the soul may give rise to an ill-considered association of abnormal

N

mental and psychic faculties with forms of insanity, when in fact they are only premonitory indications of a condition which in process of time will come to be regarded as normal.

Viewed from the point of view of numerology, we exhaust our gamut at the number 7, and Uranus will therefore be 8 and Neptune 9. But these quantities will have to be applied to the planets Mercury 5 and Venus 6, to which they are octaves, and thus we have for Uranus $8+5=13=4$, and for Neptune $9+6=15=6$. This comes into line with the statement in the *Secret Doctrine* that Uranus is the same as the Sun, for which the latter is a substitute; and we have already seen that 4 is a number directly related to the Sun in the kabalistic system of numerology. Also we have seen that Mercury is the alternate of the Sun, which answers to the number 4, while here we have Uranus in terms of Mercury represented by $13=4$ (vide *Cosmic Symbolism*, chap. xiv.).

As to Neptune, we find the ancient name for this god of the Greek pantheon was Poseidonis, and that the horse was his symbol; and further, that he was given the dominion of the seas, specifically the Mediterranean. He is symbolised as a creature having a horse's head and the body of a large fish, sometimes also as having the fore-parts of a goat and the hind-part of a porpoise. The idea of the sea-horse suggests at once the two signs Pisces and Sagittarius, both ruled by Jupiter in the astrological system (*Astrology*, p. 28), and for a long time Neptune has been associated by

astrologers with the sign Pisces, as Uranus with
the sign Aquarius.

Now Jupiter, as the ruler of the signs Pisces and
Sagittarius, is of the value 3 in the kabalistic
system, and this is the alternative of Venus 6
(*Cosmic Symbolism*). Then, if we regard Neptune
as the higher Venus, we naturally associate him
with the numbers 3 and 6, which are those of
Jupiter and Venus. Also if we regard the planet
Uranus as being the higher Mercury and this
latter as the alternate of the Sun, then Leo, the
sign ruled by the Sun, will find its negative in the
opposite sign Aquarius, which is ruled by Uranus
and here associated with the number 4, which
hitherto has been regarded as the Sun's negative
number. This opens up an entirely new system
of enumeration, and we shall find that Sun$=1$,
Lilith $= 2$, Jupiter $= 3$, Uranus $= 4$, Mercury $= 5$,
Venus $=6$, Moon $=7$, Saturn $=8$, Mars $=9$, and
Neptune, as the alternate of Jupiter and the higher
Venus, $=6$. Here, however, we are on the horns
of a dilemma, for we cannot regard Neptune and
Venus as having the same value, but we may
truly say that Venus $=6$ and Neptune $9+6=15$.
But in such case and to preserve the analogy we
should have Mercury $=5$ and Uranus $=9+5=14$,
which employs the two Sun numbers 1 and 4, and
produces something that is yet quite distinct, but
which, in its concrete expression, is 5. This seems
the more reasonable, and consequently we have to
regard our gamut as containing nine notes and not
an octave merely. In such case we must retain

N*

the negative value of the Sun =4 and consider
Uranus as of value 14. Thus :—1 Sun, 2 Lilith,
3 Jupiter, 4 Sun (negative), 5 Mercury, 6 Venus,
7 Moon, 8 Saturn, 9 Mars, . . . , . . . , . . .
14 Uranus, 15 Neptune. Here we see that Uranus
and Neptune are raised a whole nonate by the
addition of the number 9. This number stands
for the planet Mars, and denotes the power of the
will. The raising of humanity therefore is thus
symbolised numerically as dependent on the
exercise of the volitional faculty. Nothing can
raise the mind except the will to be raised. The
millennium could begin to-morrow if we willed it.
Individual progress is controlled by the power
of the individual will. The will to do, the will to
be, these are the determining factors in all human
evolution and the final factors in the process of
natural selection.

Atmane atmanam upasya, Raise the self by the
self, is the mandate of Krishna, as of Buddha and
all the great teachers. "Not everyone that saith
. . . but he that doeth . . ." St Paul exhorts
us to " work out our own salvation " and to become
" a law unto ourselves." In *The Light of Asia*,
bk. 8, it is said :—

Ho !

Ye suffer from yourselves, none else compels,
None other holds you that ye lag and stay
And whirl upon the wheel, and hug and kiss
Its spokes of agony, its tyre of tears,
Its nave of Nothingness !

CHAPTER XVIII

SOME RECONDITE PROBLEMS

THE idea involved in the preceding chapter is common to all religious systems, and consequently we may expect it to be reflected in any system of kabalism which has regard to the unfolding of human destiny. For assuredly this unfoldment is the natural means by which man draws near to the attainment of the "full stature of Christ," which, as we have seen, is kabalistically represented by the square of 12, or 144, the enumeration of the name of the primal ancestor, or of that race of humanity which became "sons of God" by the inbreathing of the Spirit (*Cosmic Symbolism*, chap. i.). What in the animal man is merely desire becomes in the Adamic race converted into will, and this same force of divine energy working in man will eventually bring him to a state where he is both mentally and physically capable of a fuller expression of the Spirit.

Doubtless it is the fact that in the process of evolution each individual goes through the whole gamut of development from 1 to 9, *i.e.* from mere vital functioning to the expression of individual will in its quest after freedom from limitation and bondage. But some study of particular cases in connection with the doctrine of spiritual hierarchies has led me to the conclusion that each individual is permanently related to some one spiritual hierarchy, which, through a dependency of states, spiritual, mental, and psychic, is ultimately expressed in a group of incarnations coming directly under the influence of some particular constellation, star, and planet.

Thus the particular destiny comes to be controlled by the asterism which is rising at the time of one's birth, that under which a person is said to be born, and this asterism is related to a particular part of the Cosmic Man and answers to some specific function in the Cosmic Mind. And this may be taken as a partial explanation of Emerson's exhortation to " Hitch your wagon to a star," which is serviceable advice if you only know which one. It explains why a variety of individuals born under the direct influence of one of the planets are found to be altogether dissimilar in their tastes and pursuits, and different in their objective. For the planet is but one and the last of a series of screens through which the spiritual monad expresses itself in the process of incarnation. It thus becomes of greater importance to know what " star " one is born under than what planet. For the planets are but seven in number, or nine if we regard the luminaries as in the category of apparent planets, while the stars are innumerable, and together as celestial molecules constitute that Grand Man or

Cosmic Body which according to all mystical philosophers is the " vestment of God."

In a true philosophical system of cosmogony we shall find that as Deity is expressed in Nature and Spirit in matter, so every physical atom is the expression of a spiritual atom, and thus there are two monads, the physical and the spiritual, the one working up through the various stages of physical evolution to the upbuilding of the human form, and the other working downwards by a process of involution for final expression in the inspiring of the human form.   The union of the two monads is the supreme fact of the alchemy of the soul, and the process of their fusing and complete interaction is represented in the unfolding of individual consciousness and the establishing of the will to be and the will to do in man.   Until this union was effected it could not be said that the human soul existed in the man-form or human animal, for the psyche is the child of Spirit and Matter.   Traced to their source, these two, Spirit and Matter, must be regarded as essentially one, although in some systems of speculative philosophy the one (Matter) is regarded as a reflection of the other.

In developing these ideas I am but extending the cosmical conceptions of Bruno into the realm of the true Kabala.   We observe one cosmic energy or life working through a variety of states of matter to the production of various kinds of forces, and we understand that essentially all matter is identical, but apparently different by reason of a variety of characteristics produced in the process known as differentiation. The various stages at which energy is arrested by matter appear to answer to states of consciousness in man, for all consciousness appears to be the result of resistance. Individual consciousness or what is called self-consciousness is thus the product of the incarnation of the monad. If we take an etheric vibration or an electric current and set up resistance to it we shall get light as the result. By slowing this down again we get a partial conversion into heat, and by further resistance we institute the phenomenon of combustion. The descent of the monad through the successive planes of matter thus gives rise to successive states of consciousness from the various degrees of resistance set up by the material conditions through which it passes. The physical body of man and the cosmic body of the universe thus represent resistance coils of the greatest power, and it is therefore in its associations with gross matter that the centre of spiritual energy we call the monad is capable of elaborating the degree of consciousness and the forms of intelligence which relate it to the material world. Thus it is that Vulcan = Mars = Will, is both the desire that tends to the forging of our material bonds and also the volition necessary for our release from those shackles. And we see that Saturn 8, the symbol of restriction, is the cause of transition to Jupiter 3, which is the symbol of expansion, and finally to 9 Mars, which is freedom.

There arises another point of some interest both

astronomical and kabalistic, which I have incidentally referred to in the foregoing chapter, where the numbers allotted to the planets require that 2 is the value of Lilith. To many of my readers this name will be unfamiliar, and I may therefore explain that among the Kabalists there is a tradition that Lilith was the first wife of Adam, who was changed into a night spectre in consequence of her refractory conduct. She is described as especially inimical to women and children, and from all accounts appears somewhat akin to the hag known as the Banshee, the apparition of whom in any house is certain disaster to its occupants.

Cosmically Lilith is the second or rather the first satellite of the Earth (Adam), and is no longer a luminous body, but revolves still about the Earth in an orbit at a mean distance of 1,040,000 miles in 119 days. Proctor in his *Other Worlds than Ours* asserts that in his opinion there is every reason to believe that there are myriads of these dead and non-luminous bodies floating about in space, any one of which may be the occasion sooner or later of a vast cosmic cataclysm as the result of a collision. The satellite Lilith is only visible to us under certain conditions, namely, when at a particular angular distance or elongation from the Sun and at the time of its transit over the disc. From observations made by Waltemath of Hamburg and various records both before and since his discovery, we are able to establish the synodical revolution of the planet as 177 days. Thus there is recorded a transit of a black spot over the disc of the Sun on 27th March 1720, by Dr Alischer at Fauer; another in the following year by the same observer on the 15th March; another at St Neots, Huntingdon, on the 6th June 1761, recorded by a writer in the *London Chronicle*; another seen by Lichtenberg and Sollnitz on 19th November 1762; another by Hoffman near Gotha on 3rd May 1764; another by Supt. Fritsch at Quedlinburg on 25th March 1784, recorded in Bode's *Astron. Alk.*, 1805; another by Dr Ritter, of Hanover, on 11th June 1855; another by Gowey on the 4th September 1879 at N. Lewisburg, Ohio; another on 4th February 1898 at 1.30 p.m., seen by Dr Zeigler and eleven other persons, and seen at Wiesbaden on the same day at 8.15 a.m.; another on the 4th February 1898. Now, as we cannot accuse these several authorities of aberration or conspiracy, we are bound to accept their statements as veridical. A cursory examination will show that every one of these dates of transit are separated by a period of 177 days to within a few hours. Then, as the motion of the Sun will be about 174 degrees in the same period, the satellite will have travelled 360 + 174 = 534 degrees in 177 days, which gives its mean diurnal motion as about 3 degrees and its revolution as 119 days. Retrogressive computation shows that the satellite should have been in conjunction with the Sun on the 13th September 1618; and 11 days before this Riccioli, as recorded in the *Almagestum Novum*, vol. ii. p. 16, saw a fiery red globe to the west of the Sun. Cassini the elder and Maraldi saw the transit on the 7th

November in the year 1700, and it was seen again
in Hungary on the 23rd December 1719, like a red
sun with a white line across it.

If the Moon, an old and worn-out body, still
perseveres in its orbit, there seems no reason why
other bodies more remote from us should not have
persisted. It is altogether probable that as the
Moon is now receding from the Earth, so formerly
the further satellite was much nearer the Earth
than now; and indeed the suggestion may be
hazarded that even before the Moon was in the
position of a prime luminary to our globe Lilith
may have been functioning in that capacity. We
have only to assume, as I think we may, that the
Sun has a direct pull on the body somewhat greater
than that of the Earth, and we at once see that at
the conjunction, when the satellite is between the
Sun and the Earth, the former pulls it a little out
of its course, so that at no successive revolution
does it return to the same relative position as
regards our globe, but is always being urged towards
a wider orbit and a commensurately slower velocity
as required by Kepler's law. This is found to be
the case in regard to the Moon, and it must be so
in regard to any other satellite of the Earth.
Possibly Lilith held the same or similar relations
to the Earth in a former period of activity (*man-
vantara*) as the Moon does in the present period of
our terrene life. For it is not believed, at all events
by the Kabalists, that this is by any means the
first period of life through which the Earth has
passed, but that it has had successive periods of

alternate activity and quiescence (*manvantaras* and *pralayas*), and emerged from its last long sleep about eighteen and a half million years ago. I have stated the case briefly in the opening chapter of *Cosmic Symbolism*, and need not therefore discuss the grounds of this belief again. Enough has been said to institute a basis for the enumeration of Lilith, which for various reasons may be regarded as of value 2, in contrast and complement to the Moon = 7, which has already been established.

Speaking of the Sun and Moon as the male and female symbols of cosmos in relation to the humanity of this globe, we are reminded that a wider interpretation was given to this symbolism by substituting the Earth as mother in place of the Moon. This leaves out of consideration the moot question as to the origin of the Moon. It is at present our satellite. That it was always so does not transpire from any astronomical evidence, and I shall not say that they are wrong who assert that the Moon was mother of the Earth and not the contrary. The fact that at the present time our globe is estimated to be about fourteen times larger than the Moon proves nothing as to seniority, for we know that the Moon is a dead world, or at least a sleeping one, and that it has gone through a process of shrinkage during the course of ages which has left it a mere remnant of what it once was. We are, of course, astronomically aware of the fact that the Moon has for many ages been receding from the Earth; and we also know that it has reached absolute zero in its axial rotation, which shows that its vitality is at lowest ebb. If it were to rotate slower than now—and it makes exactly one rotation while it revolves around the Earth— it would appear to rotate from West to East upon its axis, contrary to its present motion, and we should have the gradual revelation of a thing as yet unbeholden, the other side of the Moon !

On the other hand, if the Moon were suddenly caught in one of those great cosmic streams of energy which Sir Hiram Maxim speaks of with such remarkable intuition, the Moon's rotation on its axis would immediately be accelerated, the planet would begin to live again, and, roused from its long slumber, it would enter upon a new day of activity and development. The evolution of new forms of life would begin anew, and the now barren globe would in process of time become a centre of teeming life. Who knows how long this catalepsy may last, or how soon the sleeper may awaken ? But awake or asleep it is regarded by the Kabalists as the mother of our world, and it holds true among astrologers that " the Sun is the father and the Moon the mother of every mundane event.".

CHAPTER XIX

GOD GEOMETRISES

WHEN Goethe called architecture " frozen music," he was impressed by the same idea as that which caused Plato to define the Deity as the Great Geometer.

Whether we view a noble edifice, a magnificent landscape, or the vast canopy of heaven " studded o'er with gold," we are looking at concrete thought. The universe has been variously described as " the vestment of God," the " bodying-forth of divine Thought," and " divine Ideation in expression of form." The day of belief in the fortuitous concurrence of atoms is now far gone and possibly will never return to the human mind in quite the same positive form. Science has made vast strides towards the theological position, and philosophy in the middle ground between them is seen to be making discreet but unmistakable advances towards the argument from design. The more we learn of the laws of the universe around us the more evident to our minds does the design and purpose of creation become, the more acceptable the idea of a beneficent Creator. A man cannot be intimate with Nature, or study the laws of matter closely, without finally swerving to a belief in an Intelligence at the back of things. Everywhere on all sides, and in an almost infinite variety of forms, he beholds the Trinity of Life, Substance, and Intelligence expressed as force, matter, and consciousness. In the mutual attraction of molecules, in chemical combinations, in the building up of cells into tissue and organisms by assimilation of inorganic matter, he sees elective affinity and the operation of a magic which he does not understand. He does not pretend to know what is the nature of that interpreter which converts inorganic into organic matter, still less what it is that renders an organism the vehicle of an intelligent will. He observes, however, that faculty, function, and instrument are immediately related. He may have a conception of life apart from any particular form that lives, but there is no possible conception of embodied life apart from function, and function implies faculty, which is not merely an expression of life but also of a living intelligence. It is perhaps hardly conceivable that one should have even a broad idea of the laws of life and the constitution of the cosmos and not regard those laws and that studied order of evolution as in some intimate relations with an Intelligence of a supreme nature, and as a partial expression at least of such an Intelligence. The question then arises as to the means of this expression. It is implied in the terms "law" and "cosmos."

The terms are correlative. According to Leibnitz

there could be no cosmos apart from pre-established harmony, which harmony is the effect of intelligence in operation. Then we have Intelligence as faculty, Cosmical Evolution as function, and Cosmos as instrument. All that is possibly knowable to us as sublunary creatures concerning that Intelligence as faculty, is to be learned from a study of cosmical functions and the world about us.

The universe is not in itself a plenary expression of an Infinite Intelligence or Omniscient Being. It is not an infinite universe; on the contrary, it is in itself a comparatively small one, and our Sun, which is its gravitational centre, is a star of no great magnitude. It is, moreover, a satellite, answering to a gravitational pull from a greater focal centre in the confines of space. The solar system has an orbit, and, from the view-point of Plato, the Sun takes 25,920 years to complete its revolution. If we take the mean precession of the equinoxes, 50″ per year, and divide it into 360°, we shall have 25,920 years, which is the Great Year referred to by the great philosopher. It is suggested that the proper motion of the Sun in space is the true cause of the phenomenon known as precession. If this be so, and I see nothing against it, although I am aware it is not the argument used by modern astronomers, then the distance of the Sun from its gravitational centre is calculable in terms of a mean vector. We know nothing, of course, of the eccentricity of its orbit, but we know from observations extending from Hipparchus, through Ptolemy, to Copernicus and Kepler, and continued by modern astronomers, that the solar system is moving in the direction of the constellation Hercules, the stars of which are opening out, while the stars in Gemini are closing in.

Leaving the consideration of these higher and more speculative astronomical problems to others, we may consider the bearing of the main facts of astronomy upon the kabala of numbers. We have already seen that the universe is only intelligible because it is an expression of Intelligence. Its intelligibility lies in the fact that it responds to the law of numbers, whence we may argue that numbers are the means employed for the expression of the Divine Intelligence. The facts fully maintain this view.

A planet moves in an orbit about the Sun at a mean distance determined by its mass, volume, and magnitude. Its velocity, or mean motion, in its orbit depends again on its mean distance, and its revolution or periodic time is dependent on its velocity. The whole mechanism is unified by the law of Kepler, which requires that the planets describe equal areas in equal times by their motions round the Sun, and hence it follows that the squares of the periodic times of the planets are to each other as the cubes of their mean distances from the Sun.

From this we see that the universe itself is governed by mechanical laws which are intelligible, and therefore are expressions of Intelligence. We see, also, that this Intelligence is expressed in terms of numbers, which we use to signify quantitive relations. The same ordered and intelligible re-

lationship may be observed in regard to the properties of the elements, chemical combinations, crystallisation, etc.   The phenomena of light and
sound, as developed in colour, art, and music,
contribute to the same testimony, while telegraphy
has quite recently given us a new view of the finer
forces of Nature in the phenomena of syntonic
vibration.

There is, indeed, no coherent view of the forces
of Nature apart from an ascription of intelligence
behind them.

It is only when we come to the symbolical use
of numbers that we are faced with any degree of
difficulty.   If the Kabalist gives a characteristic to
a number, he is in the position of one who has no
other argument than that derived by experience.
He cannot tell you why 9 should be an incisive
number, or why it should signify cutting, wounding,
severance, strife, sharp words, or a sword, but he
can link it up with the planet Mars and the colour
red by a symbolism which is mainly dependent on
its universality.   But this universality is in itself
the strongest argument in favour of its recognition.
If it were an isolated experience, or one that de-
pended wholly on tradition, then we should have
good reason to question its truth.   The symbologist
is, however, supported by the empirics of all nations;
for whether as the Chinese Ho-sing, the Persian
Marduk, the Chaldean Coah, the Coptic Kham, the
Greek Vulcan, the Indian Angarika, or the Latin
Mars, the same planetary body has the same characteristics ascribed to it.   Adam, the perfect man,

made in the image and likeness of the Elohim, is
enumerated thus : 1a 4d 4m = 144 = 9.   Adam means
red.   It is also the Hebrew number of "the
fulness of stature," or 12×12.   It is, of course,
only a convenient symbolism which connects the
number 9 with this planet ; but, inasmuch as the
whole universe is a symbol of that Intelligence
which created and sustains it, we have no cause to
quarrel with the Kabalist when he, in common with
the scientist, avails himself of its convenience.   It
appears rather an advantage to designate a characteristic by a number, when the language or symbolism of numbers is known ; as if, by the physiognomy of a man, he should be described as one of
much combativeness, it would be convenient to
say that his characteristic is 9 ; or that one of much
joviality, *bonhomie*, and expansiveness should be
characterised by 3 ; as convenient, indeed, as the
geometrical formula πa^2 for the area of a circle, or
H_2SO_4 for sulphuric acid.

The point we have to bear in mind in all these
speculations is that there is a geometry in nature
which is discoverable and cognisable, but which
exists quite apart from our recognition of it.   It is
not a feature imposed upon it by our laws of thought,
but, on the contrary, our laws of thought are determined by it ; and this seems to be the reason
why the whole of our being, the incident of our
lives, and our relations to the external world,
answer to a numerical law.

When, therefore, we say that " God geometrises,"
we mean something more than the mere observance

of geometrical law in the creation and ordering of the cosmos ; we intend also the imposing of a geometrical law of thought upon humanity.   Our concepts are those of Unity, our thought is in terms of the Triad, our perceptions answer to the Septenate. We are compounded of universal elements, and respond at all points of our being to the geometrical ratios of an elemental life.   But also we are more than elemental beings, and potentially greater than the universe in which we exist; for we are in a conspiracy of thought with the divine, taking knowledge of the gods as we are able to understand their language, learning to use the elements and the forces of nature, and entering freely into the scheme of our own conscious evolution and unfoldment.

And if, in the endeavour to penetrate some of the more subtle mysteries which encircle our lives, the Kabalist makes trial of the numerical key, he has, at least, the sanction of those who are learned in the cryptography and symbolism of Oriental writings as well as the authority of traditional practice ; and should he succeed in opening even one of the seven portals which guard the Temple of Truth, he may account himself as fortunate beyond those who merely stand outside and take note only of the external lineaments of the edifice, not caring what great treasures may be displayed within.

THE KABALA OF NUMBERS
PART II

THE
KABALA OF NUMBERS
PART II

A Handbook of Interpretation

BY

SEPHARIAL

CONTENTS PART II

THE
KABALA OF NUMBERS
PART II

INTRODUCTION

THE increasing interest taken in the study of numerical ratios and the occult significance of numbers has created a growing demand for instructive works on the subject. Consequently, I have undertaken a further and somewhat more complete exposition in the present work, which may be regarded as an extension and elaboration of the principles of Numerology laid down in my first volume bearing the same title. Unfortunately, that book was hurried through press and contains some errors which have already been noticed. These were chiefly typographic errors, but there is one of authorship which certainly requires explanation. Reference to the volume will show that I have given three distinct systems of evaluation of letters, namely : the Hebraic, the Pythagorean, and the Phonetic or Universal. The idea in my mind was to present each system on its own merits and to illustrate each with some interpretations. This

1

was accordingly done, and a note of warning was given to the reader regarding the necessity of interpreting by the key belonging to the system from which the evaluation of the name was made. Thus, if the Hebraic values were used, the interpretation should be by means of the Tarot keys. If the Pythagorean values are used, the key given on p. 32 *et seq.*, which belongs to the Pythagorean system, should be used. Similarly, if the Universal alphabet is used for evaluation of a name, then the Planetary Key (pp. 45–46) is used for interpretation. Many readers, and even reviewers who should be above suspicion, have shown that they use one method of evaluation and various methods of interpretation, thus making nonsense of the whole process. They serve, however, to point out my error of authorship, which consists in giving various methods and keys in the same work. If I repeat the process in these pages, it will be with the express intention of showing that, properly worked, the methods are not in conflict but in agreement, and that each presents some aspect of the truth. Personally, I find the fullest satisfaction in the use of the Universal or Phonetic system of evaluation and the corresponding Planetary Key of Interpretation. This I have more fully developed in my *Cosmic Symbolism*, which was intended to be supplementary to the *Kabala*, pt. i., but has been found by many readers, unacquainted with astrology, to be too far advanced. So here, in these pages, I intend to give some new material on lines that are sufficiently plain to avoid all possibility of confusion, and it is believed that in following them the reader will find much that is of interest and not a little that may be rendered profitable study. My sole object in writing is to stimulate the public interest in the symbolism of numbers, and to suggest a certain necessary connection between our apprehension of things as facts of experience and the cosmic laws which underlie those facts.

I have already shown that cosmic laws are in operation whether we are conscious of them or not, and that their significance in human life, and possible utility for us, commence the moment we begin to apprehend those laws. For just as by an understanding of the forces of Nature man has been enabled to harness them to his use, so by an understanding of the laws governing the action of those forces, he may gain some further and more permanent advantage by intelligent co-operation. All the trouble in this world arises from the mistaken idea that we are surrounded by and invested with forces which have to be resisted and overcome. If, in the process, we come by any hurt, we invent a word to stand for our unconscious ignorance of natural laws, and promptly we speak of evil and the personification of evil. It is quite otherwise, however, when we happen to be going with the stream. Only the truly wise can regulate their desires and actions so as to be wholly in accord with Nature and the will of Heaven as expressed in natural laws. But all can to some extent regulate their goings and comings so as not to be in open conflict with their immediate environment, and to this end the study of the quantitive relations of things and persons, as expressed in sound, number, form, and colour, will greatly aid in the process of adaptation, by which alone security is assured to us. Adaptability to environment may, indeed, be said to be the secret of progress, success, happiness, and longevity. It represents the line of least resistance and that of greatest progress ; and it is only when we fail to adapt ourselves to our cosmic and social environment that pain and unhappiness are capable of assailing us. What we call adaptability on the physical plane finds its counterpart on the mental plane in elasticity. It is that quality of the mind which enables us to take an interest in the trivial things of life while engaging in the study of its deepest problems. It is, in a word, sympathy, the power of feeling and thinking with others, that is the sign of the most perfect sanity ; and as cause to effect, so sympathy moves us to adaptability. It is this flexibility, this roundness of temperament, that constitutes mental and physical well-being and fitness. To be wisely sympathetic would therefore appear most desirable, since it is in harmony, symmetry, and fitness that we attain the standards of goodness, beauty, and truth comprised in the triology of Plato's most desirable things. The perfect man is symmetrical, and it is by the study of our Greater Environment, of the laws that govern the universe in which we live, and of ourselves in relation thereto, that we may attain that symmetry of being which is competent for all occasions,— sympathetic, flexible, versatile, adaptable, fit.

This much for the benefit of my critic who found the *Kabala* so interesting that he regretted its application to horse-racing and similar popular speculations. For it is my purpose to further offend his susceptibilities and to assail his solitary position by fuller demonstration of facts pertaining to matters of common interest, and which are of interest solely because they are of human origin. To show that these are governed by law is to demonstrate the existence of a law of mind by which we come into relations with them and apprehend them as facts of our consciousness. It is my intention to show that the man who follows these things with an intelligent grasp of the laws that govern them is better equipped to come out successfully than one who operates in ignorance of those laws. From this as a basis of common interest and recognition it will then be possible to proceed to higher and more universal matters, but the man who would reach up to Heaven must have one end of his ladder firmly planted in his mother earth. So let us be sympathetic in matters that are commonplace, and comprehensive of that which is trivial. In such spirit I commend these pages to all and sundry in the belief that what I have written will prove useful.

SEPHARIAL.

LONDON, 1913.

CHAPTER I

THE NUMERICAL IDEA

To trace the development of the numerical idea in human thought would entail too deep a study for a work of this nature, and indeed I cannot lay claim to that encyclopædic knowledge which would be required to render such a study at all complete. It is, however, a matter of common knowledge that the development of the numerical idea was preceded by an instinctive perception of quantitive relations or ratios. Among aborigines we find no suspicion of mathematics and no nearer sense of actual values than is imported by the common needs of their existence ; economics are an instinct with them, and, like the chimpanzee, they know "how many beans make five," but not six. In other words, they have the numerical idea in germ only, and it is expressed by crude generalities. They take comfort in numbers without any true sense of their working value ; but civilisation, with a howitzer and a wireless detonator, judges two men to be better than a tribe. Quality begins to attach itself to number as soon as the primitive man is forced into the paths of civilisation. The primitive idea is persistent in the man who does not care what he eats so long as he gets enough. He is on the same mark as the aborigine who is father of ten children and owner of twenty kine, all very poor stuff, and knows not to discern that Kitmagū in the next hut is a better man than he with only two stalwart sons and three kine, all sound in wind and limb. But quantity and quality are jostling one another along our marts and boulevards wherever we may go. I have even heard a Rockefeller and a Vanderbilt envied by a man who ate four good meals every day and slept soundly for eight hours every night, and he, too, a man who really occupied more space at any one time than an average two! Now, what could a millionaire do more than he? True, he might commission any amount of labour, but he could not do the work, nor produce more than one man in one day. Economically he is not more effective nor more necessary to society than the scavenger, but he would not like you to say so. From a certain point of view your millionaire is a man who has gone a long way ahead of his fellows without making any real progress. If to the wealth of a Crœsus one could add the wisdom of a Solomon, and the compassion of a Sakyamuni, and the strength of a Milo, and the endurance of a Job, something symmetrical could be made of your plutocrat. At present he is only a man with a hump.

One can imagine, too, how the primitive man got hold of his idea of simple numbers as being invested with some strange significance—an occultism that

perhaps only the medicine-man of his tribe had any
notion of.   For, to be sure, he had his lucky and
unlucky numbers, and he counted them out in
favour of his friends or against his enemies on the
bark of trees and on flat stakes and on the smooth
surface of the time-worn rocks.   He made so many
straight strokes in imitation of rods or spears, and
lo ! the magic had been wrought !   He counted to
ten on his fingers or digits, and began a new series on
the thumb of the left hand because it was there he
began his count of One, coming as it did easiest to
the index finger of his right.   So eleven was " ten
and one," and twenty-one was " twain-ten and one,"
and none can say what tale of sheep and oxen was
counted on that distinguished digit, the first that
man ever put a number to.

Counting by rods or sticks led no doubt to the
earliest geometrical relations of human thought.
One stick would represent existence, a fact or a thing
of man's perception, maybe a woman or a child, an
ox, a sheep, a flint-head, a day or a night.   Two,
then, would stand for relative existence, and would
give use to the faculty of comparison, as by one being
longer and shorter than the other, thicker or thinner,
and thus heavier or lighter, stiffer or more supple.
What a great deal man began to know when he
counted two !   Yet not at once could he say by
how much one rod differed from the other, for
standards of measurement would come later.   It
was just the fact that one rod stood for him and
another for the woman, his mate ; one for the boy
he had by her, the other for the girl he hoped to

have. The idea was a full one for the moment. Could he not bind those two sticks together with the thread of destiny snatched from the pampas grass or the water-weed ? Things were thus as they should be ; and when he came to examine all their relations, he found he could bring their tips together so as to form an inverted Λ, and thus was evolved the first symbol of humanity—the creature with two sides, a male and a female, one that is supple and one that is strong. But he could not enclose a space between them, and this suggested an incompleteness and gave rise to a new idea, and the number Three was born in the human mind. By placing the divided ends of his two sticks upon the ground he could remedy their incompleteness by giving them a solid base on which to rest, so the Earth was called Son, child of the Father-Mother, by name Tu. Now this was a perfect thing—Father, Mother, and Child; and its perfection was made manifest under an everlasting symbol when the man walked around the woman, and a circle, of which she was the centre, was inscribed on the ground ⊙. The idea was one that fastened upon the primitive mind, and the number three was henceforth invested with a special significance, altogether wonderful, magical, divine. Then, of course, the three greatest things in Nature answered at once to the native thought—the Sun as father, the Moon as mother, and the Earth as son; and thus they have persisted through the religions of nations, in no form more familiar or less obscured by lapse of time and traditional imposts than in the trinity of the

Egyptians, known as Osiris, Isis, and Horus. Thus the story of three sticks, of the magic tripod, the fortunate triangle, and the lucky three that has universal currency.

Here are the forms which presented themselves to the wild man of the woods as he played with three sticks :—

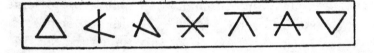

They are all primitive forms that have persisted in various of the world's scripts—Greek, Coptic, Moabite, Chinese, Latin, English,—and every one of them invested with a magical significance as primitive as the forms themselves. Look at that Delta. Who does not know it for a lucky triangle, with the child-stick lying supine at the feet of the happy parents united above? And that other triangle where the base line is uppermost and the heads of the family debased. That surely is a symbol of evil, and so indeed we find it in all the symbolism of the Hermetists, the Kabalists, and the Rosicrucians.

From the same three sticks we get the variant forms of the letter A in three different countries, the universal symbol of the Star and the Chinese symbol of Heaven. With his circle before him, suggesting the round of a tree, and his three sticks in hand, the camp-stool would soon be evolved. Home was already in sight, and soon the round sherd, supported by three sticks over a fire, would be bubbling over with the good things of the earth.   Truly the number three was a lucky one !

Four, of course, was bound to follow ; for it was the number of realisation and materiality, the symbol of possession (*Kab.*, i. 46).   The quadrate idea first took definite form when man began to parcel out the land and peg his claim.   Four rods would enclose a space convenient for allotment. Contiguous circles would leave blank spaces in between.   So four came to be associated with possession in territory, things solid and material on which the primitive idea could take a firm stand. You will find it in the earliest hieroglyphs used in this connection and continued in the records of past civilisations.   In ancient Chinese character it is a circle with a cross inside ; and the same form is found in the Egyptian hieroglyphs, standing for territory.   Without the cross it appears as a square form, signifying an enclosure, a field or plot of land —*tien*.   Astronomically it is used as the symbol of the Earth.   These are traditional values of symbols invented by our early progenitors, and they have persisted because they are natural correspondences.

In process of time calculation led to multiplication by addition, and division by subtraction, to an appreciation of fractional parts, proportional values, etc., and thus to the institution of standards of measurement.   Life soon became a serious business, and Numbers a Council of Perfection.

In the case of Meum *v*. Tuum the Court first of all impanelled a jury of ten—five men and five women. The women were afterwards expunged, leaving a *panchayat.* It was a one-handed business, with plenty of prejudice at the back of it; and when seven eggs had to be split between man and wife, or brother and sister, it always happened that the man got four and the woman three. Man's sense of equity obscured the finding of the jury, and the formula $\frac{7}{2} = \frac{4+3}{2}$ constitutes perhaps one of the most intricate problems that have been handed down to us from antiquity. Hence it is that the $4+3$ formula has come to be a bone of contention, some saying that the half of seven is three and a half, while others affirm that you cannot split seven eggs anyhow without making a lot of mess and trouble. The conventicle known as the W.S.P.U. has taken the problem seriously in hand, and probably we shall hear more of it in the near future. In the polity of nations it was not long before the Council of Twelve became a permanent institution, and the duodecimal system was applied to the world's business. Lately, however, there has been a tendency to revert to Nature's original simplicity, and counting by tens has found advocates wherever numbers are largely dealt with. In the ancient use of the Calculus—the coloured shells are still in use among the astronomers of Southern India—the decimal system was followed. Zero was represented by a coloured shell, and the numbers 1 to 9 by plain shells in a row. Ten began the second row with a shell of a different colour, and was followed by nine plain ones. Thus continuously the digits were ranged in ten rows of nine, and the power was

prefixed to each line by a coloured or marked
indicator, the form being

	0	1	2	3	4	5	6	7	8	9
1	0	1	2	3	4	5	6	7	8	9
2	0	1	2	3	4	5	6	7	8	9
3	0	1	2	3	4	5	6	7	8	9
4	0	1	2	3	4	5	6	7	8	9
5	0	1	2	3	4	5	6	7	8	9
6	0	1	2	3	4	5	6	7	8	9
7	0	1	2	3	4	5	6	7	8	9
8	0	1	2	3	4	5	6	7	8	9
9	0	1	2	3	4	5	6	7	8	9
10	0	1	2	3	4	5	6	7	8	9

and this could be raised indefinitely by shifting the
power line by the addition of a vertical line to the
right. I have seen very elaborate calculations
performed in a few minutes by expert calculators,
and I remember to have begun a kindergarten
course of study with something of the same kind,
coloured balls running on horizontal wires set in a
framework of wood ; but I do not remember to have
arrived at any stupendous results, the machine
serving principally as a weapon of assault upon
those who disputed my calculations, or otherwise
disturbed my peace.

It is difficult indeed to show any but traditional
authority for the idea that numbers carry with them
a specific meaning. The key to the position seems
to lie in the association of the number Nine with
Vulcan, he who binds and looses, and thus with the
Demiurgos the creative agent or Logos of the present

race of humanity, associated in mythology with both the principle of Good and that of Evil. Man thus numerically symbolised is the universal solvent, the maker and fulfiller of his own destiny, himself the problem and the calculator, the propounder and resolver of all questions. And here it is well to note that the questions that vex us are not universal ones, the Great Artificer has the finished work already in hand. Our race is not the first humanity to which the earth has served as seeding-ground. This seminary of Heaven has already yielded many crops. The problem of existence is solely and entirely ours, and it is for us to solve it—suitably by continued existence, for it is probably a true saying that " Life is a riddle that resolves itself." Vulcan, the forger of those chains that bind humanity to the rock of necessity, is thus seen to be Humanity itself. Thus Arnold in *The Light of Asia*, bk. viii. :

> " Ho ! ye suffer from yourselves, none else compels ;
> None other holds you that you lag and stay,
> And whirl upon the Wheel, and hug and kiss
> Its spokes of agony, its tyre of tears,
> Its nave of nothingness ! "

The number Nine as Vulcan, as Humanity, comes therefore to be symbolical of Karma, the law of retributive justice, action and reaction, the compelling force of necessity, the power of an infinite freedom. It is associated with the planet Mars (*Kab.*, i. 46, 59, etc.) and the colour red, the symbol of desire.

Now, desire is at the root of all action, and is the

fire that, acting on the fluidic body, is responsible for all forms of emotion. Working on the mental plane it produces the flame of intelligence, the flash of genius, and the will-to-do in every department of mental activity. It is the "colour" principle in the human soul, as intelligence is the "form" principle. It corresponds to heat, as intelligence to light. Without this desire-principle life would be inanimate and colourless, a valley of shadows, an Acheron. Desire it is that binds us and desire that sets us free.

Number Nine therefore has that magic in it that the Kabalists have identified it with the "Red Dragon" of Alchemy, the Universal Solvent, and the only means of transmutation. We cannot count higher than nine without falling into zero and beginning a new gamut. That and 0 are the beginning and end of existence, the Alpha and Omega of human possibility. On other planes the power is raised ; but the limitation would appear to be the same. Hence nine is symbolical of the limit of conscious activity ; zero the womb from which all life emanates and into which it all returns.

If we inquire as to the cause of this limitation of the mind by which we are compelled to count in terms of nine, we shall probably come to the conclusion that certain fixed laws of thought are imposed upon us by reason of our production from, and existence in, a world that is founded upon the cube of three. Our distance-sensation, which by continuity gives us the idea of space, is limited in three directions : as by length, breadth, and thickness. Our duration-

sensation, from which we derive the abstract idea
of Time, is also limited in three directions: as by
past, present, and future. Our sensations of duration and distance are linked together by our
perception of correlated succession—as, for instance,
that bodies are in continuous juxtaposition in all
directions of the same plane, and that events are
consecutive in similar manner. It is only when we
pierce through successive planes—as physical,
sensory, emotional, mental, and spiritual—that we
emerge upon the abstract ideas of Space and Time,
and find that they are one and the same, being, in
fact, linked together as concepts of the mind in the
consciousness of our continued existence. The
correlated succession of mental phenomena is as
much a fact in psychology as is that of physical
phenomena in physics. If we regard incarnation,
apart from its duration, as a single act, it will be
possible to relate it at once to a past cause and a
future effect. The actor becomes a necessary
permanent factor, and his embodied existence in
this world but the consequence of a past life and
the cause of that which is to be.

But I am getting side-tracked in the long grass,
and must return to the idea of numbers.

It would necessarily follow from the consideration
that a certain numerical law governs all phenomenal
sequence, that men would acquire the belief that
particular numbers have a fortunate significance
and others one that is sinister. One of the earliest
conceptions in this direction was that founded upon
the traditional belief that man was first created,

and afterwards woman. Then 1 would represent Adam or other first of a particular race, and 2 would be the symbol of Eve or other first of mothers. So numbers were alternately male and female, the odd numbers being male and the even female. Perhaps that is why Oddfellows and others of the male persuasion affirm "there is luck in odd numbers," and why also their best Seconds have sworn to be " even " with them.

In process of time, by observation of events of happy or sinister nature in connection with certain dates, days, numbers, etc., all the digits would acquire a traditional significance. Such a significance appears to have attached to the numbers 3, 7, 12, and multiples of these, in all theologies. The Masonic symbol of the eye within the triangle as the emblem of the Deity, has its counterpart in the Hebraic Yod with the triangle, and the Kabalistic talisman of the ten yods forming a triangle thus:

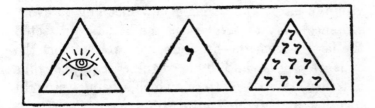

By a number of deft manipulations of figures the Rabbinical experts were able to read an entirely new and mystical meaning into the Hebrew Scripture, and this they embodied in a work which was called *Zohar*. But whereas they made use of three distinct forms of computation, they were faithful to

2

the text and to the traditional values of the Hebrew letters, and also to their methods, so that it is surprising they should have evolved so perfect a system.   Indeed it is open to us to believe either that the author or authors of the Scriptures deliberately planned the glyph and communicated the key to the Kabala, or that the writing of the Scripture was effected under the operation of the Law of Mind, which finds its interpretation in the mystical science of numbers; and I have already shown that such a Kabalism was imposed by the ancients upon cosmical phenomena, or that, alternatively, cosmic symbolism gave rise to the methods of the Kabalists. That they are in singular agreement none will dispute who have made any patient study of the subject (see *Cosmic Symbolism*).

Having given a permanent value to the letters of the alphabet, the consistent Kabalist proceeded by three methods to give a new value to every word or group of letters, and thus a new meaning to every sentence. By the *Notaricon* method he extracted the letters from the beginnings of words, from the ends of words, and by a regular sequence thus obtained certain letters which, being brought together and divided into words, gave a new sentence that was not only intelligible in itself, but apposite to the purport of the text from which it was drawn. By *Gemetria* he gave a value to each letter in a word and then reduced the whole word to its unit value, dealing thus successively with the words of the text, so that finally he had a number of figures which, being converted into letters, gave an oracular key to the meaning of the text. By *Temurah* he changed the letters of the text by the application of certain set rules embodied in the Table of Tziruph, so that a new interpretation of the text was open to him. Illustrations of these three methods will be found in *The Manual of Occultism*. I have no part in the Bacon-Shakespeare controversy, but I am prepared to show that whoever wrote the plays was a Rosicrucian and Kabalist, and an expert in the use of Kabalistic keys. For not only does he extract a truth from the symbolism of Nature and embody it in his text, but he hides a truth in the text and gives you the key in the symbol. Also, he makes use of recondite points familiar only to versed astrologers and students of alchemical literature. We cannot deny that all things are possible to genius, since it works by inspiration ; but it is more reasonable to suppose that in a studied cryptogram of this nature, conscious purpose was the moving power and experience the chief agent. The author, however, had many models upon which to frame his cryptic sentences, for secret writing of this sort had long been in use during times of wars and insurrection, and Kabalists continually use such means of conveying their teachings to those who are keen enough to perceive that an obscure sentence contains its own elucidation. Sometimes a signal is given, as by. some typographic error, peculiar spelling, or the use of an ambiguous word. The writings of Nostradamus are full of such signals, cryptograms, and anagrams.

Shakespeare abounds with them. In the *Exodus* there are three consecutive verses, each consisting of seventy-two letters, which are used for conveying the names of the Seventy-two Principalities known to Kabalists as the *Shemhamphoræ*, and they are each set over the gates of the temple, six at each gate, and three gates upon each side—one facing north, another south, one east, and another west. Astrologers similarly divide the celestial circle into four quadrants, of three signs each, answering to the four quarters of the heavens ; and each sign is again divided into three decans of 10° each, and these are split into two of 5° each, so that in all there are $4 \times 3 \times 3 \times 2$, or 72 "faces," as they are called, and each carries its own description and characteristics.

When, finally, in the evolution of the numerical idea, we come to the study of physics, philosophy, and even art, we find they are all capable of a mathematical and geometrical statement, and indeed there are some abstract ideas which cannot otherwise be communicated but by geometrical symbols and mathematical formulæ. So much is this method in vogue that it has been said that nothing is to be regarded as fact which does not admit of a mathematical statement, and yet we find that all the higher sciences make free use of symbols and formulæ in connection with them which have no existence as facts in Nature, but are merely relative truths. It would be interesting, for instance, to see a mathematical statement of the real motion in space of a body which moves in an elliptical orbit about another body occupying one of the foci, which itself moves in an elliptical orbit about a third body. This would be the moon's actual path in space as seen from a stationary sun.

But Kabalism is not concerned with such complexities. Rather it seeks to define the Universe as Symbol in terms of fixed values which have direct relation to the nature and constitution of man. Thus, although it makes use of the parabola, the hyperbola, and ellipsis, it regards man as a fixed centre of consciousness, to which all phenomena are related by a law of correspondence ; himself embodied universe in a universe that is himself, with numbers as the only key to the understanding of its mysteries.

CHAPTER II

THE GEOMETRY OF NATURE

HINTON says in one of his books on the Fourth
Dimension : " We know a great deal about the
How of things but little or nothing about the Why."
Nearer the truth, we may affirm that we know very
little of either. But what we do know is enough to
give a balance in favour of Hinton's conclusion.
We know how water crystallises ; we can make ice.
We know it crystallises always at an angle of 60°.
But why ? This beats us. We know the various
angles at which the metals crystallise, but our
science does not enable us to say why they preserve
these angles. It only enables us to recognise
them. We have learned, in fact, a great deal
of the physiognomy of Nature, but little or
nothing of its soul, of the intelligence that lies
behind its myriad marvels. Of Nature's geometry
we have learned somewhat ; of the Geometer we
know nothing but what is expressed in the work.
" Looking through Nature " is therefore the only
sane way of regarding any truths presented as
religion. If we steadily regard the geometry of
Nature in the same patient and sincere manner as

did Hipparchus, Ptolemy, Kepler, Tycho, Newton, Kelvin, and others we shall probably come to the conclusion that number, as expressed in geometrical relations, is the most intimate expression of the Soul of things.   Doubtless in the aggregate they seem to be endowed with more obvious qualities, which impress us in a more superficial way, as when we observe how beautiful, how grand and strong is Nature, how persistent and enduring.   But closer study will show that these qualities are facts of our consciousness, that the standards of beauty and strength are ours, and that what underlies all natural phenomena is the geometry of things expressed by definite quantitive relations.   Let these relations be disturbed by even a little and Nature breaks forth in fierce protest, flashing with the lightning of her eyes from beneath lowering brows, and calling with a thousand-voiced thunder across the dark abysm of night for speedy restitution.

And our study of this geometry has enabled us to understand and predict her moods, and even to utilise her magnificent strength in a multitude of ways.   It was that supreme genius John Kepler who first defined for us the relations of the various bodies in our immediate universe.   What are known as Kepler's Laws, which were later demonstrated by Newton, are the first and fullest expression of the principles of cosmology.   They reveal to us a geometry from which there is no escape, and anybody bold enough to deny the intelligence underlying them must be prepared to explain in a manner satisfactory to the scientific mind why these laws apply throughout the universe. And this is imperative, despite the fact that Science frequently makes use of a term for which it has no certain explanation or final definition. As an instance, I may cite the attraction of gravitation as one of the big labels concealing an empty bottle. For many years it has been tucked away on a dark shelf, nobody having any special concoction with which to fill it.

Kepler's Laws may here be enumerated. The first is that the planets in their motion round the Sun describe equal areas in equal times. If a line be imagined as joining the Sun with each of the planets at their several distances, then these lines or vectors will, in the same period of time, enclose triangles whose areas are all equal. Hence it follows that the nearer a planet is to the Sun the greater must be its velocity. From this proposition was derived the second, namely, if the distance of a planet from the Sun is variable so must its velocity be.

The second law is that the planets describe ellipses round the Sun, which occupies one of the foci. From this Newton derived his theory of gravitation, by which it was required that the planets were urged towards the Sun by a force inversely as the squares of their distances. The said " force " was called gravitation—a term that, as I have said, covers a great deal but conveys nothing. For Kepler's law was only true in relation to a stationary sun ; and when, as would inevitably follow from the universal application of the law of evolution, it was discovered and proved by observation that the Sun was not and never has been stationary in space, but was continually pursuing an orbit of its own, it was seen that the elliptical orbit could not be a fact in Nature, but was the expression of a relative truth only.

To illustrate this, let it be said a man on board ship walks in an ellipse around a mast. If his course were traced it would be found that, in relation to the mast, his course was elliptical, and would represent the orbit of Kepler's planet. And let it be supposed that the mast exerts a magnetic attraction on the man, constant in all directions. Now, since the mast would be in one of the foci of the ellipse, it would be necessary that, as he approached the mast in his elliptical path, he would have to accelerate his motion in order to resist being drawn into collision with the mast, since motion is our only means of overcoming the force we call gravitation. And to compensate for this hurried transit he might go slower when, at the greater distance, he was further from the centre of attraction. This is a crude illustration of Kepler's law and Newton's conclusion therefrom.

Now, of course, it will be said at once that inasmuch as the mast moves with the ship, it is possible to describe an ellipse around a moving body. In reference to the relations of the man and the mast it is so, but from the point of view of a spectator outside the ship it is not so. For let the man start on his orbital journey at the moment he is in line with the mast on board and the spectator beyond on the wharf. By the time he has completed his course and come again to the place on deck from which he started out, it will be seen that he is no longer in line with the mast and spectator, but many yards or miles away, according to the relative velocities of himself and the ship. Therefore his true motion in space cannot be an ellipse at all, neither is it a cycloid, since this infers that the body revolving round a centre in motion shall maintain the same relations with that centre. An ellipse infers that these relations shall be continually variable. Kepler therefore apprehended and formulated a relative truth only, while Newton based his theory upon it as if it were a fact. Both these great minds, however, brought us into intelligent relations with our greater environment and gave us a convenient point of view from which to study the geometry of Nature. Kepler's third law is that the centripetal (attractive) force varies inversely as the square of the distance, for any one or for all planets. From this we may conclude that the squares of the periodic times are to each other as the cubes of the mean distances of the planets. This is the converse statement of the same relative fact. Anciently it was thought that the relations of the bodies of the system were constant. Modern observations compared with ancient ones suggest that they are variable. The equilibrium of the universe is found to be unstable and in a continual state of adjustment. The universe is in a state of flux. For aught we know there may come a time when the relations of the bodies in a system become constant, but it is ᴋtremely improbable from our present point of view. Bruno evidently thought it so when he said : "Infinite variability is the eternal juvenescence of God."

From the fact that it is possible to calculate the places of the Sun, Moon, and planets for centuries in advance, we may perceive that the geometry of Nature is a fact upon which we may certainly depend with considerable security. This is the telescopic point of view. When we turn to the microscopic and examine her features in miniature, we find the same consistency, the same stability. The characteristics of a particle of iron, or of any kind of stone, or vegetable form are the same to-day as they were thousands of years ago. We recognise things by their features. The physiognomy of Nature is not evasive. It is an interesting fact that the superior metals crystallise at the angle or complemental angle of a regular polygon. If they sometimes followed one form and sometimes another we should not recognise them for what they are. We depend for the fidelity of our perceptions upon the integrity of the Great Geometer.

The fact that He never fails us has indeed led the superficial to presume that He never can, and that there is a blind mechanical law at work in the world by which things must inevitably continue as they are and always have been. " It always was and always will be " is the stock phrase of the frying-pan intellect. More depth and rotundity of mind would enable him at least to see that God is under no contract with us to complete His work. The maker of images may destroy his moulds. All the

great world-teachers have laid stress upon the
doctrine of Conditional Immortality, the condition
being obedience to the spiritual law. For aught we
know the physical stability of the universe is conditional too. Modern research would seem to
indicate that post-mortem existence is an assured
fact. But whereas we may have undeniable
testimony of survival of bodily death in some
instances, it has not been shown that even this is a
universal fact. And between post-mortem existence or continuity of personal life and immortality
there is a great gulf fixed. But this we know for a
fact, that in order to produce a chemical effect we
have to supply certain chemical conditions, and the
same may be said of electrical effects ; and if we are
disposed to regard physical existence as due to
chemical or electrical energy, we know that its
continuance depends on the maintenance of the
necessary conditions. If a personality can go to
pieces through a disturbance of the equilibrium of
its forces, why not a universe ? Indeed we have
before us, in the space between the orbits of Mars
and Jupiter, an illustration of a disrupted planet.
In the sudden flaring up of the star Nova Persei we
probably have sight of the disruption of a solar
system. Cities have been swept away, continents
submerged, valleys thrown up to the mountains,
mountains cast into the sea, planets and stars
exploded in space. Who is daring enough to affirm
the stability of the solar system ?'

But while it continues to exist it will follow the
same cosmic, electrical, chemical, and dynamic

laws as have operated from the beginning.   Why ?
Because, as Plato says, " God geometrises," and
these laws, which we apprehend and call physical,
are the numerical and geometrical expressions of
that Intelligence which constructed, animates, and
invests the physical universe.

> " We are but parts of one stupendous whole,
> Whose body Nature is, and God the Soul ! "

Providing we extend our ideas of Nature to include the whole telescopic universe, allowing that
what is perceived by us is probably but an infinitesimal part of the possibly perceptible, and what we
know of it certainly but the smallest fraction of
what is possibly knowable, we may read into these
lines, simple as they are, the most profound philosophical and religious belief that ever inspired the
mind of man.   Neither Pythagoras, nor Plato, nor
Kepler, nor Bruno taught anything that differed
from it, or was ever more profoundly true.   All
these had communed with Nature and had caught
some whisperings of the Voice of the Silence, but
who can say that any had entered into her secret
counsel or knew anything of the purpose of creation
—of the why and wherefore of existence ?   As
vessels made to honour, and bearing the inscription,
"צדק ליהוה," they carry each their quota of the water
of life, which is for the healing of the nations.
But the virtue of communion is not in the wafer or
the wine, but in the attitude of the communicant.
It is for us to study the language of Nature in a
proper spirit, if we would learn to read its symbols

and gain any practical knowledge of its secret
operations.   And the key to this study is Numbers
—ratios, quantitive relations, the geometry of
things.   But whereas it has become the fashion of
our philosophers to state their arguments and
conclusions in complex mathematical formulæ,
making of mathematics a recondite and cryptic
language that he who runs may not read, being, in
fact, in too much of a hurry to understand anything
but plain English, the ancient philosophers were
more conservative in the use of numbers, which
they used in a symbolical sense.   If it be true, as it
doubtless is, that nothing can be accepted as fact
which does not admit of a mathematical statement
—though I have tried unsuccessfully to reduce a
jumping toothache to terms of x,—it is equally true
that nothing is capable of a mathematical statement
which cannot be expressed in plain English, and
that with less chance of being misunderstood.

That quaint mystical philosopher Jacob Boehme
makes use of Numbers only in a mystical sense, and
he is worth studying.   Eckhartshausen uses them
in a symbolical sense.   Cagliostro, that genius
whom most writers have mistaken for a mounte-
bank, used them in a Kabalistic sense.   It is in this
latter that they come to have a practical value.   Of
all Numerologists he is the only one who has shown
anything to justify his teachings, and the fact that
he accidentally ran into the tail-end of the Holy
Inquisition only goes to show that the Church did
not know how to tackle the business end of a
proposition.   With a proper sense of the fitness of

things they would have given him a cardinal's cap, and left it to his artistic sense to fill the part and to his sense of gratitude to fill the coffers. I am a great advocate of Laotze's doctrine that everything exists for a purpose and that the virtue of everything is in its use. Hence I would make generals of all our bandits and admirals of all our pirates, providing they had given us enough trouble to qualify for the posts. For, after all, there is only one man who can do anything well, and that is he who knows the business. On the same principle, I think that if there is any practical good in a thing, it is good to be known. Your average esotericist would cut all his cake in a dark corner. I am well assured that there is only one cure for a hungry man, and that is a square meal of something fit to eat. Previous experience along these occult lines of study has shown me that only those who are ready for the idea can apprehend and absorb it. A good many can digest it, being of the educated-ostrich type of mind, keen on anything that means new knowledge, and punctual at meal times. But very few assimilate it. It does not enter into their constitution and become a part of themselves. It fails to affect their beliefs and their view-point in life. It is an adjunct, not a component of their mental being. Knowing this, one does not overfeed them nor put all the good things on the table at once.

Now, the connection of all this with the geometry of Nature may appear remote, but it is not really so. I have sought to show by citation of the

conclusions of great observers and thinkers tha
Nature has a geometry and that it is intelligible
only because and inasmuch as it expresses an
Intelligence. Doubtless we must finally conclude
that the geometric sense is vested in us, otherwise
we could not apprehend the geometrical. It is a
certain truth that our powers of apprehension are
limited to those things the principles of whose
existence are within ourselves. Does, anybody
think the rose is conscious of its own beauty and
blushes because we admire it ? It is we who define
our own standards of beauty, of goodness, of truth.
We are conscious of these things in proportion as
they are active principles of our own minds. They
are apprehended by the single sense of harmony.
Goodness is harmony, beauty is harmony, truth is
harmony. In what, then, consists our sense of
harmony ? It is inherent in the soul of man, in his
laws of thought, in the numerical constitution of
his being. According to his evolution and his
position in the scale of being, he embodies and
responds to a definite set of vibrations. He
apprehends number because he *is* number. The
mass-chord of all personal vibrations may be taken
as the man's physical constitution. The mass-
chord of all his emotional vibrations is the net
result of his psychic constitution. His thought-
vibrations are limited by his gamut of consciousness.
The average clodpole does not understand this fact,
but he can tell you something about pigs and
potatoes that are possibly worth knowing. He
does not understand why we are all invading his

beautiful Garden of Eden these summer days, but
he has an eye to the fact that we have brought some
money with us. He has lived fifty years in this
Paradise on earth and knows not that it is beautiful,
and that to be in it, if only for awhile, we are willing
to pay the price of many months of labour! Yet
he points with evident pride to that triumph of
porcine culture, the crown of all his labours : " That
there be a foine pig, look ye ! "

So, as Number is apprehended by us only because
it is inherent in us as a principle of being, so our
appreciation of it in Nature and in our daily life
will be in proportion to the development in us of
the numerical idea.   The man of commerce thinks
in pounds sterling, the wrestler and pugilist in
pounds avoirdupois.   The linguist thinks in words,
the geometer in forms, the mathematician in numbers.   The language we think and speak in, is the
language of our individual natures, tastes, appetites,
desires, and aspirations.   We are an embodiment of
cosmic vibrations, we make use of vibrations and
produce them in others.   But each of us has his
dominant note, colour, number, or vibration, and
answers to that note in others.   Not that we are
limited to sympathy only with those who are of the
same character and governed by the same number,
for each of us can reproduce those states of consciousness and those phases of emotion, desire,
passion, etc., through which we have evolved ; but
each of us has a basic note, a dominant which
sounds through all the movements and variations
of life's orchestration and adds its power of tone to

3

the universal harmony. This dominant characteristic or synthesis of characteristics can be
expressed as a colour or aura, by a geometrical
form, by a note, or by a number. It has been
referred to as a "signature" by Jacob Boehme in
his *Signatura Rerum*, and in this sense is a physiognomy imposed by Nature. Boehme further shows
these various types or signatures to be manifest
under Four Complexions, whereby he evolves in two
separate works a species of mystical astrology, as
if he had dealt with the planets in one book and the
four " elements " in the other. For clearly enough
he understood these four " complexions " or phrases
to be represented by the four Fixed Signs of the
Zodiac which enter into the composition of the
ancient symbols of the Assyrian Bull and the
Egyptian Sphinx, as well as the Hebrew Cherubim.
The Lion, Man, Eagle, and Bull are figures of the
four " elements " or states of Matter known to the
Kabalists as the spiritual, mental, psychic, and
physical. Two of them are light, namely, Leo and
Aquarius, the Lion and the Man, the Spirit and the
Mind ; and two are dark, the Eagle (Dragon) and the
Bull, the animal soul and body, represented by water
and earth, and the signs Scorpio and Taurus. Boehme
makes them correspond with the Four Seasons and
the four corners of the Earth or cardinal points.

So, then, if we take the nine digits as connected
with the planets (*Kab.*, i. 59–60), and consider that
these are represented on each of the four planes of
existence, then it may be that a man may be
numerically represented on the several successive

planes by the numbers 3, 5, 6, 9, making a composite total of 23, which, being reduced to its unit value =5, which brings him finally under the signature of Mercury, the colour Indigo and the note E.

Thus any horoscope may be taken showing the places of the planets in the signs, and the signs being arranged according to the "elements," the values attaching to each plane of activity may be totalled and unified, so that in the end we may obtain the "signature" or mass-chord of the man. Suppose, for example, we have a horoscope in which Saturn is in Libra, Jupiter in Scorpio, Mars in Aquarius, Venus in Aquarius, the Sun in Pisces, Mercury in Pisces, and the Moon in Leo. Here the Sun must be taken as 4, being in a negative sign; and the Moon as 7, being in a positive sign; the other planets as given in *Kab.*, i. 42.

The signs and planets involved are as follows :—

△Fire	—Leo Moon . . .	7
=Air	—Libra—Aquarius.	
	Saturn—Mars, Venus .	8 9 6
▽Water	—Pisces—Sun, Jupiter, Mercury	4 3 5
+Earth	—Nil.	

The unit values of these are :

Spiritual	7	unit value	=7
Mental	896 = 23	,,	=5
Psychic	435 = 12	,,	=3
Physical	0	,,	=0
		Mass-chord	=15 = 6 Sig.

But inasmuch as Saturn and the other planets are all represented in the horoscope at whatsoever time it is struck, we have to modify their values according to the signs they are in, since the same coloured light shining through a differently coloured medium will appear differently. For this reason certain numbers are ascribed by the Kabalists to the twelve signs and gates of the heavens (see *Cosmic Symbolism*). The number of the planet and sign being then multiplied together and reduced to its unit value, the mass-chord will be different for each combination of planetary influences, and the resultant signature will be one of the nine digits. But a more convenient method of enumerating the planetary configurations is to multiply the planetary number by the number of the planet whose sign it occupies, and then to reduce it to a unit value. Those of my readers who are interested in numerical horoscopy will no doubt take the hint and follow it out to its proper conclusion. I have here sought only to indicate that the geometry of Nature finds expression in the individual solely because he is compounded of the cosmic elements and himself a reflex of all that he beholds. For if man looks into the mirror of Nature fairly and squarely, and not obliquely or with a mental squint, he will inevitably see only himself.

CHAPTER III

NUMBER AS EXPRESSING THOUGHT

THE idea of the Universe as Divine Ideation in expression of Form leads directly to the subject of human thought in relation to number, and of number as expressing thought.

If we regard thinking man individually as a centre of consciousness in the Divine Mind we shall logically proceed to argue his physical existence as corresponding with a cosmic brain-cell, and of his consequent subjugation to a Law of Mind imposed upon him by reason of this relativity. A man cannot think as he will. If he thinks at all, he thinks as he must. He is bridled and directed by the laws of his being. It is even logical to carry the argument to the Supreme Centre and say that God is what He is by reason of His deity. According to the laws of our thought He cannot transcend the Law of His Being. He must be good, being God. He must preserve that which He has created because it is the consistent continuance of His Divine thought. Without the physical universe He can have no bodily existence. The visible universe is the vestment of God.

The man, the subsidiary agent, is what he is by reason of a preordination, and every individual unit subserves some special function of the universal economy. He is subject to the laws governing the whole body to which he belongs; he is obedient to the laws governing that organ of the organic whole of which he forms a subsidiary and integral part. Without his co-operation the economy of the universe is ineffectual. He is a cell in a brain centre. The Mind that animates him is supreme.

Taught by the experience of many incarnations to subserve the general economy of the particular function and organ to which he is related, he may even qualify for a higher function and consequent embodiment in a higher organ of the Divine Man. There is no limit to his perfectibility. He can evolve indefinitely until he reaches that supreme co-ordinating centre in the brain of the Grand Man in which resides the function of individual consciousness—the sense of the I am I,—to which all else is subsidiary.

Every individual, hence, responds to a particular number—the highest of which is Adam, אדם $= 144 = 9$ made in the "image and likeness of God." Now, God here is the Logos of our solar system, and it is not to be argued that the key number of our system is that of any other in the greater Universe. Suppose, for instance, that our solar system occupies the position of the right knee in the Grand Man—well, that is a long way from the brain, and yet so intimately linked up with it that any hurt or disturbance taking place in our system would be instantly known and provided for in the Supreme Centre.

And, according to Oriental teachings, in the *Guptavidyâ*, our humanity has not attained to a higher vibration than 5. We find man of this world blessed with five senses and five digits on foot and hand. It is a limitation imposed by correspondence, and the rest of this cycle of evolution will proceed along this fivefold line of development. Five is the number of Mercury, and its supreme function is the getting of knowledge. The quest of knowledge is therefore the key-note of our cycle. In all our Kabala we find a place for it in the centre of our scheme. In *Cosmic Symbolism* I have shown that it is the only number that is universally related and has no polarity, being itself the symbol of the co-ordinating centre of our material consciousness, *i.e.* the sensorium. All the five senses yield their impressions to the sensorium. The sum-total of our sense-impressions is experience. We are limited therefore to a fivefold apperception of things, and the development of a sixth sense lies in the experience thence derived. If now we regard all sensations as sets of vibrations, coming to us through atmosphere as sound, through light as colour, through privation of light as form, etc., then we shall come close to the perception of the numerical relations of thought. Our sense of harmony is bounded by a definite set of vibrations. We instinctively sense the fitness of certain sounds to express particular emotions. A military march,

for instance, requires the flamboyant key of G
major. To convey a sense of yearning or
regret we fall naturally into the minor. We flat
our music automatically to convey a sense of
depression.

Who taught us these things save Nature, working
through the senses. Perceive that my conception of
Nature transcends the senses. Nature does not
cease to exist where we cease to perceive her! The
limitations of the senses are part of our environment.
We know that our sense of touch is related to solids,
or bodies that affect our muscular sense ; that taste
is related to fluids ; smell to vapours ; hearing to
atmospheres ; and sight to ether. Yet all these
senses are but forms of touch. Seeing, hearing,
smelling, and tasting are all effected by contact.
It is only a matter of vibration. There are things
we cannot see because they are so fine and ethereal
we have no nerves delicate enough to register their
contact. Below our sense of touch there may be
things so solid we cannot feel them. Things
outside the gamut of our sensations do not exist for
us. We live in a world of relativity, and our relations are extremely narrow and limited. The
rotifera and other infusoria find plenty of play-
space in a drop of water that has been squeezed
quite flat between two plates of glass. From the
point of view of an Universal Intelligence our solar
system may be a mere speck upon the glass, a
microscopic culture of quite second-rate interest.
It is a good thing that we are able to regard
ourselves microscopically. We thus get a better

sense of our true relations to the infinite universe about us.

Seeing, then, that sensation follows a certain growth or development from one grade of touch to another that is finer, we may quite reasonably suppose that in a future state of evolution mankind will become possessed of yet finer faculties and correspondingly finer organisms than at present he possesses. Yet even in regard to those that we have it is seen that there is a considerable range, and only the educated sense, whether it be that of touch or sight or any other, is capable of defining our standards of perception.

The idea is that within this general fifth stage of human development in the present cycle of humanity there are nine principal modulations. They are sensory as to degree and mental as to expression. The degree of individual development will determine the particular tastes, inclinations, and habits of mind evinced by a man. One man thinks in terms of the public, and according to his degree of development he may be a caterer, entertainer, politician, writer, or teacher. Another thinks in terms of conquest, and may thus be an explorer, soldier, pioneer, or reformer. One comes under the lunar influence or the yellow ray, the other under the martian influence or red ray. One answers to the number 2 and to vibrations of that number, the other to the number 9 and its vibrations. But 2 may develop to the higher expression of the lunar ray, from yellow to white, the resolvent being, as universally, 9, i.e. strife, energy, effort. Thus :

234——567
9——18
27
——
9

The numbers 2 and 7, 3 and 6, 4 and 5 naturally balance one another, being each in combination of value of 9. To complete the series we note that 1 and 8 = 9, leaving 9 as the only digit standing unpaired.

Thought bears a definite relation to truth inasmuch as it approximates to a true expression of fact or is removed therefrom. Correct thought is formal truth, and it follows definite lines towards a conclusion involved in the premises. All consistent thought, therefore, lends itself to numerical expression because as a formulation of some truth it responds to the same test—harmony. Our thought is built up in much the same way as a material edifice. We select our ground, lay our foundations on the bed-rock of observed fact, and proceed by the addition of a variety of materials, which are fitted in their respective places, until we get a complete edifice designed and fitted to accommodate its tenant. Thus we build our thought around a central idea. It is a geometrical structure and answers at all points to the law of numbers.

The number 1 represents the straight line, whether by level or plumb; it is the symbol of integrity, of rectitude.

2 indicates parallelism, comparison, correlation, and relativity.

3 denotes mensuration and the bringing together
of things in apposition upon the common basis of
fact, as positive and negative are united in force,
force and matter in existence, man and woman in
humanity, wisdom and love in God. The Indian
Trimurti, or threefold aspect of the Deity, employs
Brahma the Creator, Vishnu the Sustainer, and
Shiva the Resolver or Destroyer of the universe.
The planets answering to these are Jupiter, Mars, and
Saturn, and their corresponding colours are violet,
indigo, and red. Violet is the combination of the
other two. So life and death are both involved in
the process of creation. We cannot add anything
to the sum-total of matter in the universe nor to
that of force. Neither can we take away from the
sum-total of either. But we can convert both.
Hence, in the building up of thought, we are
continually converting and rearranging materials
and energy we have already used. Our various
expressions of truth as we see it are merely kaleido-
scopic, and the same pieces of coloured glass go
into the making of our transformations. The
conservation of energy, the indestructibility of
matter, and the law of permutations are the
controlling factors of all human thought. Thought
is only a process of mensuration, and it is grounded
in form. For this reason we cannot ultimately
escape the anthropomorphic conception of Deity.
All thought, to be definite, must have form, and
form involves material. Hence, because the property of form is dimension, our thought is compassed
by the geometrical laws and answers to number.

Architecture, machinery, construction of any kind, as the embodiment of our thought, fully illustrates the fact that our thought is governed by geometrical laws.

Having arrived at this conclusion, we may next observe that our thought bears a definite relation to our environment. The questions that arise in our minds are in direct response to some stimulus from without. The pressure of circumstance requires a continual adjustment of our thought to our environment. The thought of others is as much a part of our circumstance as is their bodily presence ; we have to make room for it and take it into our consideration. Every man is the centre of his own universe, and no two persons can occupy exactly the same position. Consequently, he cannot hold exactly the same point of view in regard to anything except the central fact of Being. As embodied entities we occupy a position somewhere on the periphery of things and answer to a particular point in the *zodiacus vitœ* or circle of living things. In the circle here shown let A represent the central fact of Being from which, by an extension of itself in any particular plane in all directions, it eventuates in the periphery or circumference of being known as physical life, or the external world. Let B and C represent ultimate points of opposite radii, and D a point at a certain angular distance from both. Connected as they are by their radii with the central fact A, they will all regard it alike. But if we posit a relative fact F, we shall see that B, C, D each take different views of it. and between the viewpoints of B and D, and those of C and D, there is formed an angle of parallax, which from their relative standpoints gives the impression of a mental squint.

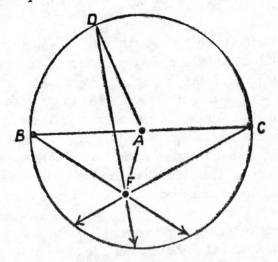

The fact that no two people look at things from exactly the same point of view is the reason why we are all so interesting to one another, and finally so necessary. It is by finding out how the facts of life strike different persons that we are able to get at the truth about it. If we want the true position of an elevated body we have to take the angle of parallax formed by looking at it from two different positions simultaneously and "splitting the difference." This method of splitting the difference is a practical means of getting at the truth about a thing when opinions differ. The difficulty is to know what obliquity is represented by each observer. But if the observers B, D, C identify themselves with the centre at A, then the fact F will appear to all alike, and its true position in the scale of things will be at once apparent by direct perception. This direct perception is only possible to those identified with the Central Fact. All else have only an oblique perception.

In meteorology we take the state of the barometer and the direction of pressure of the wind in a number of detached places throughout the country. From these we can determine the area of depression, and this, with the course of the wind, will show how the weather is travelling. We take the trend of public opinion in exactly the same way, but by different standards. The statistician reduces all his facts to the numbers, and draws his conclusions from those numbers. By the use of numbers it would be possible to make a chart of one's daily thought.

In the East they have a science of numbers which has direct reference to the things of our thought. An illustration of this science will be found in *Kab.*, i. ch. ix.; and another system of numbers by which things lost may be recovered if distinctly thought of. This latter method is based on the belief that a particular thought-form gives rise to and has definite relations with a particular number. Wherefore, if a lost article be thought of and immediately afterwards a number given, this number is a natural sequence of the thought-form, to which it is related by a law of mind. Then by the use of certain pointers or keys involved in the number, the lost article may be found. I am told by some correspondents that they cannot use the formula so as to get correct results. At the International Club for Psychic Research, three successive experiments resulted in as many successful findings. I frequently use the method for friends and associates. In one instance a legal friend had lost some valuable papers containing a precis of a case and a bill of costs wanted for immediate dispatch. In his dilemma he appealed to me, and I at once told him that he would find it on a shelf in his office among some other papers, and suggested including the mantelpiece as a shelf. Having already searched all shelves in the office, he was struck by the last suggestion and at once turned to the mantelpiece, on which stood a folding cupboard ; and on this, among papers of various sorts relating to almost everything except his business, he at once found the paper. Another reader of the *Kabala* wrote me soon after its publication informing me that by its aid he had found a valuable document which covered a considerable sum of money, and which he had long sought for in vain. Obviously, there is a certain spontaneity of mental action required. The process should be as automatic as possible. Some persons are incapable of this automatism; others cannot avoid in, being defective in the faculty of direction of thought.

There remains, however, in the presence of many failures on the part of particular individuals, quite sufficient evidence of the working of a law of mind by which numbers come to have a significance other than that of mere quantity. They are found to have direct relation to the nature of our thought by their correspondence with natural objects in which we are interested and which, as thought-forms stored in the memory, can at any time be evoked and brought forth by their numerical correspondences. That is how things suggest one another in the process known as the association of ideas. Nature would appear to be subject to the same law of numerical sequence, and in these pages I shall be able to show how numbers, or their sound equivalents, follow one another in rotation.

What we know in science as the law of periodicity is but another instance of the rhythmic sequence of vibrations, another name for the Kabalistic doctrine of numerical sequence. In astronomy we have a law of cycles by which the orderly sequence of celestial phenomena can be followed. The Metonic Cycle of 19 years gives us the dates on which the lunations will recur. The Saros of 18 years 10–11 days enables us to trace the sequence of eclipses. The cycle of 649 years gives us the entire range of all eclipses, and after this period they recur in the same order and in the same part of the zodiac. The cyclic law may also be traced in the recurrence of other celestial phenomena, such as the conjunctions of the planets and the recurrence of these in the same part of the zodiac. If Nature observes these cyclic and periodic laws, then assuredly man must reflect them in his constitution, and, through his dependence on physical conditions, in his thought also. These cycles or series of changes in man are proportioned to his average span of years, and whereas Nature has a cycle of

870 years, man has one of 8·7 years. This periodic law appears to be at the root of the old Alfridaries, of which I have given an example in *Kab.*, i. ch. xiii. An ancient Egyptian Alfridary divides the stream of life into two branches called the Sun and Moon, or the Light and Dark Paths. If a child is born during the daytime he is under the influence of the Sun and follows the Sun Path ; but if born at night he follows the Moon Path. By daytime is understood the period from sunrise to sunset, and night is the period from sunset to sunrise. Then they divide the life into periods of five years each, which they set under the planets in their Chaldean order, and from the combined action of the two sets of planetary influence, the Solar and the Lunar, they determine certain climacteric periods in the life of the child then born. The following is the Table of the Sun and Moon Paths, showing the ages at which the planets rule according to the Egyptian scheme.

The years 1, 4, 8, 11, 15, 18, 22, etc., are formative and creative, involving organic changes. The years 5, 7, 12, 14, 19, 21, etc., are chaotic and destructive. The years 8, 13, 20, etc., are increscent and beneficial. It is difficult to say how they applied these set alfridaries to individual cases, but they serve to show that a law of periodic was more than hinted at in their speculations.

[TABLE.

4

TABLE OF SUN AND MOON PATHS

Sun			Moon
☉	☉	1	☽ ☽
	☿	2	♀
	♀	3	☿
	☽	4	☉
	♂	5	♄
	♃	6	♃
	♄	7	♂
☿	☉	8	☽ ♀
	☿	9	♀
	♀	10	☿
	☽	11	☉
	♂	12	♄
	♃	13	♃
	♄	14	♂
♀	☉	15	☽ ☿
	☿	16	♀
	♀	17	☿
	☽	18	☉
	♂	19	♄
	♃	20	♃
	♄	21	♂
☽	☉	22	☽ ☉
	☿	23	♀
	♀	24	☿
	etc.		etc.

The successive periods of 4, 8, 10, 19, 15, 12, and 30 years, following the order of the planetary velocities, are well known in association with the Seven Ages of Man. They are referred to in the comedy *As You Like It,* and take the following form :—

1– 4 years,	Childhood—Variability.	☽
4–12 „	Schooling—Knowledge.	☿
12–22 „	Courtship—Love.	♀
22–41 „	Ambition—Virility.	☉
41–56 „	Concentration—Intensity.	♂
56–68 „	Fulfilment—Maturity.	♃
68–98 „	Decline—Senility.	♄

The recognition of this cyclic law in human development is a plenary acknowledgment of the fact that the phenomena of life answer to numerical sequence, and if we understand that the phenomenal world is the reflex of the numerical, we shall of course require that number is the controlling factor in the development and expression of human thought. Moreover, we cannot begin to study the laws of cosmos, nor those of any science whatsoever, without recourse to numbers as a means of expressing those laws. Therefore whatever we think of the universe or of natural phenomena must finally lend itself to numerical expression. Measure, capacity, density, bulk, gravity, velocity, weight, proportion, are all comprehended in number, the perception of which is the determining factor of mental acumen. We see therefore that mentality is grounded in the perception of quantitative relations and thus in numbers.

CHAPTER IV

NUMBER IN RELATION TO FEELING

WHEN Goethe called a cathedral "frozen music" he was expressing that sense of the relations of sound and form which invests the words of every poet. What Goethe apprehended by the instinct of poesy as rhythmic structure, science has later developed experimentally in such part that we are able to say that certain forms correspond with and are the natural embodiment of sound. The eidophone and phonograph produce definite records of sound, and it has been found that the same forms are constantly reproduced from the same sounds. By this knowledge the science of acoustics was immensely enlarged. The eidophone is a simple apparatus that anybody can construct. It consists of a tin funnel with an extended tube of the same material elbowed so as to form a stem to the funnel like that of a tobacco-pipe. Across the mouth of the funnel a sheet of thin guttapercha is stretched very tightly and tied round to keep it taut and secure. On top of this membrane is placed some podophyllin, lycopodium, or other light powder. A note being sounded down the aperture, the powder will rise into the air by the vibration of the membrane, and will fall back again in a definite geometrical form. The notes of the scale being sounded clear and strong from a cornet, each will yield its corresponding form, and a return to the same note will reproduce the same form. A more elaborate instrument employs an ink-pen turning upon a universal joint attached to a needle which is actuated by the vibrations of a wire connected with a tympanum. This instrument reproduces the most complex and beautiful geometrical forms, resulting from a scroll-work of very fine pen-lines.

If you look at the frost-ferns on a frozen pavement or window-pane, you see there the splash of the wind upon the moist surface of the hard body just at the moment when the frost seized it in its icy grip. The whole of visible Nature is an embodiment of vibrations, and the ancient belief was that the first forms were produced from plastic world-stuff by the Logos or Word, by which all things were created. " And God said : Let there be——, and it was so."

We all learn to interpret these sound-forms as soon as we learn the mother-tongue. We cannot see the atmospheric forms created by speech, but we have a sense-organ that registers them, and we read them off by sensation of hearing—at first singly, then by twos and threes, and lastly by phrases. Sound-forms that appeal to us through the sense of sight have also a meaning, but the science of symbolism is not so fully developed that we can understand this process of signalling by form so well as we do that of signalling by sound. The semaphore and helioscope are less in vogue than the telephone and phonograph, and they are very clumsy in comparison with them.   How little we take the meaning of Nature's form-message is seen by the commonplace response to a perfect conspiracy of form and colour.   " Pretty place," says one.   " Very pretty," says another—and that is an end of impressions. What it *means* is beyond them. The geologist, the naturalist, the botanist, each catch disjointed sentences. The artist may or may not apprehend its meaning, but he catches all of its feeling.   And this brings me to a consideration of vibration in relation to feeling as expressed chiefly in sound and colour.

None can listen to one of Mendelssohn's " Songs without Words " and not be impressed by a definite feeling which, by the highest science of expression, the composer conveys to us in his wonderful melodies. You know that he is portraying a definite sequence of emotions, and you feel those emotions in yourself.   He made no use of words to define them, nor have you need of words to feel them, but he nevertheless succeeds as fully in conveying his feeling by music without the use of words, as a poet does by words without the use of music. Hence we see that, as regards feeling, which in effect is all there is of life or in it, the language of music and the language of words are of equal value.   But there is this in language that does not pertain to music. It is capable of stirring up strife, which no music ever did. The nearest to it I have ever heard was produced by chromatic

discords at quick time, and was intended to indicate
a rabble.

The natural scale bears a definite relation to
cosmical factors, and because the planets correspond
with colours and numbers, there is a harmony,
through cosmic sequence, between sound, colour,
and number. Thus :

Planet, etc.	Note.	Colour.	Number.
Saturn . .	D	Indigo	8
Jupiter . .	B	Violet	3
Mars . .	G	Red	9
Sun . .	C	Orange	1 or 4
Venus . .	A	Blue	6
Mercury .	E	Yellow	5
Moon . .	F	Green	7 or 2

These colours and their planetary correlates differ
somewhat from the Table given on p. 60, *Kab*. i.,
the variants of Saturn, Mercury, and Moon, in terms
of our physical perception, being there given in
order to include the nine digits. The above Table
may, however, be regarded as correct in regard to
the primary relations of colour and number.

If we examine these colour relations—remember
always that colour is our perception of definite
rates of etheric vibration—we shall find some
interesting correspondences. Thus :

Saturn is regarded astrologically as the " melan-

choly" planet, its sobering influence when prominent in the horoscope at birth being very marked.
It was rising in conjunction with Mercury and the
Sun at the birth of Dante, "the man who went
down into hell"; and rising also in that of Edgar
A. Poe, "the night owl" of poetry.   It held
the highest position in the horoscope of Napoleon,
"the man of destiny." It is generally prominent
in the horoscopes of the philosophers, and it
induces to depth of thought whenever it dominates
the mind. Hence indigo is allied to the melancholic, and its primary significance is steadfastness.
In contra-distinction to these we find orange and
deep yellow, the vital and active colours.

Jupiter, the optimistic planet, indicating expansion, hopefulness, etc., has relation to the colour
violet. It is the colour produced by passing a
white ray through a very thin sheet of silver, and
is related to the auric envelope of the normal
man in the same way as green is to the astral body.
In the Indian cosmogony we find Brahma, the
Creator (from the root *Brih*, to expand), investing
the *Brahmándam*, or egg of the universe, wherein,
by expansion of himself, the universe is created.
Hence we trace a connection between Brahma and
Jupiter (*Deo-pitar* = the Father God), and between
Jupiter and the aura. or egg of individuality. In
esotericism this is the persistent vehicle of the
imperishable and evolving monad.   It is cosmically
referred to as *hiranyagarbha* or Golden Egg, and
represented as floating in the waters of space, while
over it is seen *Kálahamsa*, or the Swan of Time.   As

by the expansion of the One Self the universe was created, so by the expansion of the individual the fulness of life is attained. Jupiter therefore as *Brihaspati*, or Lord of Expansion, corresponds with violet, the colour of the vital optimist.

When Jupiter is prominent in the horoscope we find that optimism and power of expansion are characteristics of those then born. The planet was rising in the horoscope of King Edward VII., in that of Lord Northcliffe, and others of this temperament. The number 3, corresponding with Jupiter and violet, is seen also to represent "*ovals* and bodies capable of *expansion* and *contraction*" (*Kab.*, i. 59). Violet is essentially the colour of Hope.

Mars, the ruddy planet, is seen to correspond with the flamboyant note G, with the colour red or crimson, and the number 9. The association of Mars with all forms of hurt and strife is well known. From *marna*, to strike, we have *marta*, killing, and such derivatives as to murder, to mar, martial, etc. Among forms we have "all sharp, keen, and pointed things—spears, lances, scalpels, swords, knives, flints, and tongues of flame." The connection between "tongues of flame" and inspiration is familiar through the Pentecostal fire. Nine is the number of regeneration, of spirituality, freedom, self-extension, and pervading. Mars is associated with Vishnu, the energiser of the created universe, from *Vish*, to pervade. Fire, intensity, zeal, ardour, and keenness are all characteristic of the planet Mars so far as its cosmic qualities are represented in human character; thus its associations with the colour red are therefore so appropriate as barely to need comment. All these qualities, characteristics, colours, and sounds, that are ascribed to the planets obtain their significance for us by reason of their appeal to our feeling, through consciousness. Colour, form, etc., have no qualities *per se*. It is we who invest them with such, and we do so because of the influence they exert upon our emotions. When we listen to music we are conscious of certain emotions stirring in us, and we attribute to the music all that we experience in ourselves. The truth is that there is nothing in the music itself but the series of rhythmic vibrations of which it consists, and these are in reality perfectly noiseless atmospheric motions which attain the significance of sound only when they enter our consciousness. What we feel is what the musician felt when he was composing, and he made use of the language of music to express his feelings. If we would really know how much feeling there is in language *per se*, and beyond what we impart to it, try some Choctaw language on the first man you meet, and, unless he is an American polyglot, he will probably suggest that you ask a policeman, or tell you that he feels like that himself sometimes, and will encourage you to work it all off before going home.

Venus is the acknowledged representative of music, art, poetry, and all the finer sentiments of the human mind. It is the embodiment of the rhythmical, the sympathetic—in a word, of *harmony*. It embraces all the harmonious and rhythmic arts—

dancing, music, poetry, painting,—and all industries in which the artistic element is the principal factor. Its colour, blue, is in the nature of an anodyne— soothing, pacifying, and non-irritant. It is on the negative side of the spectrum and absorbs the yellows. Blue as a nerve-rester is well known and fully employed by chromopathic healers, such as Babbit, Albertini, and others. In the pathology of colour, blue is the tone used for allaying irritation and the effects of nervous corrosion. It answers to the note A, and by a certain fitness of things this note is used in orchestration as the pitch-note by which all instruments are brought into accord. The celestial vestment of the Madonna is that blue which represents mercy, loving-kindness, purity, and grace—in a word, harmony.

Mercury is related to the colour yellow, which is the most luminiferous of the spectrum. Mercury corresponds to the intelligence principle of the mind, the perceptive and rational faculties, and their appropriate memories. Ptolemy, in his *Tetrabliblos*, says that the Moon governs the natural or animal soul and Mercury the human or rational soul, the *epithemia* and *phrēn* of the Greek classification. Light is that which reveals all form and colour, and Mercury, as indicating luminosity, is thus the Awakener, the Anubis of the Egyptian theogony, the wolf-headed god who awakened the Sleeping Souls and conducted them to the Hall of Judgment. The Hebrew equivalent is Ish-caleb (man-wolf), from which the Greeks derived their Æsculapius, the god of medicine. Knowledge, as represented by Mercury, is the one cure for that great disease of mind known as ignorance. Man is agnostic until the messenger of the gods brings him the torch-light of revelation ; then he is gnostic, and joins the followers of Hermes. Yellow unites with blue (Venus) to form the Nature-colour, green. So Hermes and Aphrodite, Mercury and Venus, unite to form the Hermaphrodite, or natural man. So 6 Venus and 5 Mercury unite to form $11 = 2$, the number of the Moon, which corresponds in our table to green. When Mercury, the intelligence principle, is united to its ethereal counterpart, the result is enlightenment. The Gnostics spoke of two aspects of the mind, and above the sphere of the Christos, or Mercury (messenger), they placed the sphere of Eros. Mercury is represented as bearing the caduceus, the Hellenised form of the Hebrew *Qedeshi-ash*, or Fire of the Holy Ones. The idea that it is the symbol of Peace is very modern and incorrect. It represents the interaction of the *Ida* and *Pingala*, or male-female creative fires, united in the *Shushumna*, and the rod is the Brahmadandam, or spinal column, represented by the bamboo stick of the yogi, with its notches or nodes corresponding with the nervous ganglia of the spinal process. It stands for the Hermetic Art or Secret Knowledge. Mercury in this capacity of staff-bearer is akin to Prometheus, who brought the fire of the gods down in a fennel-stalk for the use of mankind. As interpreter of the gods, Mercury represents the faculty of translation By knowledge of universal symbolism we are enabled to translate form into words, colour into sound, and both into number. By the alchemy of the mind, represented by Hermetic Art, we transmute feeling into thought and thought into feeling. It is through the intelligence principle, therefore, that number as represented by Mercury is capable of a direct correspondence with feeling. The number of Mercury is 5, and it is the Nature-number which stands for embodied humanity. In the *Book of Lo* the ancient Chinese embodied the symbolism of Nature in the form of a " Square of Three " (*Kab.*, i. p. 41), where 5, the symbol of man the Cogniser, is centred, contributing to the 10 of a perfected environment the value of cognition, which converts the totality of phenomena (10) into the totality of noumena (15), and thus gives to Nature the functions of divinity, the stature of the God-man being represented by the number 15.

The *Moon* is related to two numbers, 7 being the positive aspect and 2 the negative. As 7 it is the full Moon acting in opposition to the Sun, when we get the combination $1 + 7 = 8$ sinister ; and at the New Moon the value 2 in combination with the Sun, number $1 = 3$, which is a fortunate number, being increscent, whereas 8 is decrescent, for 3 is the number of Jupiter and denotes expansion, and 8 is that of Saturn and denotes contraction. In conjunction with the Sun the Moon is negative, or female ; while in opposition it is positive, or male. Here, the Romans, following the more ancient custom of the Sabeans and Hebrews, instituted a festival to Juno-Lucina, at which the people changed garments for those of the opposite sex. So, while the Moon's body was called *Lebenah* by the Hebrews, the soul of it was *Gebur*—one being " the fair," and the other " the strong."

The number of the Moon being 2, it denotes relativity, vacillation, change ; but as 7 it denotes fulness, stability (*Kab.*, i. 8). In the Hebraic system the numbers followed the days of the week, namely :

Sunday	☉	1–8
Monday	☽	2–9
Tuesday	♂	3
Wednesday	☿	4
Thursday	♃	5
Friday	♀	6
Saturday	♄	7

And this system is interpreted in *Kab.*, i. ch. i. Here it is seen that the numbers 1 and 8, Life and Death, are vested in the Sun's influence ; while 2 and 9, denoting change and strength, are ascribed to the Moon The *Geburim* (Geber = strength) were a race of spiritual warriors, and the angel Gabriel is always represented as invested with great power. He it is who is said to have led Israel through its victorious campaign on the way to Palestine. The Kabalists, however, regard the angel as the Angel of Grace, a type of the Higher Ego, or Christ-principle in man, and in their interpretation Egypt is the physical body (Capricorn = Saturn), the House of Bondage and darkness ; the wilderness is the period of probation in the world ; the Hivites,

Perizzites, Gergashites, Jebuzites, and Amalekites are the various passions and evil principles that " he who would prevail " (Israel) has to overcome before he can pass through the baptism of Jordan (yar-din), or River of Spiritual Knowledge, and enter the Promised Land of his spiritual heritage. Therefore, in the Yetzirah, or Transformations, they trace man through the cadence of his incarnations from the Sun (the spiritual state) to Saturn (the state of spiritual darkness), and then back again from Saturn to the Sun.

The Moon has always been identified with the Earth, and in symbolical systems, which have regard to the point of view of embodied man, the Moon is set between the planets Venus and Mars. Its colour, green, is that resulting from the admixture of blue and yellow, the colours of Venus and Mercury, and, as we have seen, the numbers of these planets, 6 and $5 = 11 = 2$, the number of the Moon (negative). Now, green is the colour of the Earth's livery, and is the Nature-colour, having its place in the midst of the spectrum between the blues and yellows.

Now, if we regard the blues as denoting Thought and the yellows as denoting Feeling, we get in green a combination of the two as the colour-symbol of the natural man. In ancient belief the souls of men came to earth through the Moon sphere. Occultists do not regard this as referring to the Moon as a body, but to that circumferential sphere of the astral plane which, according to the principles of gravitation, would lie outside and around the earth as far as the orbit of the Moon. The confusion of the names Selene (the Moon) and Selinon (parsley) sufficiently explain why, according to the tradition of dames, children are born in the parsley-bed, why preparations of parsley are used as emmenagogues, and perhaps also why old herbalists call it the " lunatic herb " and place it under the dominion of the Moon.

Here I may bring out the relations of the planetary colours according to this scheme of correspondences in a diagrammatic form.

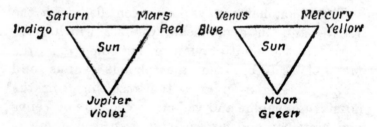

If we take a leaf out of the Hindu theogony we shall find this scheme exactly repeated, with the exception that Saturn and Jupiter change places so as to be brought into numerical order. Thus Saturn, Jupiter, and Mars represent the Trimurti or male trinity of deific aspects—Shiva, Brahma, and Vishnu ; but they are always put in this order, Brahma, Vishnu, Shiva, *i.e.* Jupiter, Mars, Saturn ; the Creator, Energiser or Preserver, and Regenerator or Destroyer.

> " It maketh and unmaketh, mending all ;
> What it hath wrought is better than had been ;
> Slow grows the splendid pattern that it weaves
> Its subtle hands between ! "

Then the S'aktis or female counterparts of the Prajapatis or Lords are set in apposition thus:

♃ Brahma—Saraswati ☿
♂ Vishnu—Lakshmi ♀
♄ Shiva—Parvati ☽

These are their cosmic gods and goddesses, but the manifestation of the Supreme Deity is Krishna, the Sun-born.

Hence it appears there are various aspects of one and the same truth, the fact being that from whatever point of view we regard Nature we shall find her full of correspondences and symbols, and at all times answering to a numerical law, because it is we who impose those correspondences and make use of those symbols, and because also they answer to a law of mind which is vested in numerical ratios, or rather in our perception of quantitive relations. Without man as cogniser Nature would hold no such significance. It is not a self-conscious aggregate. Consciousness seems to begin when Life comes into relations with matter at a certain stage of its development, and self-consciousness when Mind takes possession of the vitalised organisms. Consciousness, therefore, appears to result from the strain set up between energy and matter through resistance, and self-consciousness from the relations of soul to environment, or mind-force in association with organic matter. The first results in sensation, the last in Feeling. The position that what we call inanimate matter shows sensation-consciousness by its response to stimulus has already been argued

5

(*Cosmic Symbolism*), and there is no need to do more
than affirm it in this place. As sensation is the
beginning of consciousness, so Feeling is the end of
self-consciousness. The evolution of man is through
his sensorium, and finally he must become a perfected sensory creature capable of the highest
expressions of Feeling. The highest form of feeling
is Sympathy—another name for syntonic vibration.
Number, as represented by vibration, lies at the
root of all being, and invests colour, form, sound
with all the significance they have for us. We may
apprehend them intellectually, but they do not
become part of us until we feel them.

The scheme here presented of Colours and
Numbers in relation to Thought and Feeling may
be summarised thus :

Jupiter—Violet,   3—Hope, optimism, expansion.
Saturn—Indigo,   8—Contemplation, philosophy.
Venus—Blue,   6—Purity, spirituality, peace.
Moon—Green,   2—Sensation, variability.
Mercury—Yellow, 5—Mind, intellection, perception.
Sun—Orange,   4—Vitality, force.
Mars—Red,   9—Zeal, energy, intensity.

We may observe that Orange, the Sun colour,
becomes red, Mars, when vitality becomes concentrated. Then we get zeal, intensity, and ardour
as the effects of the vital powers being brought to a
focus and directed along specific channels towards
the accomplishment of some particular object. It
is in accord with the Doctrine of Correspondences
that we should regard Number as related to Thought

and Colour to Feeling. That one corresponds with and gives rise to the other is evident by natural science and psychology. Consequently we find Number more immediately connected with Science, and Colour with Art, the one being capable of intellectual demonstration, the other of artistic expression. Therefore, Science (Mercury) is considered as masculine and exterior, while Art (Venus) is regarded as feminine and interior. The consideration that the more interior is the more spiritual leads to the higher appreciation of Art as the expression of Feeling. From the point of view of evolution, the artist is therefore in advance of the man of science, and in all systems of symbolism Venus is placed above Mercury, and it is interesting to note that among the planetary orbits Mercury shows the greatest divergence from the circular, *i.e.* its eccentricity is greatest, while Venus shows the least, its orbit being all but a perfect circle. In days to come, when Venus makes an orbit that is perfectly symmetrical, the world will get a perfect expression of Feeling as developed in Art. The post-impressionist of modern evolution is a decadent scion of Venus. He only portrays Nature as reflected in a cracked mirror. He has no constant plane of perception and no fixed view-point. Consequently he depicts a man's left optic as in the middle of his forehead, his right ear where his nose should be, and the lapels of his coat on the back of his neck. In an age of buffoonery the effort to be original must needs lead to some strange effects; but Feeling should be the *lingua sancta* of the true exponent of Art, and reversion to standards of Beauty in colour and form—in a word, naturalness —will be his only legitimate means of progress.

Bringing our researches regarding Colour and Number into line with what has been observed regarding Sound, we find the correspondence of primaries to result as here shown :

Planet	.	☉	♄	☿	☽	♂	♀	♃
Note	.	C	D	E	F	G	A	B
Number	.	4–1	8	5	7–2	9	6	3
Colour	.	Orange	Indigo	Yellow	Green	Red	Blue	Violet

The notes C, E, G form a common chord. Their corresponding numbers are 4, 5, 9, so that $4+5$ coalesce in 9 ; also D, F, A form a chord, and their numbers are 8, 7, 6 ; thus bringing $8+7=15=6$ into harmony with 6. I cannot say where the observation may lead to, but I have noted it as suggestive ; and I may add that Saturn 8 and Moon 7 are astrologically in terms with Venus 6, inasmuch as the two signs Libra and Taurus are ruled by Venus, and are the exaltation signs of Saturn and the Moon respectively.

CHAPTER V

NUMBERS AND INDIVIDUALS

It would be possible to argue a connection between Numbers and Volition in the same way as we have seen it to exist in relation to Thought and Feeling ; but as all will is expressed in thought and feeling which ultimates as speech and action, or word and deed, it will be convenient and probably far more interesting if we trace this association of Will and Number in the ultimate fact of birth, showing the expression and limitations of the will by reference to the date of birth and other data incidental to particular cases.

It will be well, however, if we have a clear idea of the Correspondence in the Scale of Manifestation through which we argue from Divine principles to human activity, and thus from unity into diversity. Assuming the Sun, as centre of the system, as expressing the Logos, we have the two conditions of Light and Heat corresponding with Divine Wisdom and Love, the two being united in the single body of the Sun, or the Divine Substance. Things that correspond are not identical, but the material is dependent on the spiritual as body upon soul, and the inferior or dependent state of existence is the expression of the superior. The words inferior and superior may be regarded as equivalent to exterior and interior in this connection. Light reveals forms, heat gives them life. In gross darkness nothing exists as form, and in a state of ignorance there is no true definition of things. Heat animates and fills all forms of life with energy. At the poles, where there is less heat than at other parts of the earth, there is less animation. Rays of light may be artificially slowed down and converted into heat rays. By offering resistance to an electric current one may obtain light. Thought and Feeling are thus convertible. What lies at the back of Light and Heat, or Thought and Feeling, is Energy or Life, and this is the source of Volition. From these and other considerations we may derive the Scale of Correspondences as follows :—

Life
Wisdom—Love
Volition
Truth—Charity
Desire
Knowledge—Affection
Thought—Feeling
Speech—Action
Character.

Here we see Life as Volition and Desire ultimating as Character or Conduct, the expressions of human life in speech and action. The Scale of Correspondences shows the related pairs of principles on the

Divine, spiritual, and human planes. In this scheme of thought every life is a partial expression of the One Life, and every phase of human character and destiny is the reflex, under limitation, of the One Intelligence and Will. The idea is laid hold of by Armand Silvestre:

> "Thou art Cause Supreme of Life,
>   The hidden Good in every ill—
> Which even they who live in strife
>   Do serve with an unconscious will,—
> Thou art the salve of hearts that bleed,
>   The grave of every ruined creed!"

We may therefore safely explore the diversities of character and destiny from the point of view that all is subservient to the main purpose of creation, and a reflection—perhaps also a refraction—of the divine will as expressed in number and regulated by cosmic laws.

I have already shown (*Kab.*, i. ch. iv.) that man answers to a certain numerical plan known as the "Square of Three." He is embodied cosmos, and, being compounded of cosmic elements, he responds to the planets of the solar system, and to the numbers, colours, sounds, and forms associated with them.

What may be the law of the supramundane it is not our purpose to inquire. Man as we know him is such as he is by reason of embodiment. The fact of birth is the result of cosmic law acting through the individual. The evolution of an entity is wrapped up in the circumstance of birth, the time and conditions being dependent on inherent character and faculty. The making of gods out of men

is a long process, and we have no reason to suppose
that it is compassed in one life or even one hundred
lives.   But, in order to illustrate our insistent law
of numerical ratios, it will be necessary to make use
of a number of striking instances, restricting ourselves to the one life that is presently patent to us.

It has already been shown that the Moon represents the element of variability, and that its numbers
are 2 and 7.   It is proposed to show that the sign
occupied by the Moon at the birth of a person is
that which, by its planetary and numerical affinity,
controls or determines the particular characteristic
that is dominant in that person.

Granted for the moment that the premiss of
astrology is valid, and that the disposition of the
cosmic factors at the moment of birth is the key to
character and fortunes, then it will follow that,
inasmuch as the Moon's apparent motion in the
zodiac is the greatest, and that whereas the Sun
remains in the same sign for a month, and other of
the celestial bodies for many months together,
while the Moon passes from one sign to the next in
the space of only sixty hours, it must be of chief
importance in the estimate of individual faculty,
character, and even destiny.   Such, indeed, we find
it, although it is not that which finally determines
the line of individual evolution.

In order to examine these cases in the light of the
values already ascribed to the numbers 1 to 9, we
shall have to give a value to each of the signs in
terms of the planet which has affinity with each.
Thus :

Aries and Scorpio signs, of Mars, answer to number 9
Taurus and Libra,   ,,   Venus   ,,   6
Gemini and Virgo,   ,,   Mercury   ,,   5
Cancer, ruled by the Moon,   ,,   2 and 7
Leo ruled by the Sun,   ,,   1 and 4
Sagittarius and Pisces, ruled by Jupiter,   ,,   3
Capricornus and Aquarius, ruled by Saturn   ,,   8

Applying these numbers to the position of the
Moon at the birth of several notable persons, it will
be seen that there is sufficient ground for establishing an argument in favour of numerical values as
determined by planetary positions. Vibrations, of
course, lie at the back of the whole scheme. They
are Nature's expression of number, as revealed by
the various modes and rates of motion in the same
etheric medium, giving rise to as many different
natural phenomena, as electricity, light, heat, etc.
Moreover, there is nothing unreasonable in the view
that the Moon may exert a different action on us
from various parts of its orbit. Our zodiacal
divisions may be a convenient method of registering
and classifying these differences.

Take, then, the following examples from among
many at our disposal :

Napoleon I., born 15th August 1769. Moon in
Capricornus, number 8, ruled by Saturn. Saturn
in Cancer, number 7. Here we have the combination of a strong egotism, denoted by the
number 7, and fatality denoted by the number 8.
The disturbance of the equilibrium or *status quo*
in the concert of nations is well defined by the

position of the Moon in the sign of Saturn, answering to the sinister influence of the number 8. This is the number of dissolution, of cyclic evolution, reaction, revolution, fracture, disintegration, decomposition, anarchism, lesion, separation, and divorce.

The Moon being in the sign of Saturn, and Saturn in the sign of the Moon, there was a particular strengthening of the fatal egotism which determined the destinies of the great general.

King Henry of Navarre. According to Morinus the Moon was in Aries, ruled by Mars, number 9. Born 13th December (O.S.) 1553. Here we have the scion of Mars, answering to the high vibration of liberty and conquest indicated by the number 9. But Mars, being in the sign of Saturn—namely, Capricornus—answering to the number 8, there was a sinister resolution to his career, which ended in his murder at the hands of Ravaillac.

Queen Alexandra, born 1st December 1844. Moon in Leo, ruled by the Sun, number 1. Dignity, honour, prestige, success, distinction, rulership. Sun in Sagittarius, ruled by Jupiter, number 3. Generosity, expansiveness, increase, benevolence. The combination of Sun, Moon, and Jupiter is very fortunate.

"Carmen Sylva," Queen of Roumania. Moon in Aries, ruled by Mars, number 9. Penetration, incisiveness, courage, fortitude, determination, zeal. Mars in Pisces, ruled by Jupiter, number 3. Generosity, increase, and good works. Impulsiveness.

Charles I. of England. Moon in Libra, ruled by Venus, number 6. Venus in Sagittarius, ruled by Jupiter, number 3. This combination indicates a strong artistic sense, gentleness, suavity, love of peace and harmony, fondness for the play, music, dancing, etc. A sociable nature with keen sense of justice and a benevolent disposition.

Joan of Arc, born 6th January 1412. Moon in Libra, ruled by Venus, number 6. Gentleness, suavity, peace, harmony, and love of the beautiful. Venus in Capricorn, ruled by Saturn 8. Disappointment, loss, captivity. A more positive element is found in the horoscope by the conjunction of Moon and Jupiter, and the mental peculiarity is derived from the opposition of Mercury to Neptune.

Annie Besant, born 1st October 1847. Moon in Cancer, number 2. Change, variability, travelling, alternation, publicity. The more positive aspect of the Moon is related to the number 7, and denotes attainment, fulness, completion, satisfaction, equilibrium.

Kaiser Wilhelm II. Moon in Scorpio, ruled by Mars, number 9. Zeal, energy, courage, decision, strength, and endurance. Mars in Pisces, ruled by Jupiter, number 3. Generosity, magnanimity, increase, and good works. Impulsiveness.

Rudyard Kipling. Moon in Gemini, ruled by Mercury, number 5. Intellection, reason, logic, travelling. Mercury in Sagittarius, ruled by Jupiter, number 3. Expansiveness, generosity, increase, success. The horoscopical conjunction of Mercury and Venus shows clearly the poetic bias of the intellect, ruled by Mercury.

Lord Northcliffe.   Moon in Aries, ruled by Mars, number 9.   Courage, persistence, keenness, penetration, attack.   Mars in Virgo, ruled by Mercury, number 5.   Alertness, intellection, commerce, astuteness.

Now, if we take these few cases, which might have been multiplied indefinitely, and find the numerical equivalent of the Moon and planetary combination, we shall have the key to the character.

Napoleon I.   2 Moon, 8 Saturn.   Sum 10 or 1. Empire, rulership, egotism.

Henry of Navarre.   Moon, Mars, Saturn = 298 = 19 = 1.   Rulership, empire, egotism.

Queen Alexandra.   Moon, Sun, Jupiter = 213 = 6. Gentleness, refinement, harmony, charity.

"Carmen Sylva."   Moon, Mars, Jupiter = 293 = 5. Intellection, intelligence, alertness.

Charles I.   Moon, Venus, Jupiter = 263 = 2. Vacillation, variability.

Joan of Arc.   Moon, Venus, Saturn = 268 = 16 = 7. Attainment, completion, perfection, publicity.

Annie Besant.   Moon (in its own sign) = 2. Variability, popularity.

Kaiser Wilhelm II.   Moon, Mars, Jupiter = 793 = 19 = 1.   Conquest, empire, egotism.

Rudyard Kipling.   Moon, Mercury, Jupiter = 253 = 10 = 1.   Conquest, dominion, rulership.   In the case of a commoner it denotes success, distinction, and authority.

Lord Northcliffe. Moon, Mars, Mercury = 295
= 7. Perfection, completion, attainment, publicity.

It will be observed that we take the Moon as the basis of the calculation in each case and apply to it the number of the planet in whose sign it is, excepting when it is in its own sign, when it is taken by itself alone, and to these we add the planetary value for the sign in which the Moon-ruler is found.

Most frequently it will be found that people who have prominent parts to play in the world have the Moon-rulers in prominent positions at the time of birth, so that they come under that ray or vibration which at the time is the most powerful. Thus Napoleon, whose Moon-ruler was Saturn, had Saturn in the mid-heaven of his horoscope. The present Emperor of Germany, whose Moon-ruler is Mars, has Mars in the mid-heaven. But this is not always the case, and it may well be that there are other combinations of planetary influence producing vibrations in the constitution to which the singular prominence of an individual may be attributed. It is a patent fact, however, that those planets which hold the four angles of a horoscope—namely, the Mid-heaven, Ascendant, Descendant, and Nadir —have always a most marked effect in the character and destiny of individuals.

Thus in Napoleon's horoscope Saturn was in the mid-heaven and the Moon in the lower angle. In King Edward's horoscope (see *Prognostic Astronomy*) Jupiter was in the eastern angle or Ascendant. The same was the case with Lord Northcliffe (*Answers*). Cecil Rhodes had Sun, Moon, and

Venus in the descending angle. Annie Besant had Uranus rising in the eastern angle, the Moon in the north angle, Sun, Venus, and Mercury in the west angle. The German Emperor has Mars in the mid-heaven. Mr Tom Mann, the socialist, has Sun and Mercury in the east angle, Mars in the west, and Venus exceedingly weak. Mr Gladstone (Prime Minister) had Uranus in the south angle and Sun and Mercury in the east.

It may be said, in fact, that the more the planets in a horoscope are angular the more is the subject of that horoscope impressed with the peculiarities and potencies of such planets, making in effect a personality strong enough to force itself into public notice whether in good or evil. Thus, while it gives an apparent independence of character, because of marked individuality, it also brings them under greater compulsion, and thus in a sense into greater servitude. For those who attain to positions of great eminence hold them only by continual effort, untiring watchfulness, and constant anxiety. The "cynosure for wandering eyes," they must play their elected part without recess, or sink into oblivion. Those, on the other hand, in whose horoscopes the planets are in succeedent positions owe their measure of success not so much to prominence before the world or to the compulsion of circumstances, but rather to steadfast endurance and application, being by nature plodders rather than pioneers. But when the majority of the planets are cadent there is seen to be a degree of indifference to the common ambitions of life and a peculiar inconsequence of temperament, even in those whose faculties are conspicuous.

Therefore, when we speak of a person answering to the number 9, we do not mean that he is disposed to the more forceful methods of the average Martian, but that he is capable of great intensity of purpose, much zeal, independence of spirit, and freedom of opinion. Then, again, there is the abnormal aspect of this particular red ray of the " nine " vibration. In such case it produces the maniac, the firebrand, the anarchist, and the homicide—the man who " sees red." In a last analysis it will probably be found that Mars and the number 9, the colour red, and all their natural correspondences, signify merely *intensity*. It is as if the vital principle answering to Orange (the Sun) had been brought to a focus, and that from this concentration of the vital principle a species of fever had been induced. All men attain to this fervour of feeling and intensity of purpose and action in their supreme moments ; while to genius, and its near neighbour insanity, it is more or less habitual and constant.

Similarly, the man who answers to the vibrations of the planet Jupiter, the violet ray, and the number 3. He may be generous, magnanimous, benevolent, and sympathetic ; but also he may be nothing more than a bombast, abounding in excesses and extravagance, jovial, but self-indulgent, and as much indisposed to do harm as good because both entail too much effort and trouble. In either case the expression of the number 3 is *expansion*. In the one case it acts normally by sympathy and altruism, in the other by apathy and egotism. Occasionally we find that a man has nothing more to show for his Jupiterian increscence than an abnormal expansion below the belt. He represents merely the physical side of the number 3. In the two opposite expressions of this type cited above we have the distinction between the blue-violet and the red-violet rays, the limits of this particular order of vibration.

In the Venusian 6 also we have two distinct types, one of which is remarkable for its refinement and culture and the other for its licence and frivolity. Yet the love of harmony is common to both. The number 5 also has a variety of expressions, inasmuch as it primarily answers to intellection; but it divides easily into a higher and lower aspect of mind, represented by science on the one hand and commerce on the other. The co-operation of these two aspects of mental activity in modern times is a healthy feature tending to intellectual integrity. It is now rightly felt that knowledge is desirable in proportion to its practical utility.

The great range of Mercury's signification, its correspondence with the principle of Mind, and consequently with the varieties of language needed for the expression of mental phases, led to Mercury being regarded as the interpreter or linguist of the gods. Its versatility is well known to astrologers.

Saturn also has two aspects, and its number 8 may signify conservatism or privation That sequestration of the mind peculiar to all philosophers, which enables them to take a detached view of mental and physical phenomena, and so to formulate the laws of mind and of matter, is one aspect of the indigo ray and the significance of the number 8, which probably may be accounted its highest faculty. The lower aspect is that which abides in the dark and cold alleys of a cheerless misanthropy, finding occasion in the byways of life to snatch some small advantage from the forgetfulness or need of another, a sordid miserable type that finds comfort in privation in order to save expense. Between this miserable parasite of the Earth and the sublime philosopher whose seat is upon the summit of intellect and whose fearless eye looks into the very heart of the Sun, there would appear to be an immeasurable gulf. Yet it is bridged by the one word—loneliness.

This isolation, conservatism, insularity, is directly opposed to the publicity and democratic publicity of the negative lunar character, responding to the number 2.

Saturn 8, rules Capricorn ; and the Moon 2, rules Cancer, the opposite sign.

Similarly we have the dark blue of Saturn opposed to the yellow of the Moon.

Mars and its corresponding number 9 are allied to force and strife, while Venus and its number 6 to persuasion and peace. Consequently, we find Mars associated with the signs Aries and Scorpio, opposite to those of Venus, which are Libra and Taurus.

Thus, while it is extremely easy to " place " an individual by reason of his dominant characteristic, whether the intensity of Mars, the pacivity of Venus, the mutability of the Moon, or the isolation of

6

Saturn, etc., it is by no means so easy to determine the particular grade to which that individual belongs. For, as we have seen, there are extreme poles of any particular ray, colour, or planetary vibration, and between them there are many grades of expression. It would appear that each ray, colour, note, and planet contains a submerged octave in itself, or rather a septenate, so that there may be seven violet sub-rays, or perhaps one pure violet ray with its six sub-rays, making a septenate ; and similarly with the other colours.

Arranged under their planetary symbols they would therefore fall into the following order, number 1 of each series expressing the true characteristic of the particular note, colour, number, or vibration, and number 7 the extreme or abnormal aspect of the dominant characteristic, the intermediate numbers 2 to 6 indicating the variants.

PLANETARY VARIANTS

Pl.	♄	♃	♂	☉	♀	☿	☽
Col.	Indigo	Violet	Red	Orange	Blue	Yellow	Green
No.	8	3	9	1–4	6	5	7–2
1	♄	♃	♂	☉	♀	☿	☽
2	♃	♀	♄	☽	☽	♂	☿
3	♂	♄	☿	♂	♃	☽	♀
4	☉	☉	☉	☿	☉	☉	☉
5	♀	☽	♃	♃	☿	♄	♂
6	☿	♂	☽	♀	♄	♀	♃
7	☽	☿	♀	♄	♂	♃	♄

It will be observed that the several columns maintain the polarity already referred to, and that this is again repeated along the several lines,—Saturn being polarised by the Moon, Mars by Venus, Jupiter by Mercury; while the central column under the symbol ☉, indicating the vital principle, finds its modifications through the Moon, Mars, etc., and falls into extinction in its negative pole under the

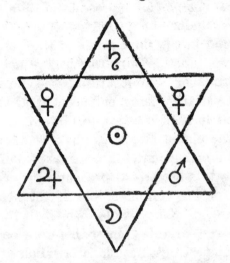

influence of Saturn.   This is conveyed by the astrological paradigm of the Seal of Solomon, which we have elsewhere considered in other relations, wherein these polarities are maintained by the interlacing of the two triangles, representing the spiritual and material, the nominal and phenomenal worlds, in which the positive trigon of Saturn-Jupiter-Mars employs the major planets, and denotes the active male principle; and the negative trigon of Venus-Mercury-Moon, embracing the minor planets, denotes the passive female principle.

From this it would appear that the individual note is that produced by the admixture of a dominant and sub-dominant vibration, as, for example, the Moon being in Taurus, ruled by Venus, answers to that planet and the number 6, colour blue. But Venus being in Pisces, ruled by Jupiter, number 3, we get a composite expression of the Venusian character, under the sub-division of Jupiter, this being found in the third grade of the Venus line of expression. In the Table the vital principle ☉ 4 is the fulcrum of manifestation, the positive and negative variants being balanced upon this centre line ; and it is of interest to observe that in this scheme the planet Mercury, which was found to be the numerical counterpart of the Sun (*Cosmic Symbolism*), is here seen to occupy the corresponding position in the fourth line of the solar gamut of expression. The Table, which I have called " Planetary Variants," may therefore be regarded also as one expressing Planetary Polarities. The mass of mankind are now in that stage or grade of expression, under these several rays, which is indicated by line 3 of the Table, having emerged from the lower or more animal stage of evolution and attained to the fifth or human stage. Thus one born under Saturn would be manifesting through the sub-ray of Mars ; under Jupiter, through the sub-ray of Saturn ; under Mars, through Mercury ; under the Sun, through Mars ; under Venus, through Jupiter ; under Mercury, through the Moon; under the Moon, through Venus.

Thus the destructive element of Saturn is expressed in warlike or martial forms; the theological Jupiter finds philosophical expression; the zealous Mars gains intellectual and commercial expression; the vitality of the Solar Man gains forceful or muscular expression in physical culture; the Venusian art applies to the ecclesiastical; the principle of intellection has expression in versatility of thought, while commerce is wholly dependent on publication and advertisement; and lastly, the lunar ray of publicity is expressed in the development of artistic effects, and principally applied to pleasure, ease, comfort, and luxury. The net result of all these manifestations of individual character may be called "the Spirit of the Age," the Demagorgon of our sublunary sphere. Of course it will be understood that these ascriptions of the character-notes, colours, numbers, etc., are applicable only to the denizens of our own sphere. On other planets the humanities, being in a more or less advanced stage of evolution, will respond to different gamuts and will be collectively in various stages of those gamuts. The cosmogonic relations of the Martians or the Jovians will place them in subjection to an entirely different astrology, and the various cosmic factors would have to be interpreted in terms of the Martian in the one case, and of the Jovian in the other. If these ascriptions were universal we should argue that the Earth sees these correspondences through a medium of green, or within the vibrations of the green ray, and thus at once partition our humanity into the yellow-green (2) and the blue-green (7), representing the naturals and the intellectuals; and all the universe would be in terms of this order of perception. But there is not the slightest ground for thinking that these are absolute cosmic correspondences. On the contrary, it is extremely probable that the Martian red bears the same relations to the constitution, physical and mental, of the Martian man, as does the terrestrial green to ourselves. Unless, therefore, we are prepared to be extremely complex, we must restrict our study of character and destiny to their expressions as they are known to us in our earth-humanity alone, and leave the wider field to those in whom the self-extensive faculty is fully developed. It may be of interest, however, to compare the statements of that great seer Emanuel Swedenborg concerning the inhabitants of other planets of the solar system with the characteristics connoted with them in this scheme, in which colour, sound, and number are seen to bear certain well-defined relations to individuals born under the influence of those planets. See therefore *Earths of the Universe*, by Emanuel Swedenborg, in publication by the Swedenborg Society.

CHAPTER VI

CO-ORDINATION OF VALUES

WE have seen that the expression of Character as
Will has a certain relation to quantitive values.
Will is the human expression of cosmic energy, the
various physical and chemical forces known to us,
and also dynamic force. It therefore has its
numerical relations, because all these cosmic,
chemic, and dynamic forms of energy, another name
for Life, have their mensuration.

If we take the numerical series as comprehended
in the numbers 0 to 9, we shall find that, by continual addition of the odd and even, positive and
negative, male and female numbers, we eventually
derive a further series in which the same values are
present, but in a varied order. In each new series the
value of nine is absent, as shown in the following form:

```
0 1 2 3 4 5 6 7 8 9
 1 3 5 7 9 2 4 6 8
  4 8 3 7 2 6 1 5
   3 2 1 9 8 7 6
    5 3 1 8 6 4
     8 4 9 5 1
      3 4 5 6
       7 9 2
        7 2
         0
```

In the first addition of the digits by pairs we get the series 1 3 5 7 9, including all the odd numbers, followed by 2 4 6 8, all the even numbers. In the next row the first and last numbers, 4 and 5, pair to nine, and so of the rest, 3 and 6, 5 and 4, etc. ; but the number 9 is absent from the series. It appears again in the fourth row, but the numbers 4 and 5 are absent. In the fifth row 9 disappears, but the equivalent value is lacking in the figures 2 and 7. In the sixth row 2 3 6 7, making two nines, are absent. In the seventh row 1 2 7 8 9, making three nines, are absent. In the eighth row 1 3 4 5 6 8, making three nines, are absent. In the ninth row 1 3 4 5 6 8 9, making four nines, are absent. In the end we have a return to the unit value of nine. Hence we see that the possible variants of the complete gamut of expression are ten in number, and that they finally resolve themselves into the number nine, which is the symbolical expression of the Adamic race, the 12×12 or 144, indicated by the values ADM = 144, according to the Hebraic Kabala.

By pairing the first two rows we have 5 nines, the next two rows yield 4 nines, the next two yield 3 nines, the next two rows give 2 nines, and last two yield 1 nine. Hence, from the ten rows we obtain 10, 8, 6, 4, 1, or 29 pairs, falling into the single unit value of nine. In this process it will be observed that the final resolution is *via* the two lunar numbers 7 and 2, one positive, the other negative, and both answering to the characteristic of variability. They are Moon numbers, representing the blue-green and the yellow-green of the spectrum, and therefore representing the two aspects of the soul in its natural or vital development and its spiritual or mental development.

In this scheme, therefore, we see that the whole gamut of human expression, so far as it can be represented by unit values, is included in the numbers 1–9, and that through successive pairings or polarisations, we arrive finally through the element of variability at the single expression of Humanity = 9. (*Kab.*, i. ch. xv.)

From this scheme also we extract the polarisations of each numerical type. For observe that whatever line we may take we shall find that the first and last, second and last but one, etc., in each line, adds to nine, and is itself an expression of the Planetary Values which have been determined by experience to attach to them, and which will be found fully explained and tested in my book on *Cosmic Symbolism.*

In this system the Sun (positive) = 1
Saturn   .   .   8
―――
9

Jupiter answers to the number   .   3
Venus to the number   .   .   6
―――
9

Mercury answers to the number .   5
The Sun (negative) to   .   .   4
―――
9

Mars, the tonic of our scale   = 9
Moon, the variable factor, 7 positive
and 2 negative   = 9

These constitute the natural pairs, and, if we regard Mars = 9 as the index of the Man or Microcosm, " made in the image and likeness of Elohim," then 7–2, the numbers of the Moon, will indicate that element of variability which makes for perfection. From this we can derive Bruno's saying : "Infinite variability is the eternal juvenescence of God."

If we take the positive values—1, 3, 5, 7, 9—we find that they correspond with Sun, Jupiter, Mercury, Moon, and Mars, all positive ; while the negative values—2, 4, 6, 8—answer to Moon, Sun, Venus, and Saturn in their negative aspects. Pairing these we get from either series the value of 10, leaving 5 unpaired. Hence Ten has been regarded as the Perfect Number, while Five is the number of discrimination, discernment, intellection. It stands for the present race-value of humanity, the Man in the midst of a world of relativity, alternation, pairs of opposites, etc.

We may give a significance to these numbers in terms of our daily life and experience, so that they shall answer to character and fortunes whenever they are applied to individuals. This has been done to some extent in the first part of this work, and may be here extended to cover particular cases which afford abnormal indications. Let us therefore presume that the following characteristics are those suited to the expression of the several numerical values :

Dignity	1	Pride.
Flexibility	2	Vacillation.
Generosity	3	Extravagance.
Practicality	4	Ostentation.
Discernment	5	Inquisitiveness.

Gentleness	6	Laxity.
Purpose	7	Prejudice.
Discretion	8	Timidity.
Zeal	9	Bigotry.

We shall then find that there are abnormal as well as normal characteristics to be accounted for. These abnormalities arise from the opposition of different planets, sets of vibrations, etc., and, as these have not been hitherto represented, they may be noticed in this place.

It should be observed, then, that numbers which enter into the enumeration of a birth-rate, as set forth in the Kabala of the Square of Three (*Kab.*, i. ch. iv.), and that are not brought into alliance by the interposition of another number, are said to be in opposition if in the same perpendicular or horizontal line.

Thus, to cite a particular instance, St Louis was born on the 23rd April 1215, and this by the Kabala is found to give the following Square of Three:

```
    3 │ 1 │
   ───┼───┼───
      │   │ 5
   ───┼───┼───
    2 │   │ 4
```

Sum = 6 Venus.

The sum is seen to respond to the value of Venus 6, which denotes gentleness. Also by the planetary conjunctions we find the Sun in conjunction with

Jupiter dominating the destiny and character. But also there is the conjunction of Mercury and the Sun on the lower planes, which would enable the benevolent character of this monarch to find a practical expression. So much was seen in the case as presented in the first part of our Kabala.

The oppositions represented here are those of Jupiter and the Moon and the Moon and Sun, since the Moon (2) and Jupiter (3) are in the same vertical line without an interposing and co-ordinating factor, which here should be Venus (6.) Also the Moon (2) is in the same line with Sun (4), without the intervening number 8.

In Napoleon I.'s scheme we get oppositions of Sun and Saturn and Sun and Mars. In Milton's scheme we have Sun opposition Saturn. In Cagliostro's we find Sun opposition Mars. In the case of Louis XVI. we find Moon opposition Jupiter, but no conjunction of Sun and Jupiter, as in the case of St Louis; but, on the contrary, there are sinister conjunctions of Sun and Saturn and Moon and Saturn, which are absent from the data of the more fortunate monarch.

Similarly, there are trines formed between the planets by the fact of two numbers holding the extreme positions in the same line of a scheme with another holding a central position in another line. Thus, in the scheme of Napoleon I. (*Kab.*, i. p. 46), the numbers 9 and 4 are in the same line, and they form a triangle with 6 in another line. Hence we have the trine of Mars and Venus, and also the Sun and Venus, on the base line of the opposition of Sun and Mars. The same combination appears in the case of Cagliostro.   In the cases of both Louis XVI. and St Louis we have the triangle of 3–5–2—namely, Moon and Mercury, Mercury and Jupiter.   This is repeated in the case of Queen Victoria.

Therefore, from a variety of considerations which employ numbers as factors for the estimating of character and destiny, we may derive considerable information if we take these numbers as answering to the various planets of the system, regard them as incorporated in the date of birth, and then find their conjunctions, oppositions, and trines, and so make account of the results attributable to these inter-actions, taking the sum of the scheme to be indicative of the particular vibration to which the whole nature responds.

Thus, in the case of Charles, Duke of Bourbonnais, Constable of Bourbon, who was born on the 25th February 1489 (converted to new style), or 16th February, old style, we have the scheme as here shown:

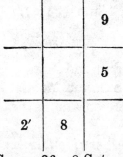

Sum = 26 = 8 Saturn.

Conjunctions.

Mars and Mercury.
Moon and Saturn.

Here the conjunction of Mars and Mercury indicated extreme mental activity and irascibility, while the Moon conjunct Saturn points to maiming and misfortune. The Key Number is of sinister import, answering as it does to the unit value of Saturn. There are no remedial trines. He was killed at the age of 38 by the bursting of a shell at the siege of Rome.

Lord Brougham had a very strong personality and a strongly set purpose, as is seen from the following scheme:

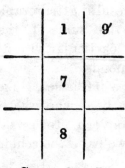

$$\text{Sum} = 34 = 7.$$

Conjunctions.

Sun and Mars.
Sun and Moon.
Moon and Saturn.

This is altogether lacking in the scheme of Charles II., which merely shows a complacent conjunction of Venus and Jupiter, indicating at best generosity and gentleness, with a material base of Saturn. This indication of the number 8 being repeated in the sum of the scheme, has a sinister import as regards material affairs.

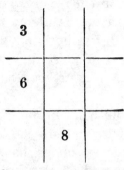

Sum, 17 = 8 Saturn.

Conjunction.
Jupiter and Venus.

It should be observed that the value of 4 is not the same as 5, though both apply to the Sun.   But 1 has direct reference to character and 4 to material prosperity.   Similarly, 7 and 2 are not to be regarded as having the same significance in a scheme, for 7 has relation to purpose and character, whereas 2 has reference to material change and circumstance.   Thus the conjunction of Sun 4 and Saturn 8 has an entirely different value to a conjunction of Sun 1 and Saturn 8.   In the first case there is material disaster, and in the other there is loss of reputation and honour.

It has been suggested that instead of taking the secular notation of the month of birth, as 1 for January, 2 February, etc., it would be more consistent to take the value of the planet ruling the sign in which the Sun is at the time. This while quite in line with the traditional methods of the Kabalists, will entail an inspection of the ephemeris, as there is a date in each month on which the Sun changes its sign, which is about the 20th of each month, though it differs by 1 to 3 days according to the month and year in question, owing to the difference between the secular months and the astronomical month.

Further, it would be in keeping with this scheme to take the actual day of the week on which a person was born and use the value of the planet ruling that day. Students should employ both these variants and observe which method gives the best results. It is admitted that there is no necessary connection between the secular dates and the characters and fortunes of those born thereon once we dismiss the idea of law and number as the governing factors in all manifestation. If, however, we see fit to adhere to these conceptions, unorthodox though they may be, we shall find occasion and reason for including all apparently chance happenings in the category of things related and designed.

For the purpose of comparing the systems of Kabala, however, it may be well to give the day and date numbers.

DAYS OF THE WEEK

The day of the week begins at noon for each day.
Sunday ruled by Sun—Number 1 when Sun is in
a male or odd sign.
Number 4 when Sun is in female or even sign.

Monday—Number 7 when the Moon is in a Male sign.

Number 2 when the Moon is in a female sign.

Tuesday—Number 9.

Wednesday—Number 5.

Thursday—Number 3.

Friday—Number 6.

Saturday—Number 8.

DAYS OF THE MONTH

January 1–20—ruled by Saturn—Number 8.

January 21–February 19 — ruled by Saturn — Number 8.

February 20–March 19—ruled by Jupiter—Number 3.

March 20–April 19—ruled by Mars—Number 9.

April 20–May 20—ruled by Venus—Number 6.

May 21–June 20—ruled by Mercury—Number 5.

June 21–July 22—ruled by Moon—Numbers 7 and 2.

July 23–August 22—ruled by Sun—Numbers 1 and 4.

August 23–September 22—ruled by Mercury—Number 5.

September 23–October 22—ruled by Venus—Number 6.

October 23–November 21—ruled by Mars—Number 9.

November 22–December 21—ruled by Jupiter—Number 3.

December 22–December 31—ruled by Saturn—Number 8.

7

Note.—In June, July, and August female births take the number of the planet agreeing with the sex—namely, 2 for the Moon and 4 for the Sun. Male births take 7 for the Moon and 1 for the Sun.

This question being disposed of by the simple expedient of giving such building material as is required for the work, and letting everybody suit himself as to the particular style of architecture he fancies, we may pass on to the consideration of

Sound Values,

concerning which there is considerable dispute. This must inevitably be the case so long as you have dialectical differences. In the Hebrew evaluation there is no such difficulty, inasmuch as the Hebraic equivalent of every English letter is well known, and the values are applied irrespective of the phonetic value a letter may have in a word. Thus, by the Table of Hebraic Values (*Kab.*, i. p. 30), we have for the name Aboyeur (Fr.) $1271562 = 24 = 6$, and there is no doubt about it. But when we come to the Universal or Phonetic Values (*ibid.*), which I have said is the most satisfactory in its general application, we are faced by the difficulty that two persons may give different phonetic quantities to the same word. Thus, Aboyeur may be coded as 126162 (A-bo-yur), but a French-speaking student would code it 226112 (A'-bwah-yĕr), though the English transliteration does not quite convey it. The evaluation of the name in the one case is $18 = 9$, and in the other $14=5$, and because 9 and 5 are taken in some systems as interchangeable, both would consider that they had coded it correctly.

A more difficult case would be the name of the Australian horse whose name is Urelia, $162131 = 14=5$ (U-reel-ya), but which the inconsequent pencillers converted by laying the stress on the penultimate, to which " You're another " appeared to be the only suitable reply.

Granted, however, that we are agreed as to our quantities, there is certainly no more satisfactory system of evaluation of names than the Phonetic. But, as I have always insisted, and here repeat, " Each system has to be employed in relation to its own method of interpretation," and to make no doubt of it, I have specifically cited two cases (*Kab.*, i. 30): " The Hebrew method is employed for the kabalistic interpretation of the Scripture, as in the *Zohar*. It is especially suited to the Tarotic interpretation by the Twenty-two Major Keys "; and " The Pythagorean alphabet is used in connection with the interpretation employed in that system." There cannot, therefore, be any doubt in the matter. If people use one method of evaluation and another of interpretation and find there is no truth in it, the fault is with them and can be easily corrected.

It is, of course, possible to apply one's own evaluation, but more difficult to find a method of interpretation which fits it. Thus I have seen some curious results derived by the use of the decimal evaluation of the English alphabet :

A B C D E F G H I J
1 2 3 4 5 6 7 8 9
K L M N O P Q R S
1 2 3 4 5 6 7 8 9
T U V W X Y Z

and when the letters are taken in connection with
the signs of the zodiac and applied to the names of
competitors to know the result of a contest, the
reading has been singularly curious.   In this scheme
the letters fall thus :

Aries	Taurus	Gemini	Cancer	Leo	Virgo	Libra
AN	BO	CP	DQ	ER	FS	GT

Scorpio	Sagittarius	Capricornus	Aquarius	Pisces
HU	IJVW	KX	LY	MZ

The day being divided into 24 hours and counted
from equatorial sunrise (which is 6 o'clock) to the
time of an event, beginning with that planet and
number which belongs to the day, as Moon 7 on
Monday, Mars 9 on Tuesday, and so on, then that
planet which coincides with the hour in which the
event took place will, by its position in the zodiac,
give a numerical value to every letter in the name of
the winning competitor. These being computed
and reduced to a unit value, they are found to
correspond with the planetary number governing
the hour in which the event took place.

But it will be found, upon examination, that
however ingeniously we labour with such cypher
alphabets we shall come no nearer than to note a

certain correspondence between the values ascribed to the letters and the planet that happens to be in rotational order at the moment.

Far more significance attaches to the language of the heavens if only we are able to read it, and in such case it gives its message clearly and without ambiguity, neither is there need to make any calculation in the matter save to find what planet holds the greatest significance by chief position in the heavens at the time, as indeed some examples will readily show.

These " pointers," as we call them astrologically, doubtless depend upon the harmony of form, colour, name, and number that is seen to characterise the whole physiognomy of Nature, so that, while one may be intent upon discovering a ruling number, another will be searching for the prevailing colour, another for the dominant sound, and so forth, while the astrologer merely seizes on the general physiognomy of the case, taking the aspect of Nature at the moment, and finding in her at all times a revelation of some hidden truth. By way of illustration I may adduce the following few examples from among a large collection of others coming under my notice from time to time.

Mars being in the ascendant in its own sign Aries, being the only planet in its own sign at the time, " Rubra " (red) won a race from five competitors. Note that the planet Mars rules red.

The Moon exactly rising in the military sign Aries, " The White Knight " won from several competitors. Here Moon is " white " and Mars is " knight."

The Moon being in its own sign Cancer, and elevated above all the other bodies, " Cream of the Sky " won a conspicuous victory in quite unexpected form.

Mars being exactly on the Mid-heaven, and therefore the most notable feature of the celestial chart, " Rubio " won the Grand National Steeplechase at the remarkable price of 66 to 1 against.

These examples will sufficiently serve, no doubt, to indicate the extremely simple method of such observations. It amounts practically to the discernment of such correspondences as may exist in any particular instance. But in the nature of the case they are not always represented, and are sometimes difficult to recognise even where present. The student of occultism is, however, always on the look-out for such " pointers," even in the affairs of daily life.

CHAPTER VII

THE LAW OF PERIODICITY

It has been shown, from a careful computation of factors involved, that as regards a pack of cards, a roulette wheel, and many other methods of employing the element of chance, a certain combination may be counted upon to recur at stated intervals; and although it cannot be shown that these intervals can be predicted, it can certainly be shown that they do recur within given limits.

But this is quite different from showing that particular factors are bound to recur at stated and predicable intervals, and, as this is my task, it will be seen that there can be only one way through, and that is by employing natural factors. For Nature undoubtedly has a periodicity which can be understood and anticipated.

Naturalists observe that certain habits of creatures are governed by the seasons, though they cannot say how the intelligence or instinct of those creatures can compass the vagaries of an English climate and yet strike true within twenty-four hours, as may be observed in the migration of birds, the various periods of nesting and hatching, the

colonising of ants, the swarming of bees, and similar
natural phenomena apparently governed by instinct—an unknown quantity to human methods
of intelligence.

Astronomers also observe that there are cycles
and periods within which Nature repeats her
phenomena, from the rising of the sun to the
apparition of a comet. These observations submit
readily to a mathematical law, and the recurrence of
similar celestial phenomena are therefore predicable.
It is from this basis that I shall be able to demonstrate that matters apparently governed by chance
are subject to a like periodicity to that which we
observe in Nature, and for the reason that they, too,
are governed by natural laws.

Let us take two factors only as the ground of our
argument—the Sun and Moon. When these bodies
are conjoined in the heavens, so as to appear in the
same meridian at the same time, we get what are
called Spring Tides. The Sun and Moon are then
acting together on the same side of the earth, and
consequently the tides are highest. But when they
are acting from opposite sides of the earth, as at the
full moon, we get Neap Tides. Now, if there were
no interaction between the Sun, Moon, and Earth,
and if, further, there were no periodicity or regular
recurrence of their mutual relations, then we could
not construct a Tide-table such as forms part of our
annual almanacs. But this we can do for years and
decades in advance, so that the common formula
$t^d_{\frac{1}{2}}$ has a numerical significance which is quite
appreciable and has a constant value for the same

day of the Moon's age for every month in the year.

To go a step further, let us suppose that the tidal energy has an equivalent in regard to animate life, as we find it to have in regard to the inanimate waters of the globe. Let us presume that it has a subtle, although as yet undefined, action upon the sap of plants, the juices and humours of animals, and the blood-pressure of human beings. And this, when carefully thought over, is not presuming very much, for it is certainly the fact that atmospheric pressure is increased at the new and full of the Moon, and that lunatics and feeble-minded persons respond to increased blood-pressure at such times. We call them lunatics simply because they are subject to this lunar influence. The Sun maintains approximately the same relations with a given meridian at the same time each day, but the Moon does not do so, and it is to her variability that the gradual recession of the tides upon a meridian is due. For if on a particular day the Sun and Moon are conjoined, the next day will see the Sun at the same hour in the same relations with the meridian, but the Moon will be about 12° to the east, having advanced about 13° in its apparent orbit, while the Sun has only advanced 1°. The following day the Moon will be a further 12° east of the Sun, and so it will continue until the two bodies are in opposition and cross the meridian on opposite sides of the earth at the same time. The distance between the Moon and Sun is called *Elongation*, *i.e.* longitude out of the meridian which the Sun holds. If we multiply this distance or elongation by 4, we shall convert degrees of longitude into minutes of time, and this time will be the time after noon at which normal high tide is due at a place ; and this would actually be the time at which it happened but for local disturbing causes. With these, however, we are not now concerned, and I only venture upon a popular explanation of the tides in order to establish the premiss of my argument, which is that the Moon as variable factor is what we must look to in connection with any periodicity we may hope to find in connection with apparently chance events.

Imagine a number of competitors in an event as having an equal chance of success. Such, for example, is the idea aimed at in the process of handicapping by distance from " scratch," or by additional weight. In the case of racehorses this is effected by allotting weight for age, plus penalties, or additional weights, for successive wins. In effect we find that we are able to distinguish the competitors by the weights they carry, but we cannot distinguish the winner because the handicapping has given to each an equal chance. Hence the grounds for speculation and wagering which is a feature of all such contests, " the spice in the pudding," as its advocates affirm.

By a comparative study of various records, I find that I am able to present the net results of my investigations in a single glyph which, from what has been said, will doubtless be appreciable by the intelligent reader.

The fact is that one may triangulate upon any series of events of like nature with an absolute certainty of gaining a majority of them by as many as seven in every ten, or seventy per cent., and that by no further trouble than is involved in the study of the tidal law we have been considering. It will be observed that the circle or sphere of action is divided by interlaced triangles into 12 arcs of 30°

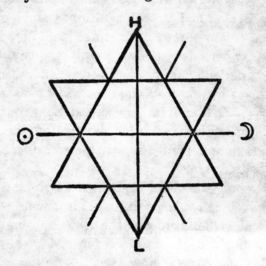

each, three being included in each quadrant of the circle. Then two divisions will equal 60°, and this gives us 6 in the circle, and 42÷6=7, which is therefore due to each of the arcs between ⊙ and H, H and ☽, L and ⊙, L and ☽. So that in taking the relations of the three factors into account and applying the tidal law, we arrive at a periodicity of results that have a direct weight relation to one another. An exposition of this law would occupy a great deal of space and would usurp the main

purpose of this work.   I have therefore only hinted
at the method of procedure.

But as soon as we come to the study of sound
values, *i.e.* the numerical value of vibrations, we
are able to exemplify this law of periodicity in a
simple and convincing manner.   This statement,
however, involves the fact of such phonetic values
having cosmic equivalents, and hence that the
planets are linked up with number and sound as
well as colour in such manner that by tracing
planetary periods we are simultaneously tracing
their numerical and phonetic correlatives.   This, I
endeavoured to show (*Kab.*, i. ch. viii.), was actually
the fact, and I so far succeeded as to stimulate
inquiry for further examples, illustrations, and rules,
and, as this is within the scheme of my chapter, I
may do so here.

It was seen that the basis of our calculation was
the Sun's true centre rising.   This means that the
astronomical longitude of the Sun is rising on the
celestial horizon of the place for which calculation
is made.   On p. 85, however, the rule was trans-
posed in error.   The ascensional difference of the
Sun must be *added* to 90° when the Sun's declination
is *North*, and *subtracted* when it is *South* ; and the
result multiplied by 4 will give the minutes in time
before noon at which the Sun rose.   The example
on p. 86 is worked correctly and will serve as a
guide.   It should be remarked, however, that the
rule should be reversed for places South of the
Equator, as for Australia, New Zealand, etc.,
and the ascensional difference *added* when the

Sun's declination is South, and *subtracted* when North.

In order to prove the periodicity of numerical values and their sound equivalents, we have only to take two consecutive days and show that the same unit values are in force at corresponding times, *i.e.* at times when the planetary periods are the same ; or, alternatively, we may take two consecutive Wednesdays, or Thursdays, and show the same results from the same or equivalent times. Let us take two consecutive days.

Newmarket—Wednesday, April 17th, 1912. Lat. 52° 15′ N. ☉'s declin. N = 10° 21′.

To find the Sun's ascn. difference, add together the logarithms of the tangents of 52° 15′ and 10° 21′. Thus :

Log. tan. 52° 15′   10·11110
„   „   10° 21′   9·26158

„   sine 13° 38½′ = 9·37268

These logarithms will be found in Chambers's Mathematical Tables. The sum of the two logs. gives us the log. sine of the Sun's ascensional difference, and, as the declination is N. and the latitude of place N., we must add 13° 38½′ to 90° and multiply by 4 in order to find the time before noon at which the Sun rose on Newmarket.

Thus, 90° + 13° 38½′ = 103° 38½′

4

414^m 34^s = 6^h 54^m 34^s

Hence the local time of sunrise was 5.5 a.m. nearly, and the corresponding Greenwich time would be 5.4 a.m.

The Sun will be 6h 55m coming from the horizon to the meridian, and the same time, approximately, from meridian to sunset. We are only concerned with the afternoon of April 17th, and so we take the semiarc of the Sun from noon to setting, viz. 6h 55m, and divide this by 6 to get the length of the planetary hour = 1h 9m nearly. As there are 6 planetary hours from sunrise to noon, the seventh hour will begin at noon, and the Horary Speculum (*Kab.*, i. p. 84) tells us that on Wednesday the seventh hour is ruled by Venus and the eighth by Mercury. Each " hour " is at this date 1h 9m in length, and therefore Venus will rule from noon to 1.9 p.m., and Mercury will begin at 1.9 p.m. and continue to rule till 2.18 p.m.

But each hour is subdivided into seven parts, and each of these sub-periods is ruled successively by the planets in rotation. Then to find the length of each sub-period divide 1h 9m by seven, which is 10m nearly. With these preliminary calculations we can set out the Table for the day, showing the beginnings of the hours or periods, and also those of the sub-periods, for Wednesday, April 17th, 1912. It will be observed that the 8th sub-period, which would be ruled by the same planet as that which governs the hour, syncopates in this scheme, and is replaced by the planet governing the next hour and sub-period in succession. Otherwise the Chaldean order is in every respect observed, thus:

Wednesday, April 17, 1912

Venus 12·0		Mercury 1·9		Moon 2·18		Saturn 3·27		Jupiter 4·36		Mars 5·45	
♀	12·0	☿	1·9	☽	2·18	♄	3·27	♃	4·36	♂	5·45
☿	12·10	☽	1·19	♄	2·28	♃	3·37	♂	4·46	☉	5·55
☽	12·20	♄	1·29	♃	2·38	♂	3·47	☉	4·56	♀	6·5
♄	12·30	♃	1·39	♂	2·48	☉	3·57	♀	5·6	☿	6·15
♃	12·40	♂	1·49	☉	2·58	♀	4·7	☿	5·16	☽	6·25
♂	12·50	☉	1·59	♀	3.8	☿	4·17	☽	5·26	♄	6·35
☉	1·0	♀	2·9	☿	3·18	☽	4·27	♄	5·36	♃	6·45
♀		☿		☽		♄		♃		♂	

The Speculum ends with the period of Mars and the sub-period of Jupiter, and this latter extends for 10^m, which brings us to 6.55, the time of sunset. Now the events of the day were as follows—

2.0	Won by Kempion	=	214825 = 4	☉
2.30	,, Thimble filly	=	9423831 = 3	♃
3.0	,, Saracen	=	6121615 = 4	☉
3.30	,, Jackdaw	=	31242 = 3	♃
4.0	,, Clay Pigeon	=	231835 = 4	☉
4.30	,, Pintadeau	=	854146 = 1	☉
5.0	,, Thunderstone	= 9254126465 = 8		♄

At first sight it may not appear that all these results are in harmony with our law. Let us, however, examine them. The first event at 2.0 falls in sub-period of the Sun = 4 negative, and is won by Kempion = 4.

At 2.30, ruled by Saturn, number 3 wins. We should have expected 1 or 8 to win. But on reference we find Saturn at this date in Taurus, ruled by Venus, whose negative number is 3 (*Kab.*, i. p. 90). We are here dealing with the afternoon, which is negative, and therefore look for negative numbers.

At 3.0, ruled by Sun, Saracen wins in correct time ; Sun = 4 negative.

At 3.30, ruled by Saturn, Jackdaw = 3 won. The same result as for 2.30, where Saturn, in sign of Venus negative = 3, was replaced by 3.

At 4.0, ruled by Sun, Clay Pigeon = 4 wins.

At 4.30, ruled by Moon, Pintadeau = 1 wins. Here the Moon is in Taurus and 3 should win.

At 5.0, ruled by Sun, Thunderstone = 8 wins. This being the number of Saturn, it is alternate to the Sun. There were no less than five competitors of value 1 = Sun positive, but none value 4, and in consequence the Sun wins under 8.

Therefore we find that out of seven events four are direct and unequivocal, being won by horses whose names are phonetic equivalents of the negative ruling number of the periods in which they won. Two others are won by the negative number of the planet in whose sign the ruler of the period is found at the time.

But, generally, it will be found that the events which do not fall into line with the law are won by the number represented by the sign the Moon is in. On April 17 it was just entering Taurus = 3. This is invariably the case when the ☽ is the sub-period planet and there is no number 2 present among the competitors.

For convenience of those who have no astrological knowledge I here give the negative values of the signs of the zodiac.

NEGATIVE NUMBERS OF THE SIGNS.

♈	♉	♊	♋	♌	♍	♎	♏	♐	♑	♒	♓
5	3	9	2	4	9	3	5	6	1	1	6

Now let us take the next day, April 18th. The Sun's declin. being 10° 42′ log. tan.   9·27635

Lat.   52° 15′   ,,   ,,   10·11110
                                ‾‾‾‾‾‾‾‾‾

Asc. diff. 14° 7½′ ,, sine   9·38745
+90° 0′
                                ‾‾‾‾‾‾‾‾‾
104° 7½′
4
                                ‾‾‾‾‾‾‾‾‾
416° 30′ = 6ʰ 56ᵐ 30ˢ.

The period from noon to sunset is thus seen to be 6ʰ 56½ᵐ, which, divided by 6, gives the *period* of 1ʰ 9ᵐ 10ˢ; and this, again, divided by 7 gives the *sub-period* of 10ᵐ nearly.

8

The events were as follows :—

1.0	—Shipshape	38318 = 23 = 5.
1.30	—Biter Bit	2142 24 = 15 = 6.
2.0	—Thrace	9216 = 18 = 9.
2.30	—Jingling Geordie	352352 32241 = 32 = 5.
3.0	—Distcha	4631 = 14 = 5.
3.30	—Tullibardine	423212415 = 24 = 6.

At 1.0 the period was just changing from Mercury to Moon, and, allowing 1 minute for east longitude of Newmarket, there was 1 minute of Mercury's period to expire at the set time of the race. Consequently we find Shipshape = 5 winning under its own number. This is irregular if a 9 was present, but it is not in contravention of the law.

At 1.30 the Sun was ruling, and he was on this date in Taurus, ruled by Venus, who won under its own number 6.

At 2.0 the Moon was ruling. 9 won, this being contrary to our rule, but in agreement with the suggestion that Mars is the alternate to the Moon (*Cosmic Symbolism*).

At 2.30 the Sun was ruling. Here the Sun in Taurus = 3, and Geordie = 3, but the full name = 5, a misfit.

At 3.0 the Moon was ruling. Winner = 5. See above where Mars (negative 5) wins in same period.

At 3.30 the Sun again rules in Taurus = 3, but the positive number 6 wins.

The results, though involved, are mainly in support of the theory we have adopted. Taken over a period, the findings are abundantly satisfactory. But this, of course, is not advanced as a system of selection. At best, and like all other systems depending on name values, it is a system of exclusion, or what is called in science a method of exhaustion. I presume it would be impossible to formulate any law which does not admit of exceptions, because our laws are founded upon observation of the direct working of one form of energy, and this may be interfered with by the operation and interaction of other forms of energy, whether by resistance or by deflection.

A method for employing the positive numbers of the planets may here be mentioned. It is based on the Hebraic view that the day commences at noon and not at sunrise, as is generally and erroneously believed. The statement in *Genesis* is, "The evening and the morning were the first day." Not by any stretch of fancy could we speak of the period from sunrise to sunset as "the evening," nor from sunset to sunrise as "morning." But we can quite legitimately refer to the period from noon to midnight as "the evening," and from midnight to noon as "the morning."

The planet giving its name to the day takes rule over the first hour after noon, and is followed in the Chaldean order by the other planets, and so on in rotation. Each hour is taken as 60ᵐ in length, and is subdivided into 15 parts of 4 minutes each, the first of which is ruled by the planet of the day, and followed by the rest in rotation. Thus Sunday is divided as follows :

        Noon to 1 p.m. Sun
        1 p.m. to 2   ,,   Venus
        2   ,, to 3   ,,   Mercury
        3   ,, to 4   ,,   Moon
        4   ,, to 5   ,,   Saturn
        5   ,, to 6   ,,   Jupiter
                etc., etc.

Then the hour of Venus, from 1 to 2 p.m., will divide into sub-periods thus:

1☉, 2♀, 3☿, 4☽, 5♄, 6♃, 7♂, 8☉, 9♀, 10☿, 11☽, 12♄, 13♃, 14♂, 15☉.

The planet ruling the day, that ruling the hour, and that ruling the sub-period, are represented by their positive numbers, and these being added together, the sum is reduced to its unit value. The winner of a race or contest taking place in the limits of the sub-period should have a name which is the phonetic equivalent of the unit value of the three factors.

The Tables of the Hours and sub-periods of the week, counted from noon each day, are as follows:

Sunday	.	1657839	recurring
Monday	.	7839165	,,
Tuesday	.	9165783	,,
Wednesday	.	5783916	,,
Thursday	.	3916578	,,
Friday	.	6578391	,,
Saturday	.	8391657	,,
Hours .	.	1234567	from noon
Periods.	.	1234567	from Hour

Example : 11 Sept. 1911—Saturday.

Saturday = 8
3rd hour   = 9
1st period = 8

_____

25 = 7, won by Countess Mac = 9.

Suggested alternative of Moon 7 = Mars 9.

Saturday   = 8
3rd hour   = 9
8th period = 8

_____

25 = 7, won by Holt's Pride = 2.

Negative ☽ period = 2.

Saturday   = 8
4th hour   = 1
1st period = 8

_____

17 = 8, won by Chasuble = 4.

Saturday   = 8
4th hour   = 1
8th period = 8

_____

17 = 8, won by Cylgad = 8.

Saturday   = 8
5th hour   = 6
1st period = 8

_____

22 = 4, won by Montmartre = 8.

Saturday $= 8$
5th hour $= 6$
8th period $= 8$

$22 = 4$, won by Wolftoi $= 8$.

The Coding used is as follows :
Countess Mac	225416 412	$= 27 = 9$.
Holt's Pride	563468 24	$= 38 = 11 = 2$.
Chasuble	317623	$= 22 = 4$.
Cylgad	613214	$= 17 = 8$.
Montmartre	425241242	$= 26 = 8$.
Wolftoi	6238421	$= 26 = 8$.

Thus it will be seen that, with the exception of the first event, all the results are in harmony with our customary evaluations, and support the scheme here for the first time advanced. In the first case it is of interest to note that the Moon 7 was, on 11 September 1911, in the sign Aries, ruled by Mars 9 ; and this fact appears to support the general ascription of "variability" applied to the Moon. Certainly it is repeatedly observed that the Moon can win in any period whose mass value (as above) agrees with the planet ruling the sign it is in, as follows :

♈	♉	♊	♋	♌	♍	♎	♏	♐	♑	♒	♓
9	6	5	2	4	5	6	9	3	8	8	3
			7	1							

Some little while ago I instituted a test with an old student of the "Mysteries of Sound and Number," a man whose patience and faculty for figures were backed by a considerable knowledge of turf matters. In making selections before the event and using the above system called "Trilogia," because it employs three arguments, it was found that I could easily double his successes, after making my selections in half the time. The reasons for this superiority were that I had not to speculate on the "off" time, but merely to use the set time of the event; that I had not to take any count of the distance to be run; and, finally, that my method of coding was simpler than his. But probably the chief reason lay in the fact that he was never correct in his times of sunrise except for places in or about the same latitude as Greenwich— and fortunately for him, and the system he followed, these included Bath, Salisbury, Windsor, Gatwick, Epsom, Kempton Park, Hurst Park, Alexandra Park, Ascot, Bibury, Brighton, Folkestone, Lewes, Goodwood, Lingfield, Sandown Park, and Newbury. This was the broad base on which an astounding fallacy was erected, and when we came to deal with Liverpool, Manchester, York, Newcastle, Ayr, and some other northern centres, the record he had been building in the South went to pieces.

We may now look at the subject of periodicity from another point of view.

CHAPTER VIII

PERIODICITY OF EVENTS

In trying to trace a law of periodicity in regard to things of chance which apparently have but small significance in the main purpose of human life, and yet which, being included, must in some way be conformable to the general plan and subject to universal laws, we may find ourselves forced to rely upon partial and sporadic successes. We may assume a broader base with more certainty of success. It is easier to indicate which way the wind is blowing on the open plains than to take our reading from the play of some little eddy in the byways of a town. Consequently, when we come to the study of the law of periodicity in relation to the broad facts of history, we find that the indications are more marked and easier to discern. We take our pointers from the same cosmic factors that have guided our investigations from the first, and trace in the mutations of the planets certain definite changes in human affairs. From like causes we argue like effects, and the fact that these effects are repeatedly observable serves not only to confirm the validity of our argument, but also enables us to establish a law of periodicity in regard to events which, if they were not disposed by superior causes, would not respond to this law, being apparently under human control.

We have already seen that Mars represents energy, executiveness, and when vitiated its abnormal expression is seen to be violence, strife, and lawlessness. Normally it denotes freedom, abnormally it indicates licence. Saturn we have found to be associated with the number 8, which indicates destruction, revolution, inversion. One is a positive planet and the other a negative. The two acting together produce outbreaks of public feeling, violence, and mortality.

Elsewhere it will be seen that the sign of the zodiac ruling England is Aries, governed by Mars, and responding to the vibrations of the number 9 and the colour red. The popular expression " the all-red " refers very aptly to the British. By some play of human faculty this has been sensed and identified with all that is British, and accordingly we find our atlas showing the Empire extending across the two hemispheres all red. Therefore we may expect that Mars stirs up strife in various countries as it passes through the signs of the zodiac governing them, and that its conjunction with Saturn in the sign ruling a country is of sinister import. We find it so, in fact. Thus there was a conjunction of Saturn and Mars in Aries in 1879, and there followed the terrible Afghan and Zulu Wars. Passing into Taurus (ruling Ireland) the planets produced the agrarian outrages in

Ireland. In 1883 the conjunction fell in Gemini
(ruling Lower Egypt), and was at once followed by
the Soudan War and the tragedy of Khartoum.
We might trace the whole circle of the zodiac, did
space permit, until we come to the conjunction of
these planets in Aquarius (ruling Russia) in 1904,
and again in 1905, which brought about the defeat
of Russia by the Japanese and the outburst of
popular feeling which culminated in the disgraceful
tragedy of " Red Sunday " ; and finally in Pisces,
which brought Portugal into startling prominence
by the assassination of the King and Crown Prince,
and the Revolution which followed it.

Thus we come to 1909–10 and the destructive
Socialist policy of the Lloyd-George clique, the
Dock and Coal Strikes, the War scare of 1912, and
the Suffragette outrages. From 1879 to 1909 is a
period of thirty years, which is approximately the
period of this conjunction as regards any part of the
zodiac. If we go back thirty years from 1879 we come
to 1849 and the Sikh War. A second conjunction
followed in 1851, and was soon followed by the
Russian War. Its immediate effect was the *coup
d'état* of Louis Napoleon and the jeopardising of
British interests by his ambitions. Then we go
back thirty years and find Saturn and Mars again in
Aries in the year 1821, which was the period of the
Cato Street Conspiracy and the suicide of Lord
Londonderry (Lord Castlereagh), then Minister of
State for Foreign Affairs.

So that whether we trace this combination of
Mars and Saturn (9+8) through the successive signs

at intervals of two years, or from one conjunction to the next in the same sign at intervals of thirty years, we find its effects disturbing and destructive.

But we may take the cycle of 265 years, which admits of many minor cycles, and we find the same planets conjoined in exactly the same part of the zodiac. Thus from the epoch 1909–10 it brings us to 1644 and the overthrow of the Royalists at Marston Moor. Then from 1644 we take the cycle again and come to 1379 and the Rebellion under Wat Tyler. From that date we go back to 1114, when England was disturbed by the wars waged by Henry I. against Robert of Bêlleme and France. Going a further cycle back, to 849, we come to the Danish invasion during the reign of Egbert. Prior to this epoch history becomes obscure in regard to British affairs, and so we may leave it. The cycle has been traced in regard to other countries ruled by other signs than Aries, and undoubtedly we have complete evidence of a connected periodicity of events due to the combined action of these two major planets.

Conjunctions of Saturn and Jupiter lead to great mutations in those countries ruled by the signs in which the conjunctions fall. The conjunctions differ from those of Mars and Saturn in this respect, that whereas the latter pass regularly through the signs at intervals of about two years, those of Saturn and Jupiter remain in the same triplicity for several decades. At present they are in the earthy triplicity, embracing the signs of Taurus, Virgo, and Capricorn, and have been so since 1842. Every twenty years these planets are conjoined in one of these signs—namely, in 1842, Capricorn; 1861–2, Virgo; 1881, Taurus; 1901, Capricorn; 1921, Virgo; 1941, Taurus; 1961, Capricorn; 1981, Libra. Thus we get a change of triplicity after seven periodic conjunctions. Hence, from 1842 to 1981, the countries ruled by the earthy trigon—among which are India, New Zealand, Greece, Turkey, Mexico, Ireland, and Persia—experience great mutations. These mutations are eventually of good effect, and always lead to a beneficial legislation and the establishment of a more solid constitution. After 1981 the conjunction will begin to affect Japan, Russia, America, and Egypt. But, so far as history serves us at this date, we find the countries named to be among those whose affairs of state since 1842 have undergone most remarkable changes, and further developments are likely to take place before the cycle is completed. It will be seen that the Indian Mutiny followed the conjunction in Capricorn, India's ruling sign; that the Russian invasion of Turkey, involving British interests, took place after the conjunction in Virgo; and the Coercion Act, the Parnell agitation, the agrarian outrages, and murder of Lord Frederick Cavendish (the Secretary of State for Ireland), took place immediately upon the conjunction in Taurus. Minor causes, the interplay of cycles according to periodic law, at times retard, and at others accelerate, the course of events; but in the end the major influence asserts itself and brings about those great convulsions in human thought and polity which we have been considering.

There are other features of this periodic law which depend on numerical sequences (*Kab.*, i. 71, 133). Some illustration of these has been given in the *Manual of Occultism*. What are called the fatal periods recur after a certain interval of years, depending on the radix. These are such as make the unit value of 13 and 16. The sequence is derived from the addition to any radical date of its own unit value, as 1870 = 16, which, being added to 1870, gives 1886 = 23, and this is repeating continuously. Thus Napoleon I. was born in 1769, and his numerical sequence would therefore be :

$$1769 = 23 \quad \text{Birth number.}$$
$$23$$
$$\overline{}$$
$$1792 \quad \text{The Revolution.}$$
$$23$$
$$\overline{}$$
$$1815 \quad \text{Waterloo.}$$

Another and more general sequence is this :

$$1769 = 23$$
$$23$$
$$\overline{}$$
$$1792 = 19$$
$$19$$
$$\overline{}$$
$$1811 = 11$$

The year 1811 corresponds with the turn of the tide in Napoleon's fortunes, for in that year Wellington

made his first victory over the French in the
Peninsula, and followed it up at Badajoz. Napoleon
attained his 46th year in 1815, and this brings out:

$$
\begin{array}{r}
1815 \\
46 \\
\hline
1861 = 16
\end{array}
$$

the fatal number, which kabalistically answers to
" The Stricken Tower " (*Kab.*, i. p. 29).

Other illustrations, taking as radix the founding
of a dynasty or some great epoch in the history of
a nation, will be found in my previous works. The
accession of George I. to the throne of Great Britain
and the establishment of the Hanoverian dynasty
in 1714 yields by numerical sequences the years
1727, 1744, 1760, 1774, 1793, and 1813; corresponding with the accession of George II., the Stuart
Rebellion, the accession of George III., the American
Rebellion, the French Revolution, and the Grand
Alliance. The Fall of Napoleon, 1815, gives 1830,
Fall of Charles X., and this latter is derived also
directly from the Fall of Robespierre in 1794.
Shelley's career shows a curious periodicity by
numerical sequence.

$$
\begin{array}{llll}
\text{He was born} & 1792 = 19 \\
& 19 \\
\cline{2-2}
& 1811 & \text{Expelled from Oxford.} \\
& 11 \\
\cline{2-2}
& 1822 & \text{Expelled from the world.}
\end{array}
$$

Here, again, the year 1822 is seen to have the unit value of 13, "The Reaping Skeleton = Death," while the age of thirty years, attained in 1822, gives 1852 =16, "The Stricken Tower." All subjects do not respond to the same kabalism, but all are subjects of some periodicity in the course of events, and frequently it will be found that, instead of the birth date, we have to take this of the first great event, and in my own case I find:

$$1868= \begin{array}{c} 1868 \quad \text{Death of father.} \\ 23 \\ \hline \\ 1891 \quad \text{Death of mother.} \end{array}$$

The House of Brunswick came to the British throne in the person of King William IV., from which we have the events:

$$1830=12 \quad \text{Accession of William IV.}$$
$$12$$

$$1842=15 \quad \text{Scinde War.}$$
$$15$$

$$1857=21 \quad \text{Indian Mutiny.}$$
$$21$$

$$1878=24 \quad \text{Afghan War.}$$
$$24$$

1902=11   Accession of Edward VII.
Boer War ended.

$$11$$

1913=14   Balkan War and (?).

The founding of the German Empire after the war with France in 1871 seems to lead to the same epoch, thus:

1871   German Empire.
  17
_____

1888   Accession of Kaiser Wilhelm III.
  25
_____

1913   (as above.)

Peter I. ascended the throne of Servia in 1903 = 13 = "Death, the Reaper," according to the Tarot. It was not until 1912 that this number recurred in the date, and then the Balkan War broke out. The horoscope is of interest :—

29 June 1844—morning = 28—6—44.

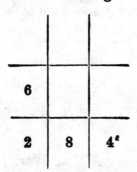

Sum, 24 = 6, Venus.

Conjunctions.

Moon and Venus.
Moon and Saturn.
Saturn and Sun.

It is an unfortunate scheme, and we may therefore expect that Servia will not come out well from the mêlée in the Balkans.

The Kabalists have cycles of 15, 34, 65, 111, 175, 260, and 369 years, which are the cycles of Saturn, Jupiter, Mars, Sun, Venus, Mercury, and the Moon respectively. An example of the constitutional effect of the Sun's period is seen in the case of Ireland:

$$\begin{array}{ll} 1801 & \text{The Union.} \\ 111 & \text{Cycle of Sun.} \\ \hline 1912 & \text{The Separation.} \end{array}$$

The Kabalists further divide the periods and also extend them, in the following manner:

Saturn	3,	9,	15,	45 years.
Jupiter	4,	16,	34,	136 „
Mars	5,	25,	65,	325 „
Sun	6,	36,	111,	666 „
Venus	7,	49,	175,	1225 „
Mercury	8,	64,	260,	2080 „
Moon	9,	81,	369,	3321 „

It will be observed that the sum of the least years of all the planets is 42, our gravity standard applied to the three triangles, or trilogia (ch. vii.). The sums of all the years are multiples of seven, namely, 6 times, 40 times, 147 times, and 1114 times. The periods differ from the astrological periods of the

9

planets according to the Chaldeans, the values of these being :

For the Moon	4	years.
Mercury	10	,,
Venus	8	,,
Sun	19	,,
Mars	15	,,
Jupiter	12	,,
Saturn	30	,,

The Kabalists, however, extract the values of the planets from these periods, giving to Saturn 6, Jupiter 7, Mars 2, Sun 3, Venus 4, Mercury 8, and the Moon 9, as radical numbers, and they are used for the evaluation of names according to the Hebraic system. By kabalistic progression the further key numbers of the planets are derived, viz. Saturn 8, Jupiter 3, Moon 7, Mercury 5, Mars 9, Sun 4, Venus 6, which, as will be seen, are the numbers already and frequently associated with them by Haydon and others, the peculiar feature being that the Sun's negative number 4 and the Moon's positive number 7 are alone employed for those bodies.

The astronomical period of 19 years ascribed by the Chaldeans to the Sun has a close connection with the periodicity of events, because every 19 years the Sun and Moon form their phases on, or close to, the same date ; and as the recession of the Moon's nodes has a period of about 19 years also, it follows that there are two or three successive eclipses of the same kind in the same longitude at intervals of 19 years. Thus, there was an eclipse of the Sun on January 22nd, 1860, in ♒ 2°, another in 1879, January 22nd, in ♒ 2°, another in 1898, January 22nd, in ♒ 2°, the difference being in their respective magnitudes. From time immemorial eclipses have been regarded as significant portents in human affairs, and their symbolical value may readily be conceded, while as physical phenomena eclipses have recently received considerable attention from men of science, it having been conclusively shown that definite physical effects have followed immediately upon the obscuration of the luminary, more particularly in those parts where the eclipse was visible, and especially where it was vertical at the time of central conjunction. It is in the symbolical sense that we regard eclipses, and this because there is a periodicity attaching to their zodiacal position which is not observed in regard to any geographical locality. This period of 19 years has been observed since the days of Meton in the fifth century B.C. as of astrological value, that is, as a means of prognosis. Ptolemy and other of the early astronomers accede this symbolic value. Kepler confirmed it by his own observations, and suggested the regulation of human affairs as being effected by means of the celestial bodies. Be that as it may, the case should be capable of proof. Take, for instance, the large solar eclipse which happened over Europe on April 17th, 1912, in ♈ 27°. It was central in latitude 43° N., and its longitude from ♈0 was 27°. In longitude 27° East, and latitude 43° N., the Balkan War broke out, the significant fact being that ♂ Mars, on the very day, 14th October 1912, was in ♎ 27°, and therefore in exact opposition to the place of the eclipse. The war ran its course, and came to an end. The Allies well knew that the intervention of the Powers was merely a moral one, and that any attempt to police the situation would be very dangerous to the Power that undertook the work; so they fought on, despite the protests of the Powers, and Turkey capitulated. But Roumania, who had taken an active part in the Alliance, was apparently to be shelved when the partition of territory came to be discussed. So it happened that in June 1913, when Mars was in transit over the place of eclipse in ♈ 27°, the war broke out again between the Allies themselves. Roumania speedily reduced Bulgaria and took the foremost position in the theatre of war, thus reversing the entire position and setting Europe at defiance. Here we see that a significant eclipse falling over Europe brings trouble upon that part of the world, and that the opening dates of the two great contests coincide exactly with the position of the martial planet Mars on the line of that eclipse.

As regards individuals, it has been found by long observation that events are repetitive in nature and sequence after 19 years in certain cases, as when the eclipses fall on significant points in the horoscope of a person's birth. Otherwise they are not so. King Edward VII. was born when the 26th degree of Sagittarius was rising. There were solar eclipses in this degree of the opposite sign Gemini in June 1852, 1871, 1890, and 1909. They were

followed by unfortunate periods, and finally by
death, as predicted, in the year 1910, within a year
of the last of the series of eclipses. In other cases
it is found that half the period of Saturn = 15 years,
which alone is the whole period of Mars, has a
sinister significance and recurs from the year in
which Saturn transits a significator in the horoscope.

The study of planetary periods in the symbolical
sense leads to a curious numerical fact which evidently has a significance in regard to the periodic
law. If we place the Chaldean period of the
planets in the order of the apparent velocity of the
planets, thus :

Saturn	Jupiter	Mars	Venus	Mercury	Moon
30	12	5	8	10	4

and divide them into their least common multiple,
120, we shall get :

4	10	8	15	12	30

the same values in reverse order. Now, as 120 is
the whole period of the planetary cycle according
to both the Chaldean and Indian systems of astrology, we may see here a definite relationship of
periods to polarities. For Saturn and the Moon are
opposed to one another in respect of their signs
Capricorn and Cancer ; Jupiter and Mercury in
respect of their signs Sagittarius, Gemini and Pisces,
Virgo ; Mars and Venus in respect of their signs
Aries, Libra and Scorpio, Taurus (*Kab.*, i. p. 81).
Then, if the circle of 120 years responds to the
circle of 360°, it follows that the periods answering

to the aspects 45°, 90°, 135°, 180°, which are regarded
as malefic, being formed upon the cross, namely,
the 15th, 30th, 45th, 60th, 75th, 90th, and 105th
years of life are adversely climacteric. On the
other hand, the years of life which answer to the
aspects 60°, 120°, which are benefic, being formed
on the triangle, namely, the 20th, 40th, 80th, and
100th years are favourable climacterics. But inasmuch as individual births do not coincide with
zero, but persons are born in all periods during the
course of 120 years, the periods will not respond to
individuals at the same ages, but at different ages
according to the period in which they were born.
This idea lies at the root of the 120-year cycle of the
Indian Dasabukthi system.

If we deal with the numbers of the planets in
the same way as with their periods, we get the basis
in the unit series :—

0	1	2	3	4	5	6	7	8	9
✳	☉	☽	♃	☉	☿	♀	☽	♄	♂
	+	−		−			+		

By adding the first and last, $0+9$, we get Mars $=9$,
$1+8=9$, $2+7=9$, $3+6=9$, $4+5=9$; and here we
find Sun and Saturn, Jupiter and Venus in combination, the positive and negative Moon numbers
$2+7=9$, and finally the negative Sun number 4
paired with the number of Mercury, which elsewhere (*Cosmic Symbolism*) has been suggested as
the alternate of the Sun negative. On this point
we shall have something more to say when we come
to the practical application of these values.

CHAPTER IX

COINCIDENCES MAKE LAWS

THE method of finding sunrise, and hence the planetary hours and their sub-divisions, has already been given, and it will be found upon examination that many remarkable effects attach to the rulership of the planets during these periods. But very frequently it will be found that the planet ruling the day, or its zodiacal alternative, will take possession of and rule the whole day. One or two illustrations of this will not be without interest, and may possibly lead to further research along profitable lines.

The planet ♃ Jupiter rules on Thursday and gives its name to the day. Its zodiacal alternative is Mercury, so called because it rules the opposite zodiacal signs to Jupiter. Thus:

♃ rules ♐ and ♓ Number 3
☿ ,, ♊ ,, ♍ ,, 5

15th August 1912, fell on a Thursday. The following events took place at Kempton:

2.0 won by Dutch Courage = 46428 2762135 = 50 = 5.
2.30 ,, ,, Jocasta = 3721341 = 21 = 3.
3.0 ,, ,, Iron Duke = 1275 4625 = 32 = 5.
3.30 ,, ,, Lomond = 374754 = 30 = 3.
4.0 ,, ,, Drawbridge = 4216221435 = 30 = 3.
4.30 ,, ,, Mesmer = 453452 = 23 = 5.

It will be seen that the Hebraic values are used
for the evaluation of the names, and that all the
events are under Jupiter or Mercury, values 3 and 5.

12th August, Monday, at Nottingham.

2.0 won by Artist's Song = 12413433752 = 35 = 8.
2.30 ,, ,, Irish Demon = 121545475 = 34 = 7.
3.0 ,, ,, Katanga = 2141521 = 16 = 7.
3.30 ,, ,, Brancepeth = 2215258553 = 5 = 8.
4.0 ,, ,, Translucence = 421533625525 = 43 = 7.
4.30 ,, ,, Grave Greek = 32165 32552 = 34 = 7.

Here the values are those of the Moon 7 and
Saturn 8, these planets being the ruler of the day
and its zodiacal alternate respectively. The Moon
rules ♋ Cancer, and Saturn rules the opposite sign
♑ Capricorn. It will be observed that the hard
final in " song " is value 2, not 3 as when soft in
such words as courage, drawbridge, etc. Also that
the final *th*, as in Brancepeth, is of value 5, while
sh in Irish is of value 5, *i.e.* s = 6 and h = 8 = 14 = 5,
while the pure S sound is of value 3.

Thus on Tuesday, 13th August 1912, the day
being ruled by Mars = 9 and its alternate Venus = 6,
events were won by Lady Frederick II. = 3141

8254521222 = 42 = 6, Venus; Thimble Colt = 514235
2734 = 36 = 9, Mars; and Dennery = 4555521 = 27 = 9,
Mars.

Peculiar sequences of weights may also be noticed
in connection with a series of events. Thus, in the
first instance, 15th August, we get the following
values :

2.0	winning weight		9·1	=1
2.30	,,	,,	8·9	=8
3.0	,,	,,	7·2	=9
3.30	,,	,,	9·8	=8
4.0	,,	,,	8·9	=8
4.30	,,	,,	7·10	=8

Here the values are those of the Sun and Saturn,
with a single interloping of Mars in the third event.
The 12th August, as given above, shows the following curious coincidence :

2.0	won by weight		8·11	=1
2.30	,,	,,	8·2	=1
3.0	,,	,,	7·12	=1
3.30	,,	,,	8·9	=8
4.0	,,	,,	8·7	=6
4.30	,,	,,	7·8	=6

Four of the events were won by the numbers
1 and 8, Sun and Saturn. On the following day
there was an alternation of Sun and Moon numbers :

2.0	won by weight		8·11	=1	Sun
2.30	,,	,,	9·7	=7	Moon
3.0	,,	,,	8·5	=4	Sun
3.30	,,	,,	8·12	=2	Moon

On the 12th, at Folkestone, the values were :
8·11 = 1, 8·11 = 1, 7·9 = 7, 8·11 = 1, 7·11 = 9, 8·5 = 4 ;
four Sun numbers out of five events. Possibly
some patient research along these lines would
reveal an underlying law. I do not propose to
suggest one here, but merely bring the cases forward
as curious and interesting. As it may be anticipated that some of my readers will take a hint from
this, I may here give a tabular view of the weights
ruled by each of the planets according to their
numerical procession.

TABLE OF WEIGHTS

Planet.	Weights controlled by Planets.
Saturn . .	8·13, 8·4, 7·9, 7·0, 6·5, 5·10.
Jupiter . .	8·8, 7·13, 7·4, 6·9, 6·0.
Mars . .	9·0, 8·5, 7·10, 7·1, 6·6, 5·11.
Sun . . .	8·6, 7·11, 7·2, 6·7, 5·12.
Venus . .	8·11, 8·2, 7·7, 6·12, 6·3.
Mercury . .	8·10, 8·1, 7·6, 6·11, 6·2.
Moon . .	8·12, 8·3, 7·8, 6·13, 6·4, 5·9.
Sun . . .	8·9, 8·0, 7·5, 6·10, 6·1.
Moon . .	8·7, 7·12, 7·3, 6·8, 5·13.

By means of this Table the weights controlled
by the dominant planet can be seen, and the competitors carrying those weights are those which

alone have the winning chances, selection being made by triangulation of the values involved. Thus : Lincoln Handicap, 1912. Dominant planet Saturn = weights 8·13 Mercutio, 8·4 Long Set, 7·9 Moscato, 7·0 Cinderello, 6·5 Ben Alder, 5·10 Warfare —weights involved 9·6–6·1. The triangulation brings out the weights 8·4 and 7·3, and Long Set, the nearest to 8·4, won, while Uncle Pat, 7·3, was second, Warfare being third. Our planetary weight would therefore have taken us directly to Long Set when triangulated.

At 3.10 on Thursday, 28th March, at Liverpool, the Spring Cup was won by Subterranean. The dominant planet was again Saturn, and among his weights we have already found 7·0, which was the weight carried by the winner of this event. The frequency with which this gravity of the planets, as determined by their respective numbers, is carried out by events is really surprising, and deserves attention. It illustrates more forcibly and conclusively than anything else could do the existence of a law of numerical ratios, a geometry which encompasses both gravity and planetary velocities. It informs us once more that the force of gravitation is inversely as the velocity of the body attracted. Thus, we see that a body moving at a tangent to the line of attraction can only overcome gravity by its velocity. If it had no motion it would be immediately impelled along the line of attraction directly to the centre ; but, in proportion as it has velocity, it is able to overcome attraction. We overcome the gravity of the earth by motion. When the propelling force of a body in flight is stayed, the body slows down, expends its velocity, and eventually falls to earth. The velocities of the planets being in proportion to their distances, they come under a law of numerical ratios. Consequently, any study of their connection with events must be founded upon their primary cosmic relations. It is by the observation of the coincidence of an event with its theoretical cause that we are able eventually to formulate a law. We may do this either by a number of direct observations all pointing to the same cause, or we may adopt the method of exhaustion, and by a process of exclusion bring ourselves at last to recognise the operative factor. Thus, if a given event can be examined in regard to the position or cosmic order of each of the planets in succession, we shall eventually arrive at the conclusion that such event can only be attributable to a particular planet, and a number of observations can then be made to establish this conclusion.

By taking the direction and force of the wind at any seaboard, and working in connection with the tidal constants, we may, after a series of observations, predict the time and height of the tide with great accuracy. The constant factor here is M–S, or the Moon's distance from the Sun. Wind pressure is a variable factor which has to be taken into account. Similarly, we may say that at a certain point of time the same factors may apply to the weights carried by competitors or to the gravity-value of certain numbers, or colours, because these latter have a gravity-value on account of their being definite vibrations, and vibration is always in terms of velocity. Suppose, now, that we say M–S=D, then it will be found the weight will depend on S+D, or S−D, where S is the horary equivalent. This is so uniformly the case that it puts the question of chance entirely out of the field. Consequently, when estimating the chances of a given event falling to a definite selection, we only employ the doctrine of probabilities in default of any certain knowledge of a Law of Values; but in knowledge of this law we wisely drop the word " chance " out of our vocabulary. It is found that every competition, no matter how many competitors may engage, can be reduced so as to divide the winning chance between two, and this will yield the winner in 80 out of every 100 events. This surely puts the case beyond doubt.

It has been suggested that the same principles might be applied to lottery numbers, and some investigations into this matter have yielded curious results. For the purpose of illustrating a successful method of dealing with lotteries, I shall have recourse to a further exposition of the " Secret Progression " (*Kab.*, i. p. 67 *et seq.*).

Having obtained the five numbers of the last drawing of the lottery, they must be set down in a line, and reduced by consecutive subtraction (adding 90 when necessary, as there are 90 numbers in the drawing), and thus a second line of numbers will be obtained, which, being similarly dealt with, will yield a third line of numbers, and these again will yield a fourth line, each line being reduced by one number, and in the result we obtain one final number.

Example.—The five numbers drawn for prizes at the Rome lottery on 6th January 1894 were 63, 48, 60, 27, and 81. These we deal with for the first reduction to obtain the Mother Number, thus :

$$
\begin{array}{cccc}
63 \\
48 & 75 & 27 \\
60 & 12 & 45 & 18 \\
27 & 57 & 87 & 42 & 24 \\
81 & 54
\end{array}
$$

The Mother Number is therefore 24. This composed of 2 tens and 4 units. We deal with the tens first of all.

Place the tens on a line to the left, with the digits following in usual sequence, until three lines are formed. Thus :

2	3	4
5	6	7
8	9	1

Here 2 is the figure representing the tens in 24, and therefore it holds the first place, and is followed by 3 4 5 6 7 8 9, when it is seen that one space remains in the square for 1, which is the completion of the series.

Now deal with the units, placing the units of Mother Number in the first square:

24	3 –	4 –
5 –	6 –	7 –
8 –	9 –	1 –

The second units are obtained by adding 5 to the units of the Mother Number, curtailed by 9, if necessary. Thus, the units of the Mother Number are 4, to which add 5, and obtain 9, which are accordingly the units of the second tens, making 39. To 9 add $5 = 14 - 9 = 5$, and we have the units of the third tens. So continue until the full series is completed, when the square will appear thus:

24	39	45
51	66	72
87	93	18

The next step is to couple the numbers, adding them together and deducting 90 wherever they amount to more than that number. The result exhibits six numbers, thus:

$$24 + 39 = 63 \qquad 84 = 39 + 45$$

$$51 + 66 = 27 \qquad 48 = 66 + 72$$

$$87 + 93 = 90 \qquad 21 = 93 + 18$$

Finally, these are coupled again, and we have three numbers, thus :

$$63 + 84 = 147 - 90 = 57$$
$$27 + 48 = 75 \qquad\quad 75$$
$$90 + 21 = 21 \qquad\quad 21$$

The three numbers, or " Daughters " of the Mother Number, are therefore

$$57, \quad 75, \quad 21,$$

and these are to be followed on five consecutive occasions, that is to say, at the five drawings following upon that of the 6th January 1894, from which we took our numbers for the extraction of the " Mother."

The following were the drawings referred to :

13th January   44— 1—63— 5—25   Lost.
20th   ,,   37— 9—39—**21**—1   Won 4th.
27th   ,,   80—**57**—15—14—69   Won 2nd.
3rd February 80—83— 4—19—78   Lost.
10th   ,,   **57**—76—59—81—74   Won 1st.

Hence the stake of $15 = 5$ times 3 will yield $42 - 15 = 27$ gain.

The Italians have many methods of dealing with these chances, the most usual being the Pyramid. For this they take the numbers extracted at the last drawing. The drawings take place weekly, and there are always five winning numbers. These they set down and reduce to unit value :

$$44\text{-}1\text{-}63\text{-}5\text{-}25$$

$$\begin{array}{ccccc} 8\text{-}1\text{-} & 9\text{-}5\text{-} & 7 \\ 8\text{-}1\text{-} & 9\text{-}5\text{-} & 7 \\ 7\text{-}2\text{-} & 9\text{-}1\text{-} & 5 \end{array}$$

$$5\text{-}4\text{-} \quad 9\text{-}2\text{-} \quad 1$$

The unit values being doubled and added together, throwing out the nines as formed, the figures 7, 2, 9, 1, 5 result; and these are added again to the two rows above, throwing out the nines, so that the figures 5, 4, 9, 2, 1 are obtained. These are written from left to right and repeated from right to left, using the last figure 1 as the turning point :

$$5\ 4\ 9\ 2\ 1\ 2\ 9\ 4\ 5,$$

which gives us the base of the Pyramid. The Pyramid is built up by pairing the numbers and throwing out the nines, thus :

$$\begin{array}{ccccccccc} 5 & 4 & 9 & 2 & 1 & 2 & 9 & 4 & 5 \\ & 9 & 4 & 2 & 3 & 3 & 2 & 4 & 9 \\ & & 4 & 6 & 5 & 6 & 5 & 6 & 4 \\ & & & 1 & 2 & 2 & 2 & 2 & 1 \end{array}$$

until the fourth row is reached, when selection is made by taking the two numbers to the left and the

10

two to the right, which here are 12 and 21, which are accordingly selected as the numbers to be followed in the next drawing.

The numbers 44—1—63—5—25 were drawn at Rome on 13th January 1894, and these, as shown, yield 12 or 21. Accordingly, the winning numbers on the 20th January were 37—9—39—21—1. As these include one of the numbers selected, the result is satisfactory. As the curious reader may wish to test the value of the method for himself, I here give the actual figures drawn for January 1894:

6th January	63—48—60—27—81	
13th ,,	44— 1—63— 5—25	
20th ,,	37— 9—39—21— 1	
27th ,,	80—57—15—14—69	

I may now give a further key to the resolution of numerical chances which will serve for lotteries.

The five numbers extracted for the first drawing each month are taken as the basis of the calculation, and serve for the remaining three weeks of the same month.

1. Reduce the numbers to their unit values. To the first add 3, to the second add 1, to the third add 4, to the fourth add 1, and to the fifth add 5. Now, compose the numbers to the total, and also their unit values. Reserve the last number, *i.e.* the total of the unit values.

2. Proceed again in the same way to add 1 to the first extraction of the month, 4 to the second, 1 to the third, 5 to the fourth, and 3 to the fifth.

3. To the same numbers add successively 4, 1, 5, 3, 1.

4. Add 1, 5, 3, 1, 4 to the same numbers.

5. Add 5, 3, 1, 4, 1 to the same numbers.

You will now have 5 totals of whole numbers and 5 totals of unit values. It will be seen that the unit value totals afford two numbers. Add these together to obtain the third.

These three numbers must be followed for the remaining three drawings of the same month.

Example.—6th January 1894, Rome. Numbers drawn—63, 48, 60, 27, 81.

1. Reduce to unit values:

	63 = 9	48 = 3	60 = 6	27 = 9	81 = 9
Add	3	1	4	1	5
Total	12	4	10	10	14 = 50
Unit	3	4	1	1	5 = 14

2.	9	3	6	9	9
	1	4	1	5	3
	10	7	7	14	12 = 50
	1	7	7	5	3 = 23

3.	9	3	6	9	9
	4	1	5	3	1
	13	4	11	12	10 = 50
	4	4	2	3	1 14

4.	9	3	6	9	9
	1	5	3	1	4

	10	8	9	10	13 = 50
	1	8	9	1	4 = 23

5.	9	3	6	9	9
	5	3	1	4	1

	14	6	7	13	10 = 50
	5	6	7	4	1 = 23

Our unit totals are 14, 23, which, being added, yield 37. These three numbers are to be followed for the drawings of 13th, 20th, and 27th January 1894. Results :

13th January   44- 1-63- 5-25
20th   ,,   37- 9-39-21- 1
27th   ,,   80-57-15-14-69

Observe also :

14 = 5
23 = 5

37 = 10 = 1 came out twice.

If to the sum of the unit values of the numbers drawn you add 14, the result will always be the sum of the unit values of the resolution. As—

$$9—3—6—9—9 = 36$$
$$\text{Add}\quad 14$$
—
$$50 = 5$$
$$\text{Chance number}\quad 14 = 5$$
$$\text{,,}\qquad\text{,,}\qquad 23 = 5$$

The numbers drawn for the 3rd February 1894 were 80, 83, 4, 19, 78.

Reduced to unit values :

$$8—2—4—1—6 = 21$$
$$\text{Add}\quad 14$$
—
$$35$$

This number 35, when resolved by its five circular parts, 31415, yields the Chance Numbers 17 and 26, which, being added together, give 43. Hence the numbers 17, 26, and 43 are to be followed for the next three drawings.   Result :

10th February	57-76-59-81-74
17th ,,	68-17-42-57-31
24th ,,	43-79- 8-13-25

Here, again, the lowest and the highest of the Chance Numbers came out according to the rule.

When the total of the unit values is also the sum of the numbers plus 14, the numbers must be reversed, and the number 14 will be a winning one. Thus, on 3rd March 1894, 30, 19, 37, 35, 73 being drawn, the unit values are:

$$3—1—1—8—1 = 14$$
$$\text{Add} \quad 14$$
$$\overline{}$$
$$28$$

But   3—1—1—8—1
Plus   3—1—4—1—5
_____

$$6—2—5—9—6 = 28$$

which is the unit value total.

But   3—1—1—8—1
Plus   1—4—1—5—3
_____

$$4—5—2—13—4 = 28$$
and $4—5—2—4—4 = 19$
$$\overline{}$$
$$47$$

Therefore 47 becomes 74, and 14 will be our other number, being a multiple of 28.

Result of the subsequent drawings :

10th March	22-**74**-44-43-81
17th ,,	36-68-**14**-25-57
24th ,,	72-**14**-36- 2-40
31st ,,	62- 6-**14**-78-26

Here our numbers come out no less than four times in as many drawings.

This kabala is not invariable, but has a basis in fact which renders it extremely valuable. The following is the paradigm.

The digits 0 1 2 3 4 5 6 7 8 9 = 45, and 4+5 = 9. Therefore 9 is the basis of the unit value of all numbers and the key to the mensuration of all chances. The value 3·1415 = 14, and is the expression of the relation of the circumference of a circle to the diameter of the same. A nearer expression is 3·14159 (*Kab.*, i. p. 13).

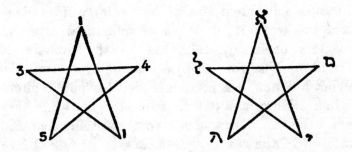

Pico della Mirandola wrote on the subject and gave a table of sympathetic numbers showing what numbers answered to those drawn, and hence were likely to be drawn in sequence. These I have tested very severely, and I condemn them utterly. It is hardly likely that a man who was known as " the scourge of astrology " should be capable of divining upon so subtle a matter.

A more reasonable method is that of the progress suggested by Benincasa. It consists in pairing numbers which have a major probability of turning up in a sequence. Thus :

81 and 72, 53 and 16, 25 and 50, 87 and 84,
59 and 28, 22 and 44, 84 and 78, 56 and 22, etc.

Applied to the year 1894, I find a stake of 1 wins 13, a stake of 45 wins 81, another stake of 45 wins

81, in the course of 19 drawings; which shows a net gain of 84, or at the rate of about 4½ for each drawing. This, however, is mere "betting to figures," and any such progressive system will yield commensurate results. My object is not to formulate a system, but to show affinity of numbers and the working of a law of numerical ratios in matters ordinarily relegated to the domain of Chance. This can always and most certainly be done, but not in a book intended for public circulation. Here it is only possible to give hints that are valuable in proportion to the intelligence and interest of the reader. One such is contained in a very astute statement by one of the old writers, who uses the pentagon in much the same way as I have used the pentacle. His key numbers are 7, 29, and 34. He arranges the five numbers last drawn at the five points of the pentagon, and successively adds together A B C, B A D, C A D, D C B, and multiplying the sum by E, and also dividing, he gets three numbers which may be used either singly or in a combination for the next drawing.

A similar idea is contained in the cross of numbers said to be appropriate to each month of the year. Thus, for January they have :

1

3 4 2

4

To these are attached certain cryptic verses, and concerning the above it says, in the last line of the

quatrain : " Dieci volte il destro ed una al lato "
—" Ten times the right and one to the side."
The right-hand number being 2, the value is
$10 \times 2 + 1 = 21$.

In addition to this, we have the numbers 14, 44,
41, 34, and a reasonable degree of success marks
the proceeding when compared with the records.
Thus, in January 1894, we have drawn 44, 21, 14 ;
in January 1895, 44 ; in January 1896, 44 ; in
January 1897, 34 and 41. But it would be quite
impossible to follow all the combinations of the
Cross of Numbers through the four drawings in
each month with hope of ultimate advantage.
The only possible means outside of the Secret
Progression, which is a kabalistic expression of the
cyclic law in numerical sequences, by which one
may determine the forthcoming numbers in a lottery,
is by reference to their gravities, as indicated by
the horary equivalents of the disposing factors at
the time of the drawing, and this method is not to
be understood by those who have had no preparation in astronomical studies. Sufficient, however,
has been said in this place to indicate the existence
of a numerical sequence by which we may argue
from coincidence to law.

CHAPTER X

SOME NEW VALUES

THE general experience of uncertainty which pervades the question of planetary periods and the mode of their reckoning, together with the yet more doubtful problem of phonetic values, has induced me to give the matter some attention. It will be convenient if in this place I indicate, for the benefit of those who have not ploughed through my *Cosmic Symbolism*, what are the points at issue.

It was the ancient astrological practice in India to count time from sunrise, and it persists to this day. Obviously, in the state of astronomical science among the populace of India, nothing but approximations could be expected. But the jyoshis and others skilled in the mathematics of the subject were, and are, capable of giving the time of apparent sunrise with great accuracy. That is to say, they could determine the apparent longitude of the Sun at any time by means of their astronomical tables, and could calculate the time at which this longitude would be on the celestial horizon of any locality. They then divided the day into 60

hours of 24 mins. each, counting from sunrise as
we count from noon. Approximately, there would
be 5 ghatikas, or 120 mins., for the rising of each
complete sign of the zodiac, or 4 mins. for each
degree, and hence a person born so many *ghatikas*
and *vighatikas* (hours and mins.) after sunrise could
be informed from the position of the Sun in the
zodiac at the time of its rising under what degree of
the zodiac he was born. But the chronometry of
the ancient astrologers was very faulty, and the
sun-dial was perhaps the most accurate means of
measuring time known to them. They had no mean
or true clock-time. But nevertheless they divided
the signs into 30 parts called *trims'âmshas*, and
allowed 4 mins. for each of these parts. They
gave the same names to the days of the week as
do we, and they recognised the same zodiacal order
of the signs and the same planetary rulerships
in those signs. European astrologers later gave
attention to the subdivision of the day, and introduced what are called " planetary hours." The
planetary hour is one-twelfth of the time between
sunrise and sunset. Now, in equatorial parts,
this would be almost uniformly 12 hours, but in
northern latitudes the length of the day would
vary according to the season of the year.

Hence the doubt has arisen as to whether the
hour should be a secular one of 60 mins. or a planetary one of one-twelfth the diurnal arc of the Sun.
My own view is that, counted from sunrise, the
hours should measure of equal length from sunrise
to sunset, six of such hours being included between

sunrise and noon, and six between noon and sunset. The mistake some astrologers have made is that they have counted the hours from midnight, making a blend of secular and astronomical measures, thereby overlapping noon by some minutes instead of completing an hour exactly at the four cardinal points of the local circle of observation.

Further, the vexed question of phonetic values in the matter of coding has given rise to serious misgiving in the minds of those who have followed the rules given in some misleading works by amateur exponents. I have only one view on this point, and it is that every letter which contributes to the sounding of a word or name, and especially if such be in a stress syllable, must be counted. In such a name as Calliope the i is not only long, but forms the stress syllabus, and to omit it would be sufficient reason for omitting anything. I always use it (*Kab.*, i. p. 30), and its value is 1.

Some other values not included in my Table of Phonetic Values (*Kab.*, i. p. 30) will be found in my *Cosmic Symbolism*.

The object, therefore, should be to find a method which, while satisfying the law of values, leaves no doubt as to the planetary period involved. Such a method I have discovered. It is based on the old view that the day begins at noon and not sunrise. That the first hour after noon is ruled by the planet giving its name to the day, and is followed by the others in Chaldean order (according to apparent velocities), and every hour is of equal length, viz. sixty minutes. Then it will be necessary to take note of the day planet, the hour planet, and the period planet.

The day includes 24 hours of 60 minutes. The hour includes 15 periods of 4 minutes. The first hour after noon is ruled by the day planet. All periods count from the day planet. Here, then, is the

Table of Periods

Noon to 7 p.m.

Planet.	Day.	Periods.						
☉	Sunday .	12 ☉	1 ♀	2 ☿	3 ☽	4 ♄	5 ♃	6 ♂
☽	Monday .	☽	♄	♃	♂	☉	♀	☿
♂	Tuesday .	♂	☉	♀	☿	☽	♄	♃
☿	Wednesday	☿	☽	♄	♃	♂	☉	♀
♃	Thursday .	♃	♂	☉	♀	☿	☽	♄
♀	Friday .	♀	☿	☽	♄	♃	♂	☉
♄	Saturday .	♄	♃	♂	☉	♀	☿	☽
Signs of Zodiac .		♑ ♒	♐ ♓	♏ ♈	♌	♎ ♉	♍ ♊	♋

This will be sufficient for purposes of a demonstration. It will be seen that the planets read from left to right in the Chaldean order, as on Saturday: Saturn, Jupiter, Mars, Sun, Venus, Mercury, Moon—these being according to the apparent velocities of the several bodies as seen from the earth. The slowest is given the first place.

Suppose I want the period ruling on Friday at 3 p.m. Under the figure 3 and in a line with

Friday I find Saturn. Therefore Saturn begins to rule at 3 o'clock, and will continue for 1 hour. The first 4 minutes, from 3.0 to 3.4, will be ruled by ♀. Hence it is a Venus period in the hour of Saturn. To enumerate this we take

$$
\begin{array}{llr}
\text{Day planet} & ♀ = 6 \\
\text{Hour} \quad \text{,,} & ♄ = 8 \\
\text{Period} \quad \text{,,} & ♀ = 6 \\
\hline
& 20 = 2
\end{array}
$$

Therefore among a number of contestants the Moon should win, but if not present by name-value the sign the Moon is in must be taken. Thus, suppose the ☽ not represented by a 2 or 7 among the competitors; then by looking in the Ephemeris we find the ☽ on that day in the sign ♈, and our Table shows that sign at the foot of the planetary periods immediately under ♂, and so Mars is the planet which disposes of the Moon or in whose "House" the Moon is that day. Hence, in default of 2 or 7, we look for 9. Some examples will serve for the purpose of clearing up any doubts in the matter and making the whole plan clear to the reader.

Plumpton, 5th January 1912. Day, Friday = 6.

Hour, 1.15—Mercury 5—Per. ♄ = 8.
   658 = 19 = 10 = 1, negative 8.
   Phyllis, 836 = 17 = 8 won.

1.45—Mercury 5—Per. Jupiter 3.

    $653 = 14 = 5.$

    Volauvent, $66366252 = 36 = 9$ **won.**

2.15—Moon 2—Per. Saturn 8.

    $628 = 16 = 7.$

    Bridge, $223 = 7$ **won.**

2.45—Moon 2—Per. Jupiter 3.

    $623 = 11 = 2.$

    Mint Tower, $454\ 462 = 25 = 7$ **won.**

3.15—Saturn 8—Per. Saturn 8.

    $688 = 22 = 4.$

    Place Taker, $8316\ 41212 = 28 = 1$ **won.**

3.40—Saturn 8—Per. Saturn 8.

    $688 = 22 = 4.$

    Wavelass, $616316 = 23 = 5$ **won.**

Here it will be seen that five out of six events are straightforwardly accounted for by phonetic values of the competitors, taking the periods of the planets in the order stated above. It will be noticed that *Volauvent*, a French name, is phonetically vŏlōvŏng $= 66366252 = 36 = 9.$

The alternates here used are :

Saturn   8—1   Sun.
Venus   6—3   Jupiter.
Mercury   5—9   Mars.

The Moon is taken as of value 2 in this case, being negative to Saturn and Jupiter. In the periods of Venus, however, it is positive. As to Wavelass, the winner of the last event, it was well

indicated by symbolism of the Moon, ruler of the
ascending sign Cancer, being exactly on the cusp
of the second House (finance) and in good aspect
to Uranus, Mars, and Venus, and conjoined with
Neptune. Here Cancer and Neptune rule the
ocean wave, and the Moon is that lass that loves—
or loveth not—a sailor, according to its fickle whim.

Take another place on the same day:

5th January 1912, Haydock Park.   Friday = 6.

1.0 —Mercury 5—Per. Venus 6.
       656 = 17 = 8.
       Claydon, 231425 = 17 = 8 won.
1.30—Mercury 5—Per. Venus 6.
       656 = 17 = 8.
       Lady Scholar, 3141 62232 = 24 = 6 won.
2.0 —Moon 7—Per. Venus 6.
       676 = 19 = 1.
       Climax, 231412 = 13 = 4 won.
2.30—Moon 7—Per. Venus 6.
       676 = 19 = 1.
       Calliope, 2131681 = 22 = 4 won.
3.0—Saturn 8—Per. ♀ 6.
       686 = 20 = 2.
       Jacobus, 312626 = 20 = 2 won.
3.30—Saturn 8—Per ♀ 6.
       686 = 20 = 2.
       Great Peter, 2214 81412 = 25 = 7 won.

Here, again, we have five out of six events clearly
in harmony with the law of phonetic values and the

periodicity of the planets. I cannot say if in the 1.30 event there was no 8 or 1 present, but I observe that, in any case, Saturn 8 was on that day in the sign of Venus 6, and that 6 won. This would only be allowable in default of 8, when of course it would be quite regular and what we should expect by the rule.

The next day at Plumpton affords further indications of the general reliability of this very simple method.

6th January 1912. Saturday = 8.

1.15—Jupiter 3—Per. Sun 1.
       831 = 12 = 3.
       Beauty Bird, 2641224 = 21 = 3 won.
1.45—Jupiter 3—Per. Venus 6.
       836 = 17 = 8.
       Penitent, 8154154 = 28 = 1 won.
2.15—Mars 9—Per. Sun 1.
       891 = 18 = 9.
       Saucepan, 62685 = 27 = 9 won.
2.45—Mars 9—Per. Venus 6.
       896 = 23 = 5.
       Early Closing, 1231 236752 = 32 = 5 won.
3.15—Sun 1—Per. Sun 1.
       811 = 10 = 1.
       Campamento, 2148141546 = 36 = 9 won.
3.40—Sun 1—Per. Sun 1.
       811 = 10 = 1.
       Snap, 6518 = 20 = 2 won.

All but the last two events are in line with the

11

principles laid down in this new theorem. It will be seen that we have held rigidly to the positive values of the planets except in the case of the Moon when operating in combination with a masculine or positive planet, such as Saturn, Jupiter, and Mars. Also it will be seen that the values of the sounds are those given in Part I. of the *Kabala of Numbers*. The whole name is used in every case. Only the schedule or set time of the event is employed, no allowance being made for a speculative " off " time. Finally, we employ all the factors, namely, the day, hour, and period planets, and the combination of the positive values of these three factors gives us 14 out of 18 events in harmony with the rules.

I will take only one more example and complete the illustration with events at Haydock Park on the same day, namely :

6th January 1912.   Saturday = 8.

1.0—Jupiter 3—Per. Saturn 8.

838 = 19 = 1.

Barnet Fair, 212514 812 = 26 = 8 won.

1.30—Jupiter 3—Per. Saturn 8.

838 = 19 = 1.

Shaun Aboo, 325 126 = 19 = 1 won.

2.0—Mars 9—Per. Saturn 8.

898 = 25 = 7.

Blunderbuss, 2325412226 = 29 = 2 won.

2.30—Mars 9—Per. Saturn 8.

898 = 25 = 7.

Borough Marsh, 2264123 = 20 = 2 won.

3.0—Sun 1—Per. Saturn 8.
      818 = 17 = 8.
      Bembridge, 214223 = 14 = 5 **won.**
3.30—Sun 1—Per. Saturn 8.
      818 = 17 = 8.
      Ilston, 13645 = 19 = 1 **won.**

Here, again, are five out of six events in accord with our simplex system. I do not think it is necessary to labour the point further. Had there been any doubt as to the values attaching to the various sounds, or if the rules for determining the planetary period in force were at all vague, then some might claim an adventitious display of proofs. But all our values are contained in previous works, *Kabala I.*, *Cosmic Symbolism,* etc., and the only new element is the introduction of the most ancient method of time divisions. One may reasonably be in doubt as to what constitutes local sunrise, but nobody can have two minds about clock time at Greenwich. The question may be asked, what allowance is to be made for E. and W. longitude ? The answer is, none at all so long as the events are timed by Greenwich. Probably the reason for this will be found in the fact that cosmic influences are distributed through centres, as, for example, in the case of planetary influence in national affairs being paramount in the horoscopes of kings. The world is governed and also timed from centres which are focal depositories of latent cosmic forces. But we cannot argue beyond facts, and these clearly show that Greenwich time serves for all events that are timed by the clock in the limits of this country.

Here, then, are nineteen out of twenty-four events in direct succession, bearing out the values ascribed to the planets, the phonetic values of names, and the alternate values of the various periods. This high record of 79 per cent. is altogether beyond the limit of a fortuitous coincidence, and hence we must conclude that our evaluations are valid, and that our rediscovery of the ancient system of time-division is upheld by the facts.

I have purposely chosen events of popular interest because they are on record and can be checked in every detail. It would have been possible to extend this survey indefinitely, and I have some months of consecutive records on hand. I am not, however, writing a book on Turf Uncertainties, but merely stating a theorem, viz. that the day begins at noon, and I am here giving a kabalistic proof that it is so.

Obviously, any system that employs name-values is comparatively useless, for the reason that there will most frequently be one or more competitors whose name-values are of equal unit significance, *i.e.* of the same or alternate values, as Velca, Remiss, Sfax, Lady Senseless, all in the same event won by Sfax. In short, a method of exclusion has no practical value, and only a scientific method of selection is at all worthy of consideration. It can be shown that a definite method of selection based on the gravity-values of the three factors, and supported by the laws of Tycho and Ptolemy in

regard to cosmic interaction, is a scientific fact
that has been under rigid test for years past, and
the average percentage of such tests is not less
than 75 continuously.

It may be of use for the testing of this method of
Planetary Periods if I here give a Table of the values
for every half-hour during the week from noon to
six o'clock.

Time.	12.0	12.30	1.0	1.30	2.0	2.30	3.0	3.30	4.0	4.30	5.0	5.30
Sunday .	2	2	7	7	6	6	8	8	9	9	4	4
Monday .	5	5	6	6	1	1	7	7	8	8	4	4
Tuesday .	9	9	1	1	6	6	5	5	7	7	8	8
Wednesday .	1	1	3	3	4	4	8	8	5	5	6	6
Thursday .	6	6	3	3	4	4	9	9	8	8	1	1
Friday .	3	3	2	2	4	4	5	5	9	9	6	6
Saturday .	7	7	2	2	8	8	9	9	5	5	4	4

These values are for the day and hour planets
combined, and the times indicate the beginning of
their influence. To these values must be added
the number of the period planet.

Rule.—Divide the minutes after the complete
hour by 4. The product will give the period planet
counted from the day ruler.

Example.—On Tuesday, what rules at 2.35 p.m. ?
$35 \div 4 = 9$. Counted from Mars (Tuesday) we
arrive at Sun $= 1$. Then $2.0 = 6$ and $2.35 = 6 + 1$ or 7.

The idea that man may compass a fortuitous
fortune by the application of numerical systems to
the chance events of life is by no means an extraordinary one. It is by means of a mensuration of

the various subtle forces in Nature that man has been able to avail himself of them in his daily life; and chemistry, among other of the sciences, only began to be properly studied when it was allied to mathematics. So far as the world in general knows anything at all about the action of the luminaries upon mundane affairs, the belief is that the Sun is the source of light and heat, and that it exerts a gravitational pull upon all the planetary bodies, including the Moon and Earth. It is further believed that the Moon is the chief cause of the tides, and that it has some vague traditional associations with lunacy. It is known to reflect light. Not everybody knows that it also reflects heat, or that of the light rays it reflects some are converted into heat rays by the earth's atmosphere. But who gave out that light, heat, and gravitation were the only forces exerted by the luminaries, or that the planets exerted none at all of their own? We cannot accuse the ancients of this exclusiveness. They fully recognised that each of the planets transmitted the vital energy of the cosmic heart in varied forms. They affirmed that the rays of Mars were irritant, that those of Venus were soothing, that Jupiter augmented the vital forces and Saturn diminished them. Thales believed that the universe was made from water, a fluid base. Doubtless he was led to this belief by the fact that water crystallises at an angle of 60°, and that this angle has first importance in the mensuration of a circle. It was observed, too, that planets at an angle of 60° or 120° affected one another in a manner which was not the case at 59° or 61°, at 119° or 121°. It has always been our fault that we have regarded the ancients as necessarily more ignorant than ourselves. As a matter of fact, however, it will be found that as to essential facts they knew as much as ourselves —I think they knew very much more,—and that only in the matter of more accurate observation we have excelled them by the use of modern instruments. Modern science has not even arrived at the conclusion that Saturn has any influence at all upon other bodies of the system, still less on human life. Ignoring the prime postulate of the solidarity of the solar system, the interaction of the planetary bodies plays no part in modern science. The idea that everything exists for use is not adequate excuse for a scientific interest in these remote bodies of the system, and, placed as they are at thousands of millions of miles from the Sun about which they revolve, they are regarded as barren wildernesses upon which no conceivable humanity can exist. And yet if they are held by the force of gravitation, the light, heat, and vital energy of the Sun must also reach them. It is rather a sorry case that men of science know so much about the microscopic germs of disease and nothing at all about a planet that is more than a thousand times larger than the Earth, and whose rays have probably more to do with pathology than all the bacteria that were ever isolated and classified. Of course, all this about planetary influence may be a mere superstition, but that does not prevent us from making a science of it by noting coincidences. The idea that the Moon has something to do with the tides may be a superstition, but it does not hinder us from noting the coincidence of its elongation with the daily recession of the time of high - water. Science is not concerned with causes, but with the tabulation and comparison of facts.   Hence we may evade the philosophical consideration of causes and apply ourselves solely to the task of noting the coincidences between sound, number, and planetary velocities, and thereby establish what we may call the science of phonetic values, of numerology, and of planetary symbolism.   It may well serve as a working hypothesis for a very much wider view of cosmic and human relations than has yet been adopted.

CHAPTER XI

COLOUR VALUES

So far we have been dealing principally with numbers and their significance in human affairs. It has been suggested that Sound and Colour have their numerical relations. So far as Sound is concerned we have, I think, consistently shown that phonetic values are linked up with planetary influence, or at least that there is a correspondence between the unit value of a name and the planet which, in the Chaldean scheme of astronomy, answers to a particular time when that unit value is conspicuous. We may now deal with Colour values.

According to the scheme already propounded, the planets are each related to one of the primary or prismatic colours. In this scheme

Violet	is related to	Jupiter.
Indigo	,, ,,	Saturn.
Blue	,, ,,	Venus.
Green	,, ,,	Earth's satellite.
Yellow	,, ,,	Mercury.
Orange	,, ,,	Sun.
Red	,, ,,	Mars.

In this scheme Venus denotes the Intuitive or Spiritual Intellect and Mercury the Rational or Material Intellect. They are united temporarily

in earth-life, indicated by the Earth (for which the
Moon stands proxy) and the colour Green. The
permanent union of the lower and higher phases
of the mind, through the experience of incarnation,
is an amalgam which, according to the Hermetic
Philosophers, changes copper into pure gold. In
all these philosophical speculations we find that
mercury is the active principle. It stands for
experience, and when this is properly digested in
the " egg philosophical " and united to copper, the
mercury is entirely absorbed and the copper is
changed to gold. The philosophers speak of the
perfect man as Hermaphrodite, that is to say, a
permanent blend of the two natures, Hermes =
Mercury, and Aphrodite = Venus.

Changing our theme we may change our colours,
and find them thus related to numbers : Violet = 3,
Indigo = 8, Blue = 6, Green = 7, Yellow = 5, Orange
= 1, and Red = 9.

Arranging the digits in their numerical order,

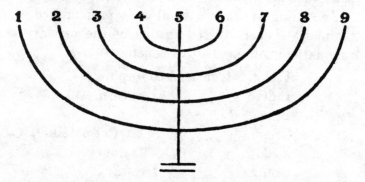

we find that when the opposites are united from
either end we get the unit value of 1; as 1 + 9 = 10

$=1$, $2+8=10=1$, $3+7=10=1$, $4+6=10=1$, and the unpaired number is 5. Now, 1 is the *ens* or vital principle in man, energy in the cosmos; and 5 is the experience principle in man, intelligence in the cosmos. These two principles of life and consciousness answer to the gold and mercury of the alchemists; the desirable thing and the means of its attainment. Mercury 5, therefore, was regarded as the universal solvent. Its symbol is compounded of the Circle, the Crescent, and the Cross, the three great religion symbols of the world. Hermetically, they stand for the Spirit, Soul, and Body, the Sun, Moon, and Earth, and are comprehended only in Mercury, the principle of consciousness. But when, by means of the "Red Dragon," the planet Mars, the number 9, which are symbols of the Will, the *ens* had been incorporated with the quicksilver = Mercury, then we might look for the realisation of our quest in the production of the material gold. Thus:

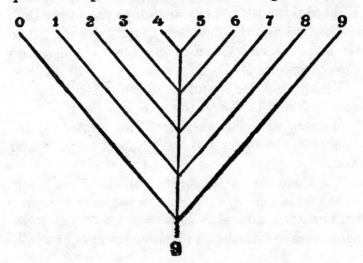

Intelligence therefore arises from experience, and is the only true solvent of our problems. By intelligence, impelled by the power of the will, the *magnum opus*, or great work, can alone be brought to a satisfactory conclusion. When, therefore, we seek to bring our speculations to a satisfactory conclusion, we must make prime use of experience.

Now, we have seen that certain numbers or unit values of sounds answer to planets, and therefore to colours, for Sound, Number, and Colour are bound up together in the universal expression of the Law of Vibrations.

Saturn and the number 8 are thus related to all sibilant sounds, such as S, Sh, and Z. They answer to the colour Indigo.

Jupiter and the number 3 are related to all palatals, as Ch, J, and soft G. They correspond with Violet.

Mars and the number 9 are related to the sounds K, hard G, and R. They answer to the colour Red.

The Sun and the numbers 1 and 4 are related to the sounds A and I, and to the colour Orange; also the consonants M, D, T.

Venus and the number 6 are related to the vowels O and UW, and to the colour Blue.

Mercury and the number 5 are related to the sounds E, the aspirate H, and N, and to the colour Yellow.

The Moon has relation to the numbers 7 and 2, and to the labials B, P, F, V, and to the colour Green.

It may be said that some writers fix the correspondence of letters and planetary numbers entirely by their numerical values : thus Saturn, whose number is 8, is said to govern all letters whose phonetic value is 8, as Ch (guttural), Ph, P ; Jupiter, whose number is 3, would thus govern the letters or sounds G (soft), L, Sh ; and so of the rest. But to this arrangement experience offers some exceptions, especially regarding initials.

Returning now to our colours, we have found that there is a gamut of colour as well as a gamut of sound and number related to the planets. In order to make a test of the colour values it will be necessary to introduce some elements of astrology. A figure of the heavens being set for the time and place of an event in which contestants may be known from their colours, it will be found that three specific points or parts of the heavens will give a clear indication of the dominant or winning colour. In the case of the Wars of the Roses, we had but to decide between the relative strength of the red and the white, *i.e.* Mars or the Moon. But in a mixed field, where the colours represent a financial as well as a sporting interest, the variety may be so great as to require some discrimination. It will be found then that the body colour which is dominant is that chiefly to be regarded. The head or cap is related to the first House, which corresponds with the sign Aries, and is that section of the heavens immediately below the horizon of the East. The body colour, which is the principal one, is determined by the fifth House, the part of the heavens which is from 120° to 150° from the East horizon, and which corresponds to the sign Leo.

These Houses, of themselves, answer to the colours White and Gold; but when occupied by any sign they take the colour of that sign, which is determined by its ruling planet. Thus, if Saturn were in the fifth House at the time, we must look for Indigo or Black to win, or if Capricorn were there it would be the same, because Capricorn is ruled by Saturn. If Mars were just rising, or the sign Aries was on the East horizon, a red cap would fit the winner very well indeed.

So, according to the signs and planets occupying the fifth and first Houses, we judge of the body and cap colours of the winning competitor. But if a single planet be conspicuous in the heavens, either by its exact rising, culmination, or setting at the time, or by its being in elevation in its own sign, then that planet will give its note of colour, to the exclusion of all others. In this connection it should be noted that the Moon, when in a watery sign—Cancer, Scorpio, or Pisces—shows green; but in other signs it shows straw colour, pale yellow, or cream. The colours of the planets are variously :

Neptune—Lavender, lilac, heliotrope.
Uranus—Stripes, grey, black and white.
Saturn—Indigo, dark blue, black, or chocolate.
Jupiter—Violet, purple.
Mars—Red, scarlet, crimson.
Sun—Gold, orange.
Venus—Primrose, turquoise, pale blue.
Mercury—Yellow, sometimes pink.

Some useful examples of the working of this

colour scheme in matters of selection will be found in *The Silver Key*.[1]

Let us now examine the working influence of colour in daily life. Red is perhaps the most striking colour it is possible for a man or woman to wear. It immediately arrests attention, and generally excites comment. The pathological effects of colour must have been noted by the publisher who first blazed into public notice by using red covers for the display of his books. Red is an irritant to all but Martians, and to them green probably means the same thing as does red to us Terranians. The pathology and psychology of colour are things to be noted in daily life. Green has a soothing effect, as all know who have lived long upon the sandy plains of the tropics. It conveys a sense of refreshment and acts as an anodyne. The red hair of the true Martian is always accompanied by the steel-grey eye : " An eye like Mars to threaten and command." Soldiers whose regimentals are red attract general notice—too much so in action,—and "one drunken soldier damns the army" because of this conspicuous colour. The rank and file are getting a better reputation since they went into khaki. We never imagine how much influence colour exerts upon us until we study it in a critical manner. We are affected by scenery without understanding art ; we are moved by melody without a knowledge of music ; and, similarly, we are influenced by colour without any idea of what chromopathy may mean.

[1] Foulsham & Co., London.

The young lover who is scrupulous about the setting of his cravat has a fancy for colour, the science of which altogether escapes him. Neither does he know that the colour of his cravat, the carpet on which he stands, and the wall-paper which forms a background to his figure, have quite as much to do with the success of his campaign as any undiscovered traits of character of which he may imagine himself to be possessed.

Black, which is defined as the absence of colour, arises naturally from the privation of light, either radial or reflected. It is universally associated with evil and death. Its influence is depressing, and the pathology of colour has been so far apprehended by the poets that they uniformly picture despair as black. Disaster has produced a " Black Monday," disease has made " the Black Death " famous throughout Europe, and what are known as " the Black Assizes " are so characterised by reason of the outbreak of jail-fever. What was formerly known as Merrie England has been transformed into Melancholy England since Puritan methods obtained in regard to dress. But, according to *The Tailor* and the *Fashion Book*, we are beginning to wake up and find that life has some joy and colour in it.

Purple and gold belong to royalty, because they are the colours of Jupiter and the Sun, the two greatest bodies of our system and the symbols of opulence and grandeur. The Order of Melkizedec arose from the association of Jupiter (Zadok) with the priestly kings, and they are represented as clothed in purple.

The fire and energy of Mars is well expressed in the properties of the colours red, crimson, and scarlet. It is the planet of Freedom, answering to the number 9. The Red Cap, or *Bonnet Rouge*, of the Revolutionists is the Cap of Liberty, or shall we say, in this case, of licence. In its sinister aspect Mars is the symbol of carnage, fire, and the sword. Its conjunctions with Saturn (symbol of Death) in the various signs of the zodiac have been seen to coincide with bloodshed and carnage either by international or civil war in those countries ruled by such signs (*Kab.*, i. 78–80). In 1792 Mars was stationary in the sign Virgo, ruling Paris, and in that year the Revolutionaries established the Republic. In the cyclic revolution of the universal horoscope the present age comes up under the dominion of the sign Aries, ruled by Mars. Consequently it has been called the Iron Age, because steel and iron belong to Mars by tradition and to the great cosmical artificer Vulcan. After the Iron Age is the Copper Age, then the Age of Amalgams, then the Silver Age, and, lastly, the Golden Age. These are under the dominion of Venus, Mercury, the Moon and Sun respectively.

Blue is akin to green in that it acts as an anodyne. It is a true nervine, and restores the equilibrium of the nerves produced by the effects of light and activity. Consequently it symbolises Peace, Purity, Truth, and Grace. It is the vesture colour of the Madonna in combination with white.

Yellow is a laxative colour and acts as a purgative, like mercurous chloride. It corresponds to the

12

stage between disease and health when Nature is
putting off effete tissue and impurities of all kinds.
It also responds to the state of Purgatory, which is
that between the worlds of Death and Life, of
earth and heaven.   In medical practice it is customary after disease to employ purgatives before
administering tonics.   Mercury, as related to the
colour yellow, is also the cosmic symbol of experience, which is the means used by the Spirit to
purge the mind of errors and delusions.   We do
not therefore need to subscribe entirely to the
verdict of Solomon that this world's experience is
"vanity and vexation of spirit."   Vexation of
spirit it may be ; but it is not in vain, since it forms
a natural and necessary part of the process of
evolution.

Red is a stimulant and tonic, and purple increases
blood - pressure ;   black, brown, and indigo are
depressants.   The mental atmosphere of the pessi-
mist is brown, and even black; that of the philosopher and deep thinker is indigo.   Indigo is
intensified blue, the deep well of truth into which
the speculative soul gazes when contemplating
universal problems.

If any doubt exists as to the actual influence of
colour on the human system, it is only necessary
to take a number of coloured glasses—red, yellow,
and blue,—fill them with pure distilled water, and
expose them for twenty-four hours to the sun's rays.
It will be found in effect that if the contents of the
red glass are taken on an empty stomach they will
act as a tonic, those of the yellow glass as a purga-

tive, and those of the blue glass as a nerve tonic, of particular use in neuritis. By combining the red and yellow, the red and blue, the blue and yellow in equal proportions a variety of effects will be observed. Temperature rapidly decreases under a combination of the yellow and blue waters. Anybody experimenting along these lines will be convinced of the chemic action of light upon water through coloured media. In New York there was established some years ago a hospital for fevers, in one ward of which all the smallpox cases were treated. The window-glass of this ward was of a red colour, and none of the cases showed any "pitting." Prof. Babitt and Dr Albertini have written extensively on the pathological effects of colour, and have adduced numerous instances of cases successfully treated. In acute cases of neuritis and mania the use of "all-blue" surroundings has repeatedly proved to be efficacious. A correspondent informs me that he has repeatedly dreamed of persons dressed in grey, and in every case they have met with accidents immediately afterwards. I have personal experience to the same effect. It is obviously Uranus at work.

These remarks refer to the pathological effects of colour. In material affairs the colours appear to be transmitted through a coarser medium than the astral body, for we repeatedly find that Mercury (yellow) is represented by the Moon, that Mercury takes up pink as if it were tinctured by Mars. On the other hand, green is often represented by the Moon in certain zodiacal positions.

These things being duly observed, it will be possible to institute a chromoscopic science in regard to matters in which colour variations are apparently of significance. Patrons of sport appear not altogether indifferent to the influence of colour, and "owner's colours" have before now been consulted in regard to speculations of this kind with commendable success. One system presents a colour for each House, another for each sign, and a third for each planet. But sometimes, as I have shown, all the colour is in the name, as, for example, Rubio = red, White Knight = white in red sign, Cream of the Sky = yellow in green sign, Grey Barbarian = grey (black and white) in white sign. The colours attaching to the Houses will be found in *Cosmic Symbolism*. Those of the planets are already known, and will be found in *The Manual of Astrology*. The sign colours are Aries, red ; Taurus, pale blue ; Gemini, yellow ; Cancer, green ; Leo, orange ; Virgo, dark green ; Libra, pale yellow; Scorpio, black ; Sagittarius, purple ; Capricorn, white ; Aquarius, blue ; Pisces, grey.

Many of these colours are modified by the amount of light they reflect. Thus Pisces is a shining grey or pearl grey, not a dead ash colour. The green of Cancer is a shining green ; that of Virgo a dead green. I have also found that Scorpio is sometimes related to a deep blood-red, the colour of the carbuncle, as contrasted with the red of Aries, which is bright red like a ruby. Here it would seem that there is a red which is equivalent to black, and that both are related to the sign Scorpio. From some experience in this direction of colour significance, I have not the slightest doubt that a consistent study of winning colours in relation to dominant planetary influence would lead to an orderly science of chromoscopy which could be profitably followed out.

CHAPTER XII

PHRENOSCOPY

IT is not usual for the common-sense man, the spinner and toiler in the workaday world, to reflect upon his relationship to the universe of which he is an integral part. It is exceptional that he should consider anything of greater importance for the moment than the man who elbows him in the street or those with whom he is immediately concerned in business. But merely because he does not reflect upon this relationship of himself to his greater environment, does not alter the fact in itself. He is, nilly willy, an integral part of the great universe around him, and, all unconscious though he may be of the sources from which he is impelled to think and act, they nevertheless continue, without interruption, to influence him in every decision of his life, every project of his conception, every undertaking in which he may engage.

Man thinks himself independent of his environment, and able at all times to act with perfect freedom. This is the conceit and vanity of human nature. It is not a fact. As long as man is dependent on the very air he breathes, the quarter whence the wind may blow, and the light and heat which stream towards this our earth from the central luminary of the world, so long is he physically bound to respond to his environment in terms of his own nature.

But man is not a body only. He is not even essentially a body. Rather is he a mind possessed of a body. And equally by his mind man is related to the greater world around him. By the incident of birth he is already endowed with a definite character, a number of specific tendencies ; and these, being related to an environment already in existence, must constitute for him the sole means of relative expression by which he is known to the world for what he is. Except in the few very rare colourless and inept characters which one may meet in the course of a long experience, it will be found that everyone is possessed of some dominant characteristic which enters into the expression of his nature in every single act of life. He has some dominant passion which controls his actions, shapes his ideals, and determines his attitude towards the world around him. He has some special aptitude which, unsuspected though it may be, finds illustration in every act of daily life. Seeing, then, that everyone has a predisposition, more or less strongly marked according to the inherent force of his nature, towards definite modes of thought and feeling and volition, we may inquire how he comes to be possessed of this individual accent ; and how, being in possession of it, he can render it purposive instead of automatic in expression; consciously directing his powers towards definite and predetermined ends, always following the line of least resistance, which is ever that of greatest progress, instead of blundering through the world half his time trying to find a place that fits him and one that he himself can fill.

The human brain, or that part of it which we employ in the process of thinking, is a congeries of minute cells which collectively constitute a species of galvanic battery, which is capable of generating waves of electrical energy, differing in intensity and in mode of vibration according to the basic constitution of the mind itself, and the efficiency of its instrument—the brain. Brain-cell vibration is at the root of every thought, every act, every effort of the will. The brain, as the root of the whole nervous system, is endowed with the power of affecting and of being affected; and it is a matter of daily experience that very few brains exactly syntonise or show responsiveness to one another. If two persons live together for any length of time they become syntonised automatically, the more powerful of the two bringing the brain of the other down to the frequency and mode of vibration proper to itself. Thus they arrive at a sort of understanding which is a tyranny of the mind on the one side and a slavery on the other. Occasionally, as by nature endowed, we find two persons who are capable of entering into immediate sympathetic relationship, who understand one another instinctively, so to speak, and are in such perfect

" rapport " as to be able to impress one another even at a distance. This is the mystery of telepathy—feeling at a distance—which has recently engaged the minds of those interested in the study of psychological phenomena and mental science. The sympathy exists in the dominant *mode* of vibration, not in its frequency alone, though this is necessarily syntonised where such telepathic communication is possible. It may be produced automatically, as by hypnotism and other means.

The dominant characteristic, the ruling passion, the special aptitude is ever that which controls the greater issues of life and renders the individual effective for good or evil in the world. For although the whole brain is not employed in any single operation of the mind, yet those parts of the brain which are the more active claim an allegiance and a support from all other parts, so that if acquisitiveness or money-making (avarice) be the dominant passion, even love will be subservient to it, and a " marriage of convenience " will follow. This is what phrenology would teach us. But we are not immediately concerned with it or its problems.

How do we come possessed of certain characteristics, certain dominant passions and special aptitudes ?

Some may say it is hereditary influence, atavism. In such case the natives of India, and other countries where the caste system prevails, and where the individual is thereby relegated to a particular sphere of work and to a particular grade of social life, should for that reason be a specialist. Emphatically, he is not. The Brahmin ryot is not an expert agriculturist. He can learn in our colleges what his ancestors have never dreamed of nor taught him. The soldier (kshetrya) is not a specialist. He is better trained by our English officers than ever he was by his forebears, and better equipped for warfare in every direction. Even the ghariwan, or professional coachman, has never attempted the coach and four. Yet his fathers for generations before him were charioteers and ashvakovidhas (skilful horsemen). In such case, too, butchers and housewives would not unite to produce poets, nor would the homely farmer and his wife number among their progeny the reformer, the statesman, and the explorer. In everything except mere physical tendency the supposed law of heredity breaks down at every point, and is all but abandoned by scientific men. The evolution of the genius is not deducible from the laws of hereditary transmission as hitherto explained and understood.

The reason of individual variants, according to the science of Phrenoscopy, is this : Every person is endowed with a brain of a definite constitution ; but that which determines its development, and the mode of activity in its cells, is nothing else than the electrostatic condition of the earth's atmosphere which obtains at the moment of birth. In other words, the moment a child is born and assumes independent existence, his first breath puts him into sympathetic relationship with his environment, and thenceforth his particular mode of brain activity is determined. And by this circumstance also he is rendered sympathetic or antipathetic to others born under similar or diverse conditions. But if we inquire what it is that controls the changes in the electrostatic condition of the earth's atmosphere, we shall inevitably be led by the *principia* of the Newtonian Philosophy to refer to those bodies which, together with the earth, constitute the Solar System—the Sun, the Moon, and the seven planets.

Now, we are informed by the study of embryology that the segmentation of the ovarian cell, the microscopic world in which organic life is commenced, is cruciform. That is to say, the cell, which consists of a wall enclosing a space, is first of all bisected by a direct line or wall of matter, and afterwards by another that is transverse to it. We learn also from a study of the tides that the attraction of the earth's mass is greatest when the luminaries are acting along the same meridian, and next when they are in quadrature; and further, that the local influence of any celestial body is greatest on the meridian and on the horizon of a place. And since the meridian and horizon are planes at right angles to one another, we are led to the conclusion that there may be an analogy and a correspondence between these two orders of fact, the physiological and the astronomical. Experience shows this to be the case.

When at the moment of a birth the meridian or horizon is occupied by any one of the nine celestial bodies—when, in fact, the celestial influence is acting directly or transversely in regard to the place of birth, the individual then born is impressed with the particular kind of electrical energy generated from that planet in the earth's atmosphere. The nervous matter infilling the brain cells immediately takes up and becomes responsive to that particular mode of etheric vibration which is dominant at the moment of birth.   But this does not hold good with respect to the whole of the cerebrum.   There are definite tracts or areas which are naturally allocated to the functions of the different orders of faculty, and there is a certain interdependence between these parts of the brain by reason of which they are capable of affecting one another.   It is here that Phrenoscopy comes into direct touch and conformity with the established principles of modern Phrenology.   The following diagram shows at a glance the particular areas of the brain which are responsive to the action of the various planets.

Here it will be seen that the planet Mercury is related to the Intellectual faculties—perception, memory, comparison, reason, etc.   Jupiter has influence over the Sympathetic group of faculties —benevolence, suavity, imitation, wit.   Saturn governs the Devotional group, consisting of veneration, ideality, etc.   Mars controls the Self-regarding faculties—execution, destructiveness, combativeness, self-defence.   The Sun rules the Governing group — firmness, self-esteem, conscientiousness, love of approbation.   Venus has relation to the Affectional group, comprising continuity, adhesiveness, friendship, and inhabitiveness; and the Moon relates itself to the Instinctual group, common to man and the lower animals, including conjugality, amativeness, love of offspring, love of life. Uranus is related to the medulla and spinal cord, and Neptune to the more interior parts and processes

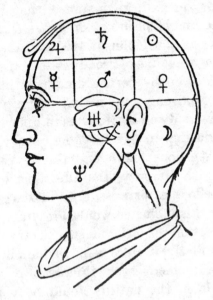

of the brain comprised in the pineal gland, the pituitary body, and the corpora quadragemini.

Suppose, then, for the sake of illustration, that a child is born when the influence of Venus is predominant, and the local mode of etheric vibration is what may be termed Venusian. That child will be dominated in all the affairs of his life by the affections and those things which appeal to them or are capable of stimulating that particular tract of brain to which Venus is related. But this is not the whole of the matter, for it will be seen that, in order to dominate the thought, feeling, and action of life, the Venusian influence must have access, through the nervous matter of the brain, to every group of faculties located in, or functioning through, other tracts of the cerebrum.

Let it be supposed, for instance, that Venus was in the same line of position, or in the same part of the ecliptic, as the Moon at the moment of birth. Then, from what has already been said, it will follow that if Venus be the dominant influence it will act more strongly upon that group of faculties which are related to the Moon than upon any other group, producing, in effect, strongly marked affections and sensuous instincts. But if Venus were conjoined with Mercury, the affections would find a more intellectual expression, and the individual born under this influence would gravitate naturally in the direction of art, music, poetry, and the drama. Similarly, if Mars were the dominant influence at the moment of birth, and were conjoined with the Moon, the nature would be violent and destructive rather than executive and constructive. If acting in the same meridian or horizontal line with the Sun, the commanding and governing faculties would be stimulated and energised by the action of Mars towards the production of the soldier, the pioneer and explorer—the man in whom abundant energy and spirit are allied to a thirst for glory, mastery, and rulership.

Then, again, in accordance with this theory, which I claim to be invariably supported by facts,

it becomes a matter of extreme interest and personal
advantage to know what the dominant influence of
one's nature may be, in what direction the natural
powers will be most easily and effectively expressed,
and in what particular line of life success will be
assured.   The Key to this information is contained
in the following

PHRENOSCOPIC CHART

Neptune acts upon the mind of man to produce a
highly-strung nervous temperament, often allied to
either insanity or genius ; neurosis, aphasia, etc. It
produces complications in business and an involved
state of affairs generally.   Disposes to fraud, double-
dealing, and irresponsible actions.   In the body it
produces waste of tissue and a consumptive habit.

Uranus gives an eccentric mind, waywardness,
originality, inventiveness.   Acting on the affairs of
business, it produces sudden and unexpected developments, irregularities, rapid rise and fall, instability, unexpected turns of good and bad fortune.
In the body it has relation to the nervous system,
and its diseases are those of paralysis, lesion, and
nervous derangement.

Saturn produces a thoughtful, sober, ponderable
mind ;   steadfastness, patience, and endurance ;
disposition to routine and habit, method.   In
financial affairs it gives steady results commensurate
with labour, success that is slow but sure, durance,
hardships, privations.   In the body it is related to the
osseous system, and its ill effects are brought about
by obstructions, chills, and inhibition of function.

Jupiter gives joviality, optimism, bountifulness, generosity, a rich and fruitful mind. It renders the subject fortunate in his affairs, giving success and frequently opulence. With this planet strong, a person never "goes under." In the body it has relation to the arterial process, and its diseases are those which arise from surfeit, congestion, and plethora.

Mars confers a sense of freedom, much ambition and executive ability, frankness, truthfulness, and scorn of consequence. It renders the mind forceful and militant, stimulates to new projects and enterprises, and in the body of man has relation to the muscular system. Its diseases are those which arise from inflammatory action in the tissues.

Venus confers poesy, good taste, fine feeling, artistic powers, gentleness, docility, dalliance, and love of pleasure. It renders the affairs pleasant and prosperous, giving profit from both artistic and rustic pursuits. Next to Jupiter it is the most benefic of the planets in its action on mankind. In the body it has relation to the venous system, and its diseases are those which arise from impurities of the blood, scorbutic and zymotic diseases, eczema, smallpox, measles, etc.

Mercury renders its subjects active, versatile, apt and business-like, disposed to much commerce, whether of the mind or the market, and eager in the pursuit of knowledge ; alert, and well-informed. Its influence on affairs of life is variable, for it always translates the nature of that planet to which at birth it is in nearest aspect. In the body it is related to the sensorium, the centres of sensation, and reflexly controls the nerves of action.

The Moon gives gracefulness of manner and suavity of speech, softness and adaptability of nature, variableness, love of change, romance, and adventure ; disposed to exploration and voyaging. In the body it corresponds to the glandular system, and its diseases are those incidental to the lymphatic glands and vascular tissue.

The Sun renders its subjects magnanimous, noble, proud, despising all mean and sordid actions ; loyal, truthful, and fearless. It produces honours and the favour of dignitaries, and renders the subject fortunate in the control of his affairs. In the body it controls the vital principle.

SUMMARY

	NORMAL.	ABNORMAL.
Neptune	Genius, inspiration.	Insanity, obsession.
Uranus	Originality, invention.	Obstinacy, eccentricity.
Saturn	Steadfastness, fidelity.	Deceitfulness, suspicion.
Jupiter	Benevolence, joviality.	Ostentation, profligacy.
Mars	Energy, executiveness.	Impulse, destructiveness.
Sun	Dignity, independence.	Vanity, egotism.
Venus	Affability, art.	Self-indulgence, disorderliness.
Mercury	Alertness, ing nuity.	Inquisitiveness, meddling.
Moon	Grace, idealism.	Inconstancy, awkwardness.

CHAPTER XIII

PLANETARY HOURS

HAVING shown that planetary hours count from noon in the most ancient system of time-division, it may now be of interest to learn of what use this knowledge is to us and how it can be turned to account in daily life.

For the sake of convenience to the reader I have here set out the numerical values of the twenty-four hours counted from noon of Sunday, which, by the same system, was always the first day of the week, as Saturday was the Sabbath (seventh) or last. To these values we have to add those due to the minutes past each hour. Thus we find that on Saturday at 2 p.m., which is the beginning of the third hour from noon, the value is 8, and if we want the value for 24 minutes past 2 o'clock, then we have to divide 24 by 4=6, and count to the sixth period from Saturn, which is Mercury=5, and by adding this to the day and hour value in the above Table, namely 8, we get 13, the unit value of which is 4. This responds to the negative Sun, the significance of which will be found in the following pages.

I. TABLE OF PLANETARY HOURS AND VALUES

Hour.	Sun.	Mon.	Tues.	Wed.	Thur.	Frid.	Sat.
Noon	2	5	9	1	6	3	7
1 p.m.	7	6	1	3	3	2	2
2	6	1	6	4	4	4	8
3	8	7	5	8	9	5	9
4	9	8	7	5	8	9	5
5	4	4	8	6	1	6	4
6	1	3	3	2	2	7	6
7	2	5	9	1	6	3	7
8	7	6	1	3	3	2	2
9	6	1	6	4	4	4	8
10	8	7	5	8	9	5	9
11	9	8	7	5	8	9	5
12	4	4	8	6	1	6	4
13	1	3	3	2	2	7	6
14	2	5	9	1	6	3	7
15	7	6	1	3	3	2	2
16	6	1	6	4	4	4	8
17	8	7	5	8	9	5	9
18	9	8	7	5	8	9	5
19	4	4	8	6	1	6	4
20	1	3	3	2	2	7	6
21	2	5	9	1	6	3	7
22	7	6	1	3	3	2	2
23	6	1	6	4	4	4	8

Here follows the

II. TABLE OF HOUR DIVISIONS AND VALUES

Day.	4	8	12	16	20	24	28	32	36	40	44	48	52	56	60
Sun.	1	6	5	7	8	3	9	1	6	5	7	8	3	9	1
Mon.	7	8	3	9	1	6	5	7	8	3	9	1	6	5	7
Tues.	9	1	6	5	7	8	3	9	1	6	5	7	8	3	9
Wed.	5	7	8	3	9	1	6	5	7	8	3	9	1	6	5
Thurs.	3	9	1	6	5	7	8	3	9	1	6	5	7	8	3
Frid.	6	5	7	8	3	9	1	6	5	7	8	3	9	1	6
Sat.	8	3	9	1	6	5	7	8	3	9	1	6	5	7	8

The significance of the above Table is that it has
to be employed in finding the value due to any
number of minutes. Each hour is divided into
15 parts of 4 minutes each, counting from the
planet which rules the day. Thus on a Saturday,
ruled by Saturn, the whole day has the value of 8,
and the hours count from noon, which is ruled by
Saturn for one hour and is followed by Jupiter,
Mars, etc. Then the value for each succeeding
hour has to be added to the Day Planet's value, as
shown in the first of these Tables.

The Period Planet is also counted from the Day
Planet, as shown in the second Table, and its value is
to be added to the value derived from the first Table.

Example.—What is the value for Tuesday, 2nd
September 1913, at 5.25 in the afternoon?

Table I. shows the hour from 5 to 6 p.m. to be
    ruled by 8
Table II. gives for 24–28 minutes on a
    Tuesday 8

        The total of these is . . . 16

Thus we obtain at once the unit value of 7, which
is the number of the Moon, and we therefore know
that the value 7 is ruling for 3 minutes after 5.25
p.m., and that it is under the direct or positive
influence of the Moon. Again, supposing that
the time given were 3.45 on Wednesday morning.
Let it be supposed that a child were born at
that time. It is required to know under what
number and Star it was born. According to
Table I. it is seen that Tuesday, at 15 hours
after noon, is under number 1, and Table II.
informs us that on a Tuesday 45 minutes after
the hour is under 5. Therefore we have 1 plus
5 equal 6, which is the number of the Nativity,
and hence the child would be born under the
planet Venus.

Supposing that there is a competition which
begins at a particular time, as, for instance, a race
of any description. By means of these Tables we
may at once decide upon the numerical value of
the winning competitor's name, or number if he
carries one. For in a very large majority of cases—
so large as to preclude the idea of a fortuitous
coincidence—it will be found that the planetary
value of the time of commencing the competition
or race will coincide with the value of the name of
competitor or the number he carries.

But it is found that the hours have a significance
which is dominant during their rule or sway, and
the use to which this can be put is in the selection
of the times for performing any work according to
its nature, and also a knowledge of the influence

of the ruling planet enables us to make forecast of the result of any effort, the contents of letters, the nature of messages, etc., that may be received under their rule.

For this purpose Table I. is alone to be used.

The influence and signification of the planets are as follows:

PLANETARY INDICATIONS

1. In the hour ruled by this number. Persons indicated by this number will be independent, proud, and magnanimous, scorning deception and meanness of every sort. They are bold and fearless, and capable of governing others and taking positions of trust and authority. Subject when ill to defects of the heart and circulation, and to hurts and diseases of the right eye.

Things sought for in this hour should be found in the East, and are brought to light at the full of the Moon.

Persons applying to one in this hour are ruddy, with grey or blue eyes and strong active bodies.

Letters received during this hour are relative to affairs of credit and position, honours, dignities, public persons, places of government, etc.

2. This hour is ruled by the Moon in its negative aspect, and is unfortunate, especially in regard to all matters having to do with females, changes, etc. Things lost will not be found. Persons applying are shifty and unreliable. Journeys are unfortunate. Letters refer to changes and misfortunes, and are often of the nature of evasion.

3. Ruled by Jupiter. A fortunate hour. Persons indicated by this planet are generous and even extravagant, disposed to help others, to their own detriment. Fond of good living and very grandiose in their ideas, pompous, but kind. They usually have full foreheads and protruding eyes, large teeth and plentiful hair, waving or curling, but in mature years they are disposed to baldness.

Things sought for in this hour may be recovered by searching in the N.-E. direction. If stolen, they will be restored if notice is given, with a reward.

Complaints to which the subject is predisposed are those of the liver and spleen, congestion and surfeit, sometimes flatulence.

It is a fortunate hour in which to avail oneself of legal advice, to consult churchmen, and to obtain favours from judges and magistrates. It is fortunate for all financial transactions and for general commerce, also for advancing one's interest in any direction. It is unfortunate for sailing or for dealing in cattle.

Letters received during this hour will have reference to money, trade, justice, and are always indicative of some advantage to the person receiving them. Information given at this time is reliable.

4. This number is ruled by the Sun, but is negative and unfortunate. Persons applying to one during this hour are haughty and proud, conceited and overbearing, fond of display and bigoted.

Things sought for in this hour are seldom recovered, but may be so at the New Moon if sought for in the N.-W.

Letters received relate to loss of position, defects of credit and esteem, and sometimes they are threatening and blatant.

The diseases of those born under this number are those of the blood, and generally arise from lack of tone or vitality.

It is an unfortunate hour in which to do anything of importance or to approach persons in authority, or to go a journey or enter a house for the first time.

5. Ruled by Mercury. Persons applying in this hour are usually tall and thin, but, if short, will be extremely wiry and active, and rather wizened in appearance. The eyes are small and sharp, and the appearance very alert and businesslike. The hands are slender, and the step quick and nimble.

Things lost generally prove to have been stolen, but they are usually recovered if sought for in a Northerly direction.

Messages received relate to writings and to papers, to business and trade, and to educational matters, books, and matters affecting young children. Sometimes to short journeys and to health.

The diseases of those born under this influence are chiefly nervous, affecting the brain and the organs of speech, and sometimes the limbs. Various forms of neuralgia, vertigo, brain sickness, pellagra, epilepsy, and defects of the senses and memory are the chief ailments of Mercury.

6. Ruled by Venus. Persons applying at this hour are of a kind, gentle, docile, and amiable disposition, disposed to the arts and culture of various forms. Sometimes easy-going and lovers

of pleasure, to their own hurt and detriment. The body is well favoured and fully fleshed, the limbs round and supple. The hair fine and of a light brown or flaxen colour, sometimes very black and abundant. The eyes may be either dark and sloe-like, or of a fine blue colour, as suits the complexion. Generally good-looking if male, and pretty if female, but always attractive.

The hour is good for all matters pertaining to the sexes and for the pursuit of things of beauty, fashion, and pleasure. It is good at this time to prefer a suit, and to become engaged or to marry. A good hour for domestic affairs and for entering a new home. Good for journeys and for taking trips, but not for setting out on a long voyage, and principally for matters of a domestic and social nature—visiting, shopping, calling on friends, etc.

Things lost in this hour are to be found in the West.

The diseases to which those born under Venus are subject are those arising from the morbid expression of the passions, sexual complaints, and diseases of the throat and kidneys ; skin diseases, phlebitis, etc.

Letters received at this time relate to pleasure and to domestic and social affairs, and sometimes to affections.

7. Ruled by the Moon. The person applying under this number is usually of full body, fleshy and pale, with rounded features and colourless complexion. Hands and feet small, head large. In character the individual is self-assertive and fond of praise.

The Moon governs all persons attached to public service. It denotes public bodies and Government or municipal servants.

Things lost or observed to be lost in this hour will be recovered if public notice is given of the fact. The thing should be looked for in the North, and will come to light in the full of the Moon.

The diseases to which those born under this influence are subject are chest affections, diseases and complaints of the stomach and breasts, bad digestion, injuries or bad defects of the left eye and the brain.

The hour is good for dealing with matrons and all public concerns, municipalities, affairs of public interest, journeys, voyages, changes of all sorts, advertising, etc.

Letters and messages at this time relate to journeys and changes, and there are female influences involved. The hour is good in contradistinction from the hour ruled by Moon under number 2.

Nevertheless it is best not to take any important steps under this influence, as changes of plan and arrangement are apt to intervene to spoil the best results. It is especially good for dealing with all matters affecting the public, and also public bodies of government.

8. This number is ruled by Saturn. It is an evil hour, and bad for almost all affairs, but singularly good for dealing in land and the produce of the earth—minerals, crops, etc.

Persons applying are usually of a dark and lean

visage, sinister in appearance, and stooping in gait. Hardly to be trusted, because selfish and material to a degree.

The hour is good only for dealing with the aged and infirm, and for matters connected with the produce of the soil, such as crops and minerals; but also for any matter in which time is a prominent factor, as in the case of contracts reaching over many years.

Things lost during the hour of Saturn are seldom if ever regained, but should be looked for in the South, and they may be found, but only after long delay.

Letters in this hour relate to death, sickness, misery, disease, misfortune, darkness, mourning, and delays.

It is not a good hour in which to deal with anything, as it shows delays, deceptions, treachery, and loss. The Hebrews made the whole day, so far as it related to business, a holiday and period of rest.

A person falling sick in this hour will have a long period of illness, and will only recover after much care and expense. Mental impressions received during this hour should be carefully thought over before being acted upon, as they are generally faulty.

The diseases of Saturn are those of the bones and articulations, morbid decay, consumption, melancholia, and religious mania.

9. This number is ruled by Mars. Persons applying during this hour are such as have a sandy or ruddy complexion and grey, steely eyes. They

are usually strong and muscular and very militant in their manner. It is better to placate them than to oppose. They are petulant and fiery and very impulsive, yet frank and outspoken, and easily dealt with on that account alone. You know what they mean and intend to do as soon as they speak.

Things that are lost in this hour are usually found almost at once or not at all. They are to be sought for in the West.

The diseases of Mars are those that are incident to the head and face, and also the excretory system. Fevers, accidents, and affections of the skin; itchings, swellings, and blains; cuts, burns, scalds, and corrosions.

Letters received during this hour are such as relate to disputes, frauds, thefts, lying, fire, accidents, fevers, operations, and tragedies.

Do not trust news that is received or impressions that come to the brain during this hour; do nothing hurriedly, but test all communications and act deliberately after mature thought.

The above indications are useful in regulating one's affairs and making decision in matters that are productive of doubt in the mind. The ancients paid great attention to these Elections, as they were called, and seldom did any work of importance without regard to the current influences as expressed in the hour of the day.

Some writers have used the Planetary Hours as beginning at midnight in a conventional manner not at all known to the ancients, while others have

used them as from the time of sunrise, always
omitting to say what is meant by that very am-
biguous~term. Sunrise may be upon the local
horizon or upon the celestial horizon, and may be
apparent or true sunrise. If sunrise is to be taken
at all, it should be taken astronomically, that is to
say, by the conjunction of the Sun's apparent
centre with the celestial horizon of the place for
which calculation is made.

I have found that the ancient method of using
the hours is in close agreement with the events of
daily life, and for that reason alone have adhered
to it in practice. Elsewhere in the pages of this
work I have given examples of the manner in
which the evaluation of names by the Phonetic
alphabet brings them into accord with the value
of the Day, Hour, and Period involved, and these
examples will be sufficient proof of the integrity of
the system. We have now to consider one or two
propositions of a more recondite nature connected
with the subject of planetary influence in human
life, and these will suitably conclude the second
part of the Kabala.

CHAPTER XIV

SCIENCE AND SUPERSTITION

IN the foregoing pages we have seen that there is a Law of Values attaching to Form, Sound, Number, and to all expressions of the universal vibration of the etheric agent. It has been demonstrated in other places that the planets deflect and transmit the Solar rays in altered magnetic and electrical conditions, differing as does the nature of the planet transmitting them. Those who are disposed to regard the conclusions of astrology as fanciful and inconsequent should reflect on the fact that the planet Mercury is second to none in importance among the spheres, which would certainly not be the case had the ancients judged by appearances only and not by experience and reason. Here we have a planet which is about 22,500 times smaller than Jupiter, and so near at times to the Sun as to be seldom visible; indeed, I believe I am right in saying that the great astronomer Copernicus confessed never to have seen it. Yet this planet above all others is taken to be the specific significator of man, inasmuch as it is related by astrology to the intellectual and reasoning faculties as distinguished from the emotional and passional common to man and the lower animals. With thinking people this fact will weigh very heavily, and in the scientific mind it may serve to remove the prejudice which has long existed against the science on account of immature presentation and frequent misrepresentation at the hands of critics who are wholly ignorant of the subject.

It is a matter of considerable satisfaction to me to know that Mr George F. Chambers, F.R.A.S., in his admirable little work, *The Story of Eclipses*, has admitted that there is *prima facie* evidence for scientific inquiry into the connection between eclipses and earthquakes. He says : " Perhaps this may be a convenient place to make a note of what seems to be a fact, partly established, at any-rate, even if not wholly established, namely, that there seems some connection between eclipses of the Sun and earthquakes. A German physicist named Ginzel has found a score of coincidences between solar eclipses and earthquakes in California in the years between 1850 and 1888 inclusive. Of course, there were eclipses without earthquakes and earthquakes without eclipses, but twenty coincidences in thirty-eight years seems suggestive."

Had Ginzel taken the trouble to extend his observations beyond California, and to include eclipses of the Moon as well as those of the Sun, and further, had he taken note of planetary transits over the places of eclipse, his coincidences would have been considerably amplified. The fact is that you cannot get the average astronomer to

recognise the working value of the fundamental
concept of Newton's *Principia*, that of the solidarity
of the Solar System.   Beyond the fact of planetary
perturbation'caused by the interaction of the large
bodies of the system they do not care to inquire
whether there may not be other forces than the
attraction of gravitation at work in the system.
In this they err very greatly. It was by the
recognition of the law of planetary interaction as
implied by the concept of the solidarity of the
system that Laplace discovered the great perturbation of Saturn by the planet Jupiter, and paved
the way to the discovery of Uranus by Herschel,
the discovery of which was a unique performance
in the history of astronomy.

Sir David Brewster was more catholic in his
ideas, and fully admitted that if the Sun's rays were
necessary for the development of chromatic effect
and the faculty of vision, there may be other rays
which enable us to hear, to taste, and to smell.
I would go further and say, without any reserve
whatsoever, that there are rays, more subtle than
those of light, more far-reaching than the force of
gravity, which impel men to think and to act,
which create disasters, produce various forms of
sickness, inspire ambitions, and dispose men to
definite lines of conduct.   And I say this with as
much authority and from as weighty an experience
as any which at any time has been adduced in
support of a scientific proposition.   In line with
me are such men as the astronomers Tycho, Kepler,
Newton, Wichell, Wing, Flamsteed, and Christie;

the writers Sir Thomas Browne, Dryden, Varley, and Garnett, and a host of others whose names and works have embellished the records of antiquity.

In these pages I have not advanced any one of the more weighty arguments, nor adduced any part of the voluminous body of proofs which might be urged in favour of an *astrologia sana* such as that to which Bacon subscribed, for it has been my express purpose to entertain the popular mind with such material as can legitimately be advanced as a part of the Kabala. Incidentally, however, this matter goes to prove that there is a definite law of correlation at work in the universe, and that, whether we regard the cosmic as embodied Force or merely as a symbol of Mind, it submits equally to an orderly and systematic interpretation.

I have purposely refrained indeed from making any specific references to the scientific and philosophical value of astrology as a system of interpretation. This is not from want of any material, but from lack of space in which to deal fairly with it. But yet I have felt that there is a subtle connection between numerology and the various branches of kabalism, and astrology, which renders the development of the one almost impossible without the introduction of the other. Certainly, without a knowledge of astrology one cannot go very far in kabalism, and I think that symbolism of any sort, whether it be religious, Masonic, Rosicrucian, or pure Art, cannot go far without coming into direct relations with astrology.

For purely forensic purposes it may be conveni-

14

ent to regard all celestial configurations as merely
symbolical. It is a somewhat difficult matter,
apart from the introduction of a species of occultism,
to argue a connection between the presence of Mars
in a particular degree of the zodiac and a blood
temperature of 105°, between the passage of Uranus
over the place held by the Moon at a birth and the
presence of the subject in a motor smash-up, or
between the transit of Venus over the place of the
Sun at birth and the marriage of the person at an
age exactly corresponding to the interval of time
between the birth and the transit at the rate of a
day for a year. Yet these are among the common
observations of the student of astrology. If,
however, we regard the planets as symbols, the
argument rests solely in the correspondence of
symbol and event, and the man who would talk
them out of existence must inevitably fail.

In seeking for purely physical connections between earthquakes and eclipses, we may consider
the fact that the lifting power of the Moon over
all fluidic nature is exceedingly great, so great
indeed as to raise millions of tons of water several
feet in the course of a few hours. There are various
means by which this may be effected, and the
popular view is that it is caused by the attraction
of the Moon upon the particles of water composing
the ocean. When the Sun and Moon are conjoined,
and both pulling in the same direction, we have
what are called Spring Tides, when the effect is
greatest. When pulling from opposite sides of the
earth, the same bodies produce Neap Tides, when

the effect is not so great.   Now it is known that the
period from one high tide to the next is 12 hours
25 minutes, and this interval comprises a half
revolution of the earth on its axis plus the 25
minutes represented by the meridian passage of the
Moon's elongation (increase of Moon's longitude over
the Sun's) during the interval.   We are able therefore to link up the tides with the Moon's elongation
and to define the joint action of the luminaries as
greatest at conjunction.   But all conjunctions of
the Sun and Moon are not eclipses of the Sun, the
reason being that the Moon's path does not lie in
the same plane as that of the earth, and consequently crosses it at an angle, which is found to be
about 5°.   The point of intersection is called the
node, and it is only when the luminaries are conjoined on, or close to, this node that there can be
an eclipse of the Sun.   They are then pulling in a
right line together on the same side of the earth,
and the visible effect is that the sun's rays are cut
off from the earth in that region where the eclipse
is central at noon, that is to say, where the centres
of the Sun and Moon appear to coincide when they
are exactly on the meridian.   At the eclipse of the
Sun on 12th April 1912, and in other cases, the fall
of temperature at the moment of greatest obscuration was such as to be a matter of general comment.
What would be the effect of this sudden disturbance
of the temperature ?   Obviously there would be an
immediate uprush of heat from the interior parts
of the earth to counteract the chill and to restore
the equilibrium.   Further, the electrostatic con-

dition of the atmosphere would undergo a sudden change, and a similar outburst of electrical energy would be required to compensate it. The earth's crust at this part of the globe may or may not be strong enough to withstand the strain, and the effect is in the latter case a violent earthquake shock. Consequently we only look for violent earthquakes at or immediately after the time of an eclipse in those parts that are volcanic, or within what are known as the earthquake areas. Similar effects, due entirely to the strain set up between the contending forces of the Sun and Moon, may be observed at an eclipse of the Moon. In the case of the solar eclipse we have the interposition of the actual body of the Moon, whereas in a lunar eclipse it is only the shadow of the earth that is the cause of obscuration. In this connection it appears to me essential to the purposes of physicists that the static effects of solar and lunar eclipses should be carefully observed before we can argue much concerning the nature of the forces that are impeded in either case. But it may be remarked that such study and observation will inevitably lead to a re-modelling of our ideas regarding the nature of the forces transmitted by the luminaries. For whereas it is generally conceded that the Sun is the source of all light and heat, and that the Moon merely reflects these, it would seem that the effects of lunar eclipses are just as conspicuous as those due to solar eclipses. Ricciolus has observations of earthquakes following both eclipses of the Sun and Moon, and Morrison in recent times made similar observations and records. In one instance, at all events—that of the Cumana earthquake,—he specifically predicted and located the disturbance. It does not appear to have arrested scientific attention, however, and probably because at that date no scientific authority had argued a connection between earthquakes and eclipses. It is well to keep these facts warm, however, for it is commonly observed that the folly of to-day is the science of to-morrow. A hundred years ago you could not photograph a body through a brick wall, or fly in the air, or communicate with a person a thousand miles away in a few minutes ; nor, for that matter, could you predict the time and place of an eclipse with any certainty, and, with the exception of the latter, any talk of doing these things would have been a " sure sign " of enfeebled intellect.

When, therefore, we hear people talk of the folly of planetary influence in human life, which is the description of what astrology imports to us, we get impatient, first because they are inconsistent, and next because they are presumptuous in pretending a knowledge they do not possess. For, beyond all human cavil and controversy, there is the fact that we are creatures of the Earth ; the further fact that the Earth is an integral part of the Solar System ; and, moreover, the fact that every atom exerts a direct influence on every other atom throughout the system to which it belongs. When, therefore, we are asked to believe that cosmical conditions, at a time when the Sun, Mars, Jupiter, and the Earth are all in the same line, are exactly the same as when these bodies were not so placed, we are entitled to conclude either that Newton was a great dreamer or the speaker a greater fool. We prefer the latter conclusion as more in harmony with our estimate of the facts. Elsewhere I have proved that the periodic times of the planets Mercury, Venus, Earth, Mars, and Jupiter, when taken together, average exactly to the periodicity of sunspot maxima ; and Sir Norman Lockyer has shown a connection to exist between maximum sunspot periods and high Nile tides, droughts, and other physical phenomena, so that, by purely scientific means, we are coming to the point where it will be not only possible but only rational to argue a connection between the planets and mankind. For a long time it may be called " physics " or " physical astronomy," but when it gets its right name, that under which it has survived the ages in face of all the ridicule and persecution of the sceptic and the tyrant, it will be known as Astrology, the science which, in the opinion of Newton, was committed to primeval man by direct revelation, since by no other means could he account for its great antiquity and the universality of its principles. I doubt not that the astrology of Newton was of that rational kind to which modern science is steadily approaching, but what he knew of it was grounded in the traditions, incorporated in the *Tetrabiblos* of Ptolemy, and confirmed from experience by Kepler. To such studies we may profitably apply ourselves without, at this day, incurring either much ridicule or much persecution, and in this connection the present effort may be of service as showing the existence of many curious coincidences which can hardly be accounted for except on the grounds of a universal physiognomy, a symbolism that touches all phases of human experience and vaguely approaches the cusp of science. In connection with it we have been able to trace the Law of Vibrations, that of Periodicity, and the relations of both to matters of common human interest. A kabalism that is so inclusive can hardly lay claim to be considered in the light of a science, but it leads directly to the study of the problems of science which we have touched upon in this chapter, and perchance it may extend to that region of Higher Physics which pertains to the science of Mind. That it is not wholly without interest is sufficient excuse for its publication. If it should also be found to have a use, so much the better for the patient reader, to whom my thanks are due.

THE HISTORY AND POWER OF MIND, by Richard Ingalese.
"The history of mind is the history of man." So states the author of this remarkable book, which went through multiple printings in its first edition. Lea meditation, creation, and concentration, the art of self-control, the cause and cure of disease, the law of opulence; discover the colors of thought vibration. Now available for the first time in decades.
P-037-2   284 pages $4.95

THE ROMANCE OF CHIVALRY, by A.R. Hope-Moncrieff.
Here for the first time in a popularly-priced edition is a comprehensive and authoritative study of chivalry and romantic history, profusely illustrated, with the greatest tales of the knights and heroes of yore retold in clear, exciting prose.
M-038-0   439 pages $4.95

JORIS OF THE ROCK, by Leslie Barringer (The Neustrian Cycle, Book Two). With a new introduction by Douglas Menville.
This stunning sequel to *Gerfalcon* includes many of the same characters and settings. The infamous outlaw, Joris of the Rock, becomes embroiled in the intrigue surrounding old King Rene, who has a legitimate nephew, Prince Thorismund (the heir), and an illegitimate son, Conrad (who wants the throne). The King dies, Conrad's partisans revolt, and the great battle is joined! With a wraparound cover by George Barr.
F-108-5   318 pages $3.95

HEART OF THE WORLD, by H. Rider Haggard.
The great master of fantasy adventure returns to the Newcastle line with the story of an amazing lost city in the Mexican jungles, and a people who have been cut off from civilization for over a thousand years. The Indians are plotting to restore their great empire, and seem on the verge of success when Princess Maya, daughter of the ruler, falls in love with an English explorer. Don't miss the stunning conclusion!
F-109-3   347 pages $3.95

Borgo Press Originals

ALISTAIR MacLEAN: THE KEY IS FEAR, by Robert A. Lee (The Milford Series: Popular Writers of Today, Vol. 2)
Alistair MacLean is without doubt the premier adventure and suspense writer in the world today. His first success, *The Guns of Navarone*, make his byline a household name throughout the world, and he has continued to build on this reputation with such bestsellers as *Ice Station Zebra, Force 10 from Navarone, Bear Island, Breakheart Pass*, and many more. Dr. Lee examines MacLean's career in detail, beginning with his first novel, *H.M.S. Ulysses*, and including his 1976 thriller, *The Golden Gate*.
B-203-0   64 pages $1.95

THE ATTEMPTED ASSASSINATION OF JOHN F. KENNEDY, by Lucas Webb.
Dallas, Texas. A sunny November afternoon. Suddenly, a shot rings out: two men slump over in their seats. A Governor is wounded, and a President dies. Or was it the other way around?
B-204-9   48 pages $1.95

THE FARTHEST SHORES OF URSULA K. LE GUIN, by George Edgar Slusser (The Milford Series: Popular Writers of Today, Vol. 3)
Twice winner of double Hugo and Nebula Awards for Best Science Fiction Novel of the year, Ursula K. Le Guin is one of the fastest rising stars on the science fiction horizon. With each new book, her fame continues to grow, and her critical reputation increases. Dr. Slusser, author of *Robert A. Heinlein: Stranger in His Own Land*, discusses her writings in depth, from her obscure beginnings in the SF magazines, to such triumphs as *The Left Hand of Darkness* and *The Dispossessed*.
B-205-7   64 pages $1.95

Newcastle Publishing Company Inc.
P.O. Box 7589
Van Nuys, CA 91409

I. THE GLITTERING PLAIN, by William Morris.
This is the book that reestablished adult fantasy as a distinct category of modern literature. A story of love and immortality, it ranks with the best of Morris's medieval romances. For all lovers of stirring heroic adventure.
F-100-X   174 pages $2.95

II. THE SAGA OF ERIC BRIGHTEYES, by H. Rider Haggard.
Although Haggard is better known for his African romances, this Viking adventure has all of the Master's trademarks: rousing action, bloody battles, unforgettable heroes, romance, and a story that just can't be put down. If you liked *She* and *King Solomon's Mines*, you'll love *Eric*. Illustrated.
F-101-8   304 pages $3.95

III. THE FOOD OF DEATH: FIFTY-ONE TALES, by Lord Dunsany.
(Original title: *Fifty-One Tales*). It's been said that Dunsany, like the writers of ancient Greece, makes his gods human, and his men divine. As any reader will testify, he also writes some of the finest fantasy ever penned. Here's a collection of his best, with a beautiful cover by S. H. Sine.
F-102-6   138 pages $2.95

IV. THE HAUNTED WOMAN, by David Lindsay.
The author of *A Voyage to Arcturus* has written another book as eerie and strange as any fantasy you'll ever read. Put together a ghostly mansion with three rooms that somehow don't exist (or do they?), a piper 1500 years old, reincarnation, love, and supernatural mystery, and you've just begun to explore Lindsay's mystical vision. A superb romance.
F-103-4   178 pages $2.95

V. ALADORE, by Sir Henry Newbolt.
Here's a book that William Morris could have written. Set in a medieval-like world, *Aladore* is the heroic quest of Sir Ywain, who renounces his fiefdom, and sets out to discover his place in the world. How he finds Aithne, the lovely enchantress of Paladore, and all the battles and magic inbetween, is a story that every fantasy lover will want to read. Illustrated.
F-104-2   363 pages $3.95

VI. SHE & ALLAN, by H. Rider Haggard.
The two main characters from *She* and *King Solomon's Mines* finally get it together in this epic sequel of adventure and romance. Ayesha, She-Who-Is-To-Be-Obeyed, calls upon Allan Quatermain to save her from a 2000-year-old mortal enemy. Beautifully illustrated.
F-105-0   302 pages $3.95

VII. GERFALCON, by Leslie Barringer (The Neustrian Cycle, Book One).
In the mythical medieval kingdom of Neustria, Raoul of Ger fights for his life and fortune in a stirring tale of action and adventure that will leave you riveted to your suit of armor. Don't miss the first book in this thrilling series.
F-106-9   310 pages $3.45

VIII. GOLDEN WINGS, and OTHER STORIES, by William Morris. With a new afterword by Dr. Richard B. Mathews.
Although Morris wrote these beautiful little tales quite early in his career, they include many themes present in his later work. "The Hollow Land," "Gerda's Lovers," "Lindenborg Pool," and many other stories are represented. This is fantasy of the first rank.
F-107-7   168 pages $2.95

IX. JORIS OF THE ROCK, by Leslie Barringer (The Neustrian Cycle, Book Two). With a new introduction by Douglas Menville.
This stunning sequel to *Gerfalcon* includes many of the same characters and settings. The infamous outlaw, Joris of the Rock, becomes embroiled in the intrigue surrounding old King Rene, who has a legitimate nephew, Prince Thorismund (the heir), and an illegitimate son, Conrad (who wants the throne). The King dies, Conrad's partisans revolt, and the great battle is joined! With a wraparound cover by George Barr.
F-108-5   318 pages $3.95

X. HEART OF THE WORLD, by H. Rider Haggard.
The great master of fantasy adventure returns to the Newcastle line with the story of an amazing lost city in the Mexican jungles, and a people who have been cut off from civilization for over a thousand years. The Indians are plotting to restore their great empire, and seem on the verge of success when Princess Maya, daughter of the ruler, falls in love with an English explorer. Don't miss the stunning conclusion!
F-109-3   347 pages $3.95

OTHER TITLES OF INTEREST

A. GHOSTS I HAVE MET, by John Kendrick Bangs.
A delightful collection of humourous ghost stories by the author of *A House Boat on the Styx*. Illus.
P-005-4   191 pages $2.45

B. THE BOOK OF DREAMS AND GHOSTS, by Andrew Lang.
The author (with H. Rider Haggard) of *The World's Desire* explores the world of ghostly and occult lore in eighty different tales of the fantastic. A gorgeous cover by George Barr.
P-010-0   301 pages $2.95

C. THE QUEST OF THE GOLDEN STAIRS, by Arthur Edward Waite.
This strange allegorical fantasy tells of the quest of a noble prince of Faerie in search of fame and fortune. Waite is better known for his works on alchemy, magic, and the tarot. For lovers of the arcane.
X-028-3   171 pages $2.95

D. CELTIC MYTH AND LEGEND, by Charles Squire.
Admirers of Evangeline Walton, Katherine Kurtz, Lloyd Alexander, and other fantasy writers will find this massive compendium of Celtic mythology an essential guide to the gods, heroes, giants, and other legendary figures of early Gaelic and British lore. Copiously illustrated.
M-030-5   492 pages $4.95

E. THE ROMANCE OF CHIVALRY, by A. R. Hope-Moncrieff.
Here for the first time in a popularly-priced edition is a comprehensive and authoritative study of chivalry and romantic history, profusely illustrated, with the greatest tales of the knights and heroes of yore retold in clear, exciting prose.
M-038-0   439 pages $4.95

DOCTOR NIKOLA, Master of Occult Mystery, by Guy Boothby $4.95

#1. ENTER DR. NIKOLA! (original title: *A Bid for Fortune*)
A curious chinese token is the key to Nikola's ambitions, and Nikola will have it, whatever the cost. And if Wetherell refuses to sell, perhaps a suitable trade can be arranged: Whetherell's beautiful daughter for the strangely-inscribed stick. Only Richard Haterass can foil the Doctor's nefarious schemes, but Hatteras is being held captive in Port Said, and Nikola has already fled with the girl to the South Seas. Can anyone stop Doctor Nikola?
X-032-1   256 pages $2.95

#2. DR. NIKOLA RETURNS (original title: *Dr. Nikola*)
In his second exciting adventure, Nikola infiltrates a mysterious Chinese sect to gain the secrets of eternal life. With his new assistant, he penetrates the deepest regions of hidden Tibet, where he convinces the princes that he is the newest member of their triumvirate. As the installation begins, the real priest appears, and Nikola is unmasked. The lamas sit in judgment, and the verdict is death!
X-034-8   256 pages $2.95

NEWCASTLE ARCANA

1. **RITUAL MAGIC, by E. M. Butler.**
   Originally published by Cambridge University Press, this classic study of magic, conjuration, Satanism, and Kabbalistic rites amongst primitive people is the standard work in its field. Includes many texts translated from the original languages.
   W-001-1   **329 pages**   **$3.45**

2. **MAGIC WHITE AND BLACK, by Dr. Franz Hartmann.**
   First published in 1895, and long unavailable, Hartmann's work is the classic treatment of theosophy and spiritual law in the natural world. Many scholars consider it to be his best book on the occult.
   P-003-8   **298 pages**   **$3.95**

3. **FORTUNE TELLING FOR FUN, by Paul Showers.**
   The future's an open book for those in the know. Discover the secrets of your destiny by peering into the crystal ball of fate! Learn how to make prophecies from handwriting analysis, tea leaves, Ouija boards, charms, cominoes, fire, names, and cards. Illustrated.
   T-007-0   **349 pages**   **$3.95**

4. **THE DEVIL IN BRITAIN AND AMERICA, by John Ashton.**
   By far the best book ever written on Satanism, Ashton's superb study of witchcraft and demonology is now available in paperback for the first time. A comprehensive collection of case histories, dialogues, poetry, and other writings dealing with the Devil and his minions. Illustrated throughout.
   P-008-9   **353 pages**   **$3.75**

5. **NUMEROLOGY MADE PLAIN, by Ariel Yvon Taylor.**
   Numerology, the science of numbers and their rates of vibration, is as old as the pyramids, and is relevant as tomorrow. Discover the laws that govern your life and destiny! With an index of 1500 names and their numerical values.
   P-012-7   **148 pages**   **$2.45**

6. **AN INTRODUCTION TO ASTROLOGY, by William Lilly.**
   Lilly, who cast horoscopes for King Charles I of England, wrote this classic text in 1647, and it remains one of the high points of astral research and scholarship. An essential guide for the devotee. Illustrated from the 1852 edition.
   P-014-3   **346 pages**   **$3.75**

7. **PRACTICAL ASTROLOGY, by Conte C. de Saint-Germain.**
   A survey of basic astrological principles and practices, Saint-Germain's book illustrates the fascinating relationship between astrology and the tarot. Includes charts, illustrations, and tables.
   P-018-6   **257 pages**   **$2.95**

8. **THE PRACTICE OF PALMISTRY, by Conte C. de Saint-Germain.**
   Perhaps the simplest, most comprehensive work on palmistry ever written, this popular manual includes a palmistic dictionary, model charts, and over a thousand illustrative diagrams. An unabridged reprint of the original two-volume set.
   P-019-4   **416 pages**   **$4.95**

9. **THOUGHT VIBRATIONS, by A. Victor Segno.**
   The mind is the greatest power in the universe! Discover its secrets, and learn how to cultivate your will power, in Segno's fascinating guide to the amazing law of mentalism. For the serious student only.
   G-020-8   **208 pages**   **$2.95**

10. **LOST ATLANTIS, by James Bramwell.**
    This fresh and unusual survey of the Atlantis problem carefully examines the writings of Plato, Donnelly, Lewis Spence, and others, setting forth the chief modern theories, and providing a clear and unbiased look at this fascinating mystery. With a stunning cover by Cindy Rucker.
    P-023-2   **288 pages**   **$3.45**

11. **THIRTY YEARS AMONG THE DEAD, by Dr. Carl A. Wickland.**
    There is no death! This is the conclusion of Dr. Wickland's amazing researches into spirit communication and life after death. Page after page of fascinating testimony.
    P-025-9   **390 pages**   **$4.95**

12. **THE ARCANA OF ASTROLOGY, by William J. Simmonite.**
    (originally: *The Complete Arcana of Astral Philosophy*). One of the most avidly sought astrological texts, the *Arcana* is designed for the serious student of the stars. It provides the fundamentals of astrology clearly and logically, with questions and problems to help you absorb the material. Crammed with tables, diagrams, and examples.
    T-026-7   **428 pages**   **$4.95**

13. **THE KABALA OF NUMBERS, by Sepharial.**
    The clear and original revelation of the Kabalistic doctrine of numerals can be used by both the beginning and advanced student of numerology. Profusely illustrated with descriptive diagrams and tables, the Newcastle edition includes both volumes of the original work.
    P-027-5   **421 pages**   **$4.95**

14. **ASTROLOGY AND THE TAROT, by Dr. A. E. Thierens.**
    (orig. title: *The General Book of the Tarot*). Dr. Thierens offers a clear, concise explanation of the Tarot, both the Greater and the Lesser Arcana, and sets forth for the first time a carefully-arranged system of correspondences between Astrology and the Tarot. Introduction by A. E. Waite.
    P-031-3   **160 pages**   **$2.95**

15. **YOUR PSYCHIC POWERS AND HOW TO DEVELOP THEM, by Hereward Carrington.**
    A true classic of psychic phenomena and spirtualism by a pioneer in occult research, this challenging book shows you how to become a medium and harness your own psychic powers.
    P-033-X   **358 pages**   **$3.95**

16. **ASTROLOGY: ITS TECHNIQUES AND ETHICS, by C. Aq. Libra.**
    Originally published in the Netherlands, this important astrological treatise has long been unavailable to those interested in the stars. The book covers such topics as Karma, reincarnation, horoscopic calculations, the Zodiac of the head, and much more. This is the first American edition of a fascinating text.
    P-035-6   **272 pages**   **$3.95**

17. **THE HISTORY AND POWER OF MIND, by Richard Ingalese.**
    "The history of mind is the history of man." So states the author of this remarkable book, which went through multiple printings in its first edition. Learn meditation, creation, and concentration, the art of self-control, the cause and cure of disease, the law of opulence; discover the colors of thought vibration. Now available for the first time in decades.
    P-037-2   **284 pages**   **$4.95**

HEALTH

VICTOR H. LINDLAHR means HEALTHFUL LIVING

i. YOU ARE WHAT YOU EAT.
This classic revelation of diet and nutrition tells you how to balance your meals, where to find vitamins and minerals in natural foods, how to prepare dishes without destroying nutritional content, and much, much more. Includes complete nutritional tables for all fruits and vegetables.
H-004-6   128 pages $2.45

ii. THE LINDLAHR VITAMIN COOKBOOK.
Fresh foods contain all the vitamins and nutrients needed by the human body. The key to preserving these essential constituents lies in the proper preparation of meals and food dishes. Learn how to cook the vitamin way! Complete with vitamin balance charts and recipes.
D-011-9   319 pages $2.95

iii. EAT AND REDUCE!
Diet the Lindlahr way, as America's leading nutritionist outlines a safe and healthy method of getting rid of those exttra pounds. The right kind of reducing diet just can't fail! Includes diet plans and calorie tables.
H-015-1   194 pages $2.45

iv. THE NATURAL WAY TO HEALTH.
Here is Dr. Lindlahr's own story of his research into the natural values of organically grown foods. The secret of good health lies in living a balanced life and eating natural foods. For anyone interested in healthy living.
H-017-8   255 pages $2.95

i-iv. All FOUR books for just $10.00 postpaid!

Other Titles of Interest

v. ROMANY REMEDIES AND RECIPES, by Gipsy Petulengro.
Originally published in this country by E.P. Dutton & Co., Petulengro's book is a classic compilation of Gypsy health foods and medicines, painstakingly discovered by trial-and-error over many centuries of wandering the countrysides of Europe and America. Profusely illustrated.
H-016-X   128 pages $2.25

vi. VIEWPOINT ON NUTRITION, by Dr. Arnold Pike.
Taken from the TV show of the same name, Dr. Pike's book includes interviews with Gaylord Hauser, Dr. Linus Pauling, Eddie Albert, Julie Harris, Sugar Ray Robinson, and many others. Discover the celebrity way of keeping fit! With the Dept. of Agriculture report, "Human Nutrition No.2." An original Newcastle publication.
H-021-6   232 pages $2.95

SELF-ENRICHMENT SERIES

a. FORTUNATE STRANGERS, by Dr. Cornelius Beukenkamp Jr.
This pioneering study of psychology and group therapy has justly been regarded as a classic monograph in its field. "An interesting demonstration — and documentation — of this method in the words of the participants" —*Kirkus Review.* Originally published by Rinehart & Co.
S-000-3   269 pages $2.95

b. LOVE, HATE, FEAR, ANGER, AND THE OTHER LIVELY EMOTIONS, by June Callwood.
A study of human emotions, and how they master, or are mastered by, the individual, *Love* tells us how to use our feelings to our own advantage, and how to maintain a healthy mental outlook on life. Part of this book was accepted in the October 1974 issue of *Reader's Digest.* First published by Doubleday & Co.
S-002-X   170 pages $2.45

c. THE IMPORTANCE OF FEELING INFERIOR, by Marie Beynon Ray
This inspiring book shows how your feelings of inferiority can be used to propel you to greater heights of achievement, and to guide you to a richer, more productive life. Ms. Ray cites many examples from history in demonstrating that self-deprecation is common to us all, and especially to the great achievers in life. Published by arrangement with Harper and Row.
G-006-2   266 pages $2.95

d. THE CONQUEST OF FEAR, by Basil King.
Inspired by the author's incipient blindness, this reprint of the Doubleday edition provides a practical guide to overcoming the fears all of us must face in our everyday lives. A perennial bestseller.
G-009-7   270 pages $2.95

e. MARRIAGE COUNSELING: FACT OR FALLACY? by Dr. Jerold R. Kuhn.
Dr. Kuhn provides a scholarly and timely treatment of a most vital and pressing subject, as drawn from actual case histories in the files of the American Institute of Family Relations. The situations covered range from relatively minor communication problems to more serious difficulties, including incompatibility, sexual disfunction, and money worries. An original Newcastle book.
W-022-4   146 pages $2.95

NOSTALGIA

f. THE ORIGINS OF POPULAR SUPERSTITIONS AND CUSTOMS, by T. Sharper Knowlson.
Knowlson's fascinating account of the follies of human belief includes sections on amulets, charms, divining rods, drinking customs, dreams and omens, crystal gazing, lucky stars, vampries, and more. Complete with index.
W-013-5   242 pages $2.95

g. YOUR HANDWRITING AND WHAT IT MEANS, by William Leslie French.
(originally: *The Psychology of Handwriting*).
An uncomplicated survey of the techniques of handwriting analysis, and how it can be used to reveal hidden character traits in yourself and others. Many signatures of noted personalities included.
G-036-4   228 pages $2.95

h. SECRETS OF STAGE HYPNOTISM, by Professor Leonidas.
The good Professor provides a charming look at the days when hypnotism was a fascinating and mystifying part of stage entertainment. Illustrated with period photographs.
P-029-1   160 pages $2.95

BORGO PRESS ORIGINALS

ROBERT A. HEINLEIN: STRANGER IN HIS OWN LAND, by George Edgar Slusser (The Milford Series: Popular Writers of Today, Vol. 1).
B-201-4   64 pages $1.95

THE BEACH BOYS: SOUTHERN CALIFORNIA PASTORAL, by Bruce Golden (The Woodstock Series: Popular Music of Today, No. 1).
B-202-2   64 pages $1.95

Available September 1976:

ALISTAIR MacLEAN: THE KEY IS FEAR, by Robert A. Lee (The Milford Series: Popular Writers of Today, Vol. 2).
B-203-0   64 pages $1.95

THE ATTEMPTED ASSASSINATION OF JOHN F. KENNEDY, by Lucas Webb.
B-204-9   48 pages $1.95

THE FARTHEST SHORES OF URSULA K. LE GUIN, by George Edgar Slusser (The Milford Series: Popular Writers of Today, Vol. 3).
B-205-7   64 pages $1.95
